Geography, Education and the Future

Geography, Education and the Future

Edited by
Graham Butt

continuum

Continuum International Publishing Group
The Tower Building   80 Maiden Lane
11 York Road   Suite 704
London SE1 7NX   New York, NY 10038

www.continuumbooks.com

British Library Cataloguing-in-Publication Data
A catalogue record for this book is available from the British Library.

ISBN: 978-1-8470-6498-1 (paperback)
       978-1-8470-6497-4 (hardcover)

Library of Congress Cataloging-in-Publication Data
Geography, education and the future / edited by Graham Butt.
    p. cm.
  Includes bibliographical references.
  ISBN: 978-1-84706-498-1 (pbk.)
  ISBN: 978-1-84706-497-4 (hardback)
  1. Geography–Study and teaching (Elementary) 2. Geography–Study and teaching (Secondary) I. Title.

  LB1583.G46 2011
  910.71–dc22

                                                    2010023570

Typeset by Newgen Imaging Systems Pvt Ltd, Chennai, India
Printed and bound in India by Replika Press Pvt Ltd

Contents

Notes on Contributors

Each of the contributors listed below – except for Jessica Pykett and the discussants Clive Barnett, Pat Thomson and Michael Young – is a member of the Geography Education Research Collective (GEReCo). GEReCo was formed in 2007 as a group of research active geography educationists based in English universities.

Clive Barnett is Reader in Human Geography at The Open University in Milton Keynes. His research interests are focused on understanding the geographies of democracy and public life, and his current teaching centres on the development of distance-education courses in urban studies, human geography and interdisciplinary social science. He is author of *Culture and Democracy* (Edinburgh University Press, 2003), co-author of *Geographies of Responsibility* (Wiley-Blackwell, 2010), and co-editor of *Spaces of Democracy* (Sage, 2004), *Geographies of Globalisation* (Sage, 2008), and *Rethinking the Public* (Policy Press, 2010).

Mary Biddulph is a Lecturer in Geography Education in the Centre for Research in Schools and Communities at the University of Nottingham. Her research interests centre on the geographies of young people and how disciplinary research in this area can be utilized to shape and inform the school geography curriculum. With Roger Firth she is project leader for the 'Young People's Geographies' Project, a project funded by the Action Plan for Geography seeking to bring young people, their geography teachers and academic geographers into conversations with each other. Mary is an experienced teacher educator and is also an active member of the Geographical Association; she is editor of the journal *Teaching Geography*, a professional journal for geography teachers.

Clare Brooks is Senior Lecturer in Geography Education, and Course Leader of the MA in Geography Education at the Institute of Education, University of London. Her research interests include geography teacher's subject knowledge and development, and expertise in geography education. She has recently edited *Studying PGCE Geography at M level* (Routledge, 2010), and is Editor of *GeogEd*, an e-journal for geography education research. Clare has been awarded

Chartered Geographer Status by the Royal Geographical Society (with IBG) and is a member of the Geographical Association and the British Sub-Committee of the International Geographical Union Commission for Geography Education (IGU-CGE), and is a founding member of GEReCo.

Graham Butt is Reader in Geography Education, Director of Academic Planning and Deputy Head of School in the School of Education, University of Birmingham. He is a founding member, and currently Chair, of the Geography Education Research Collective (GEReCo). Graham's research is predominantly in the field of geography education, although he has also published on assessment, teacher workload and modernization. Recently published books for Continuum include *Modernizing Schools* (2007, with Helen Gunter), *Lesson Planning* (3rd edition) (2008) and *Making Assessment Matter* (2010). Graham is a long established member of the Geographical Association and an invited member of the British Sub-Committee of the International Geographical Union (IGU).

Simon Catling is Research Leader for Early Childhood and Primary Education in the Faculty of Humanities and Social Sciences, Oxford Brookes University. He is the Honorary Secretary of the International Geographical Union Commission for Geographical Education and the Chair of its British Sub-Committee. Simon's research and scholarship is in geographical education with a particular interest in geography in primary education policy and practice and younger children's geographies. With more than 200 publications for children, teachers, teacher educators and researchers, his books include the *Mapstart* series (Collins-Longman, 2010, 3rd edition), *Placing Places* (Geographical Association, 2002), *Researching Primary Geography* (edited with Fran Martin, Register of Research in Primary Geography, 2004) and *Teaching Primary Geography* (with Tessa Willy, Learning Matters, 2009). Simon is a Past President of the Geographical Association and has been involved with their early years and primary committee for many years. He has held the posts of Assistant Dean and Acting Dean for Education at Oxford Brookes University since the mid-1990s.

Roger Firth is a Lecturer in Education at the University of Nottingham and a member of the Centre for Research in Schools and Communities. He is Course Leader for the Professional Doctorate (Ed.D.) in Teacher Education, teaches on the PGCE Geography course and also supervises Doctoral students. Roger's main research interests lie in geography and environmental education and in curriculum design and change. Current research projects are concerned with how young people's lived geographies can support collaborative (students and teachers) curriculum innovation in secondary schools, the relationship between disciplinary knowledge and curriculum design and what a curriculum might look like that is designed with young peoples' epistemic and social agency in mind.

Nick Hopwood is a Chancellor's Post-doctoral Research Fellow at the Centre for Research in Learning and Change, University of Technology, Sydney. From 2006–2010 he was a Research Fellow at Oxford University Department of Education. His doctorate focused on school pupils' experiences and learning of geography, and has been reported in a number of journals and chapters alongside a book which combines findings with two other theses (*Environmental Learning: Insights from Research into the Student Experience*, with Mark Rickinson and Cecilia Lundholm, Springer Press, 2009). Nick was Evaluator for the Young People's Geographies Project and has conducted research on graduate education, including a study in collaboration with the Association of American Geographers' EDGE project.

David Lambert was a comprehensive school geography teacher for 12 years, until 1986 when he joined the Institute of Education (IoE), University of London. At various times he was course leader for the PGCE and the MA Geography in Education, becoming Assistant Dean for ITE in 1999, and leading the introduction of the MTeach an innovative Masters programme which now has over 200 students. In 2002 he left the IoE to become full-time Chief Executive of the Geographical Association, the UK's leading 'subject association' for teachers of geography. The GA has co-led (with the RGS-IBG) the Action Plan for Geography, a government funded project (2006–2011) to support the development of geography in primary and secondary schools in England. From September 2007, he has combined this role with a return to the IoE (part-time) as Professor of Geography Education. He has written widely on the curriculum, citizenship and assessment. His inaugural lecture titled 'Geography in Education: Lost in the Post?' was in June 2009, and his most recent book is with John Morgan: *Teaching geography 11–18: A Conceptual Approach*, from Open University Press.

Fran Martin is Senior Lecturer in Education in the Graduate School of Education, University of Exeter. Fran's research is in the areas of primary geography, global education and school partnerships, with an emphasis on teacher development. She is currently leading an Economic and Social Research Council (ESRC) funded project: *Global Partnerships as Sites for Mutual Learning: Teachers' Professional Development through Study Visits*. The research investigates the learning of professionals in the United Kingdom, Gambia and Southern India. The project runs from October 2009–September 2012. Fran is a long-standing member of the Geographical Association (GA), editing Primary Geographer between 2006–2009; she is a corresponding member of the British Sub-Committee of the International Geographial Union (IGU).

Alun Morgan taught geography in secondary schools in England and Wales for ten years before becoming a teacher advisor in 1999. In 2002 he moved into Higher Education first as Lecturer in Geography Education at the Institute of Education, London and then as Senior Lecturer in Education for Sustainability at London South Bank University. He is currently a Research Fellow in the Graduate School of Education, University of Exeter. Alun is a member of the Geographical Association and the British Sub-Committee of the International Geographical Union. His research interests include geography education, Education for Sustainable Development and Global Citizenship and Place-Based Education.

John Morgan is Reader in Geography Education at both the Institute of Education, London and the University of Bristol, where he undertakes work on initial teacher education, Masters' courses and doctoral supervision.

His research interests are in curriculum studies, education and cultural change, and social and cultural geography. He has published widely in academic and professional journals and has recently co-authored 'Teaching Geography 11–18: A Conceptual Approach'. He is currently completing 'Teaching Geography as if the Planet Matters' (Routledge).

Jessica Pykett is currently a post-doctoral Research Associate at the Institute of Geography and Earth Sciences, Aberystwyth University where she is researching the politics of governing through 'behaviour-change' policies and the ascendance of libertarian paternalism in the United Kingdom. Prior to this she was an ESRC Research Fellow in the Geography department, The Open University, working on the pedagogical nature of state practices. She studied for her Ph.D. on the geographies of education and citizenship at the University of Bristol. She was co-chair with Helen Griffiths of the Geographical Association Citizenship Working Group from 2006–2009 and has written articles for *Teaching Geography* and *Geography*. Recent publications include 'Making Citizens in the Classroom' in *Urban Studies*, 'Personalisation and De-Schooling' in *Critical Social Policy* and 'Pedagogical Power' in *Education, Citizenship and Social Justice.*

Charles Rawding is Geography PGCE Course Leader at Edge Hill University. His main research interests lie in curriculum innovation in school Geography and the links between school and academic geography. He has published extensively on geography education, his most recent books have been: *Reading Our Landscapes: Understanding Changing Geographies* (Chris Kington, 2007) and *Understanding Place as a Process* (Geographical Association, 2007). He is currently completing a three-book series for Chris Kington Publishing on Contemporary Approaches to Geography.

Eleanor Rawling is a Research Fellow at the University of Oxford Department of Education, and an independent researcher and consultant. She was formerly (1994–2005) Geography Adviser with the Qualifications and Curriculum Authority. A book titled *Changing the Subject: The Impact of National Policy on School Geography 1980–2000* resulted from a Leverhulme Research Fellowship in 1999–2000 and the topic of curriculum change continues to be one of her main research interests. Recently Eleanor has extended her research into cultural and literary geography and a forthcoming book about the poet, Ivor Gurney, will explore the relationship between poetry and place. Eleanor is an active member of the Geographical Association, a former President and currently co-editor of the journal, *Geography*.

Margaret Roberts, until her retirement in 2006, was Senior Lecturer at the School of Education at the University of Sheffield where she coordinated the PGCE course and was Director of PGCE. Margaret's research and publications have focused on the geography national curriculum and geographical enquiry, but she has also published articles on geographical education research and on geographical representation in museums and textbooks. Her book, *Learning through Enquiry*, was published by the Geographical Association in 2003. Margaret has been involved in the work of the Geographical Association for many years, on committees, as Editor of *Teaching Geography*, as project leader for producing web-based resources for teacher educators and as President (2008–2009). She is a member of the IGU and has contributed to conferences in Finland, Portugal, South Korea, Australia and the United Kingdom. She will chair COBRIG (the Council of British Geography) from 2010–2013.

Pat Thomson is Professor of Education and Director of the Centre for Research in Schools and Communities in the School of Education, The University of Nottingham. A former headteacher, her research is in three main areas: the arts, creativity and school and community change; doctoral education; and the work of school leaders/managers. She brings questions of power, place, image and identity to bear on these fields of study. Recently published books for Routledge include *Doing Visual Research with Children and Young People* (2008); *School Leadership – Heads on the Block?* (2009); *The Routledge Doctoral Student's Companion* and *The Routledge Doctoral Supervisor's Companion* (with Melanie Walker, 2010) and *Researching Creative Learning: Issues and Methods* (with Julian Sefton Green, 2010).

Michael Young began his career as a secondary school chemistry teacher and is now Emeritus Professor of Education in the Faculty of Culture and Pedagogy at the Institute of Education, University of London and is Visiting Professor of Education at University of Bath. He gained degrees from the universities of Cambridge, London and Essex and was awarded an Honorary Doctorate by the University of Joensuu, Finland. He is an Honorary Professor at Capital Normal University, Beijing, and the University of Pretoria, South Africa and is a Visiting Professor at the University of Witwatersrand, Johannesburg. He is a Fellow of the City and Guilds of London Institute. His recent books include *Knowledge, Curriculum and Qualifications for South African Further Education* (with Jeanne Gamble, Human Sciences Research Council Press, 2006) and *Bringing Knowledge Back In* (Routledge, 2009). Michael is a sociologist with a particular interest in the role of knowledge in education. He has also been engaged in research on qualifications and qualifications frameworks.

Introduction

Graham Butt

Geography, Education and the Future was conceived as a writing project in 2008 by a small group of geography educators working in English universities who had joined together in the previous year to form the Geography Education Research Collective[1] (GEReCo, pronounced 'Jericho'). This Collective felt strongly that geography educationists – in schools, in teacher education institutions and in university geography departments – should be able to offer helpful perspectives on the changing relationships between geography and education at the start of the twenty-first century.

Studying geography – 'one of humanity's big ideas' (Alastair Bonnett in Geographical Association, 2009, p. 7) – provides students with dynamic, inspirational, relevant and powerful ways of visualizing the world. Its contribution to education recognizes that all children's development involves discovering the world around them and understanding the significance of this planet as our home. Geography critically explores the processes that fashion both societies and environments at a range of spatial scales, with particular reference to major contemporary issues such as climate change, sustainable development, energy use, migration and shifts in employment patterns. Within schools there is also a growing expectation that geography education should be 'futures oriented', acknowledging that our experiences of the present and past must inform decisions that affect all our futures.

Geography remains a popular option for students in many schools, a point which is reflected annually in pleasing levels of engagement and academic performance in the subject in public examinations (JCQ, 2009). In English schools most geography students experience high standards of teaching post 14, which continue forward to impressive levels of student satisfaction on geography courses at undergraduate level (Unistats, 2009). Recent revisions to the public examination system and national curriculum have provided opportunities for innovation – for example, through new General Certificate of Secondary Education (GCSE) specifications (some of which have been influenced by a successful and popular pilot GCSE), new Advanced and Advanced Subsidiary (A and AS) level syllabuses, and a reconfigured Geography National Curriculum (GNC) based on a conceptual approach to learning. The current GNC has clearly moved geography education further away from the content-dominated curriculum first taught almost 20 years ago. In a sense the door to 'curriculum making' has been thrown open, if geography teachers choose to walk through it – something the Geographical Association (GA) has been urging through its contributions to the Action Plan for Geography (www.geographyteachingtoday.org.uk) and 'manifesto' (www.geography.org. uk/adifferentview).

However, the quality of geography education experienced across the range of English schools and educational phases is not uniformly high. Indeed in some schools the responses of teachers and senior managers to recent curricular changes, assessment reviews and policy initiatives have almost certainly threatened the future of geography education in their institutions. Many 'foundation subjects' in the English National Curriculum, and in the school curricula of other countries, have been exposed to increasing pressures (Gerber, 2001; Rawling, 2004; Butt et al., 2006). The particular circumstances of geography's apparent decline in a substantial number of English schools, both in terms of the perceived value of its curriculum contribution and its uptake by students, have been highlighted through official documents. In 2008 the schools' inspectorate, the Office for Standards in Education (OfSTED), branded school geography as a subject in difficulties – much of the teaching and learning they observed were deemed 'mediocre', while students' achievements were supposedly 'weaker than in most subjects' (OfSTED, 2008). With little to stimulate them in geography lessons many children were already 'voting' with their feet, choosing options that would take them away from geographical study at the ages of 13, or 16. This trend is verifiable with reference to statistics on examination entries for geography at GCSE level and at A level since 2000, with some 20 per cent fewer candidates sitting public examinations in geography at the end of the first decade of the twenty-first century compared to the beginning (Butt, 2008). The knock-on effect of declining numbers of students subsequently applying for geography, or geography related, courses in higher education is predictable.

Although a direct causal relationship between the decline in geography student numbers, poor teaching and uninteresting subject-matter is not proved – the rise of vocational options and the widening of curriculum choice are also factors drawing students away from studying geography – there is much here to concern any community of geography educators. This invites us to also consider the widening gap between geography in schools and geography in the academy (Castree et al., 2007; Johnston, 2009; Hill and Jones, 2010). At a time when student numbers in higher education are increasing, the declining proportion who opt for geography (or related) degree courses signal that any further uncoupling of school and university geography would be mutually damaging.

Motivations for writing *Geography, Education and the Future*

While the dilemma of geography's future as both a school and university subject discipline forms an important backdrop to why *Geography, Education and the Future* was written, it is not the sole stimulus for the book's conception. We started primarily from considerations of what the learners of today and tomorrow – in rapidly changing, globalized societies – would need from their (geography) education. In this respect there was an awareness that geography education should:

> prepare young people for living in the communities they are growing up in, and which they will both shape and be shaped by. Geography should also help young people understand the world around them, make informed decisions about issues that affect them at a variety of spatial scales and develop their sense of identity within a world of multiple cultures. It must offer something meaningful to both the learner and the citizen, while being confident in its response to developments in the subject discipline and in the wider world of education. (Butt, 2008, p. 158)

But what should be the role and function of geography educators, and of the subject they teach? As a preparation for life in our super-complex worlds (Lambert, 1999), we question whether the most appropriate forms of primary and secondary education are *really* those that favour the teaching of literacy, numeracy and generic 'thinking skills'. Our choice is for curricula that embrace the more targeted and meaningful contributions of the subject disciplines. Both Lambert (2009) and Morgan (2008) question school curricula that are now based on 'post-disciplinary' approaches, which appear to lack any notion of human agency and seem to legitimize the very neoliberal orthodoxy that has led to the recent global economic recession. With its particular conceptualizations of places and spaces, employment, leisure, citizenship, domestic life, sustainability, interdependence, identity and consumption (to list but a few!) geography, and geographers, can help to provide young people with a passport to their lives. The goal must surely be to create autonomous and responsible global citizens – who are capable of 'thinking geographically', possessed of the ability to both pose and answer geographical questions.

A further, related aspect of the contributions made to this book is their recognition that geography educators should adopt a 'futures' perspective to their teaching, and to their students' learning. One of the most trenchant criticisms of school geography is that it is too static and 'backward looking'. This is an issue which is arguably most keenly felt by children in schools, who may legitimately ask us: 'what has this subject got to say to me that is relevant to my future and for getting a job?' A conception of the curriculum as 'futures oriented' should go to the very heart of our educational philosophy – rejecting notions that academic subjects should primarily focus on largely fixed, given, content to be 'passed on' to the next generation (as expressed through classical humanist and cultural restorationist approaches), while embracing an ideal that knowledge should be (re)created by each generation (as in the progressive educational and (re)constructionist traditions) (see Rawling, 2001). Knowledge and understanding must be created *from and about* something: it is here that strong subject disciplines are essential.

The subject-based curriculum is under greater pressure now than at any time since the launch of the national curriculum in 1988. *Geography, Education and the Future* makes a fresh case for the role of the subject discipline – a role which has moved on from the one it served during most of the last century (see Bailey and Binns, 1987). Big questions arise – what are the subject disciplines for? How can subjects contribute meaningfully towards the education of all young people? How should subjects respond to constant change? We have seen how attempts to closely define the content of school subjects have previously failed – witness the early versions of the national curriculum – especially if we want the curriculum to remain fluid and dynamic. This suggests that overly prescriptive national curricula are unhelpful, while 'curriculum making' is best achieved when teachers and students have a clear conception of their subject, some agreed criteria for selecting content, and a shared understanding of what is to be achieved.

This book will help geography educators, at whatever stage of their career and in whichever institutions they work, to assess the relevance of the geography they currently teach. It focuses on a range of tensions within the current geography curricula taught in schools and the academy – primarily by seeking to explore 'what really matters' in terms of the geography that is studied and by considering whether young people currently gain a worthwhile appreciation of this. Some of the geographical concepts covered here are arguably under-represented in the geography taught in schools – such as 'children's geographies', young people's conceptions of geography, environmental change, the personal relationships expressed through conceptions of place and space, the status of geographical knowledge, global ethics and citizenship.

The organizational structure of *Geography, Education and the Future*

As a stimulus to their writing each author was asked to consider three important questions:

- How can geography education prepare young people for the places, environments and societies they will inhabit in the future?
- How should geography be reframed to take into account – and have something significant to say about – the major social and environmental changes wrought by growing consumption, restructuring of economies and technologies, and the dynamic connections between local and global?
- How can geography and geography education present an agenda that can be taken seriously and implemented in the twenty-first century?

Their themed responses – presented in four parts, each of which is briefly summarized by a 'discussant' (Pat Thomson, Charles Rawding, Michael Young and Clive Barnett) – address a range of pertinent issues. The opening part contains three chapters on 'Children, Young People and Geography' and has been coordinated by Mary Biddulph. The key question pursued here is 'How can the geography curriculum be reconfigured to ensure that the insights, perspectives and potential of children and young people are integral to the design?' Acknowledging that children experience the world in different ways to adults, this part highlights the spaces, places and environments they live in. It discusses how teachers and policy practitioners might seek to accommodate, through education, the participatory roles of young people in society. Simon Catling's chapter explores children's geographies in the primary school exploring ideas about the ways in which young people learn about the world. He poses the question of whether the current primary geography curriculum focuses on what should be central to children's geographical studies, while also exploring issues for children's involvement in futures-oriented primary geographies. With reference to his recent research, Nick Hopwood considers young people's conceptions of geography, how they make sense of the discipline and how the geography curriculum relates to the rapidly changing worlds they encounter. The importance of learners' conceptions of school geography are stressed with reference to issues deemed important by practising teachers. Children's own views about whether they think geography helps them to be global citizens, its relevance to their lived experiences, and their perception of the nature and status of geographical knowledge are also considered. Concluding the first part, Mary Biddulph explores the impact of the 'Young People's Geographies' Project by considering the spaces, places and environments children inhabit, their social networks and daily routines. She acknowledges that academic geography is now focusing on more research and scholarship in this area, but notes that until recently 'children's geographies' have been largely ignored within the school geography curriculum. Here the capacity of young people to utilize their own lived experiences to actively participate in curriculum development and to support their geographical learning is acknowledged.

In the second part the focus shifts to 'Place, Space and Change' under the direction of John Morgan. The three chapters in this part seek to develop geography educators' understanding of the role of place and space by responding to the question: 'To what extent are sense of place and understanding of space crucial to our changing lives and identities in the twenty-first century?' Geography education has always claimed to help students develop a 'sense of place' – an increasingly challenging task in the face of the processes of globalization, which can create the impression that we now live in 'placeless times'. The chapters in this part seek to develop a more complex and nuanced understanding of the role of place in geographical education. Thus, Eleanor Rawling's chapter explores the way in which place-based writing has increasingly engaged with the processes of environmental change. She argues that it may be valuable to reclaim place study for educational purposes, drawing on human-istic, phenomenological and representational approaches and reconfiguring these in the light of our responsibility to the environments and peoples of the world. Focusing on literary responses to change, as expressed through 'ecocriticism', she makes important linkages with an older strand of humanis-tic thinking in geographical education. Geography educationists, she believes, need to engage with these debates and develop a geographical approach to 'reading and writing place' as a key element of a future education. Alun Morgan's chapter picks up these threads and develops them in a wider context – exploring the question of whether school geography is preoccupied with a narrow definition of experience. Highlighting other countries' teaching of cross-curricular formulations, such as 'social studies' – where such a 'meta-subject' represents an amalgam of approaches drawn from disciplines such as history, economics, sociology and citizenship/civics, as well as geography – Morgan notes that place as a concept is not confined to one discrete subject discipline. This may imply that a more holistic educational approach to place is required. Underpinning both chapters is a concern that places are being eroded and challenged by processes that operate across larger spatial scales. The final chapter in this part, written by John Morgan, explicitly seeks to engage with the relationship between place and space, and to show how ques-tions of identity – who we are, and where we belong – are wrapped up with processes of modernization, marketization and change. Together, the chapters in this part make a significant contribution to the debate about the role of place and space in contemporary geography education.

Part 3 considers 'Mediating Forms of Geographical Knowledge'. Here Roger Firth draws together chapters which highlight how education policy makers and schools have neglected debates about knowledge – specifically the conceptions of knowledge that underpin curriculum and pedagogy. The key question here is: 'What role can and should the discipline (geography) play in the processes that define and redefine knowledge in the school curriculum?' Traditional assumptions about the production and status of knowledge are challenged within a critique about the nature of truth, what counts as reality, and the social nature of knowledge: that is, the ways in which the world may be known. Geography, like other disciplines, has engaged with this debate and has seen a productive rethinking of the epistemological basis of research and knowledge. David Lambert considers the reframing of school geography from a 'capability approach' – developing the capability of young people through the subject discipline. The potential of the capability concept in education, Lambert believes, is that it allows us to develop subject disciplines in schools in a way that both enables us to respond to the knowledge explosion *and* takes into account the skills agenda (and 'personalization') – without having to choose between one or the other. By considering the place of geographical knowledge within society, Roger Firth looks at a variety of issues concerning knowledge: its production, status and acquisition. Placing this within the curriculum debate in education, he argues that young people need democratic access to disciplinary knowledge. By looking back at the way in which knowledge in general, and geographical knowledge in particular, has been conceptualized, Firth identifies its significance for the school curriculum. Clare Brooks explores geographical knowledge and professional development and considers to what extent school geography is still related to its academic discipline (and whether it should be). Teachers are clearly influential in the process of geographical knowledge transfer, as the gatekeepers to the academic discipline, but what forms of knowledge do geography teachers need to mediate this process effectively? Drawing on Dewey's conceptualization of subject-matter for teaching, the chapter explores what teachers can do to ensure that students develop the geography education they need. This part is therefore focused on the importance of knowledge in education, considering its place in societal, disciplinary and educational contexts. The authors pose some important educational questions: What is it that we want young people to know in the twenty-first century? In what ways do teachers need to engage with epistemological developments in the academic discipline? In what ways do subject disciplines matter in teachers' work and in shaping the students' experience? What geographical knowledge do teachers need to mediate students' learning?

The final part, Part 4, considers 'Global Ethics, Environment and Citizenship'. Here Fran Martin draws together chapters that highlight how issues of sustainability and environmental protection have come to the fore in geography education in the past 20 years. The main question pursued can be phrased as follows: 'To what extent are issues of environmental change, global citizenship and sustainability resulting in a reconsideration of strategies for moral and ethical education through geography?' Alun Morgan considers morality and geography education, asserting that very many, if not all, ethical issues have a crucial geographical dimension. Many of these issues – referred to by some as being 'geo-ethical' – are now on the agenda of geography education and also, crucially, on wider educational agendas associated with 'spiritual, moral, social and cultural' (SMSC) education and 'education for sustainable development and global citizenship' (ESDGC). This chapter considers the relationship between ethical issues which have a decidedly geographical dimension in the light of thinking in moral and educational discourses. Global ethics, sustainability and partnership are considered by Fran Martin as she analyses the political and educational discourses implicit in policies that promote the global dimension. Students' understanding of development and sustainability are explored using post-colonial theory to make sense of how these are interpreted at school level. Through consideration of the contribution of study visits to the professional development of teachers, the input of geography to the themes of sustainable development and global partnerships is explored. Jessica Pykett concludes the part by considering Geography, Citizenship and Ethical Geocitizens. With the introduction of compulsory citizenship education in schools in England in 2002 teachers and students were encouraged to think critically about the ways in which they were made governable, while also being encouraged to exhibit the behaviours and dispositions of 'active' citizens. This chapter outlines the relationship between geography education and citizenship education, and highlights opportunities and challenges faced by teachers responsible for tackling citizenship issues through geography. These themes have significant links to morality and ethics, both of which can be explored through the lens of geography education. The chapter explores not only the theoretical basis for relating ethics, environment and citizenship to geography education, but also issues arising from the professional development of teachers within different contexts to promote the understanding and teaching of these themes. In conclusion Margaret Roberts adds her thoughts on the previous parts and draws together the main themes that have emerged from our exploration of the questions we have set ourselves.

Conclusions

The drive to construct geography curricula for young people that are forward looking, relevant and stimulating must continue apace. Unfortunately, in recent years, governments and their policy makers have seemingly lost interest in many subject disciplines – with the possible exception of the sciences and technology – being more exercised by the desire to establish national strategies for the delivery of core skills, or the provision of 'learning to learn' and 'thinking skills' programmes for children. Coupled with the slow demise of the national curriculum a growing number of schools in England only teach geography at early secondary level (Years 7 and 8), consigning the compulsory teaching of geography at Key Stage 3 to either a short course or an adjunct to an integrated humanities programme.

The contributors to *Geography, Education and the Future* believe that young people should be able to use their geography education to help them become more autonomous decision makers, better citizens and more enquiring individuals. They view the learning of geography as a motivational activity, far removed from the rote memorization of chunks of content. Our belief is that geography education not only changes the individual, but may also change the nature of the subject as well. As such this book seeks to question what is currently considered to be educationally worthwhile in the school geography curriculum. It has at its heart a conception of geography as a way of seeing, placing considerable weight on the importance of promoting children's abilities to think geographically so that they can make sense of the world. We would argue that this vision needs to be clearly transmitted, not only to the learners themselves but also to a wider group of 'stakeholders' in education – parents, teachers, employers, politicians and the general public.

The case for school geography has to be constantly restated. As the subject is squeezed by a constant stream of new education initiatives, the rise of vocational courses, increasing demands for curriculum space and declining student numbers, those who have a professional responsibility for the future of geography and geography education must respond. As Lambert (2009) correctly states, it is timely to rehearse

> how geography contributes to an idea of education that is ambitious, sophisticated and multidimensional, and which has roots in the notion of human potential – to become self-fulfilled and competent individuals, informed and aware citizens and critical and creative 'knowledge workers'. (p.17)

Note

[1] GEReCo was formed in January 2007 following a meeting at the Institute of Education, University of London, as 'a collective of individuals dedicated to the promotion of geography education through research and publication'. It has a number of aims:

1. to undertake research and publication in geography education,
2. to develop critical thinking, critical perspectives and new knowledge in geography education,
3. to produce high quality research and publications that are valued by different target audiences, but particularly by policy makers,

4. to actively pursue research projects/tenders from educational and/or governmental organizations and sources,
5. to establish a regular research and publication forum which meets once each term, rotating between members' institutions,
6. to publish three academic journal articles, or equivalent, each academic year,
7. to establish a clearly identifiable 'brand' for the Collective.

GEReCo has a website at http://www.geography.org.uk/gtip/gereco/

References

Bailey, P. and Binns, T. (eds) (1987), *A Case for Geography*. Sheffield: Geographical Association.

Butt, G. (2008), 'Is the future secure for geography education?' *Geography*, 93, (3), 158–165.

Butt, G., Hemmer, M., Hernando, A. and Houtsonen, L. (2006), 'Geography in Europe', in J. Lidstone and M. Williams (eds), *Geographical Education in a Changing World: Past Experience, Current Trends and Future Challenges*. Dordrecht: Springer, pp. 93–106.

Castree, N., Fuller, D. and Lambert, D. (2007), 'Geography without borders', *Transactions of the Institute of British Geographers*, 32, 129–132.

Geographical Association (GA) (2009), *A Different View: A Manifesto for the Geographical Association*. Sheffield: Geographical Association.

Gerber, R. (2001), 'The state of geographical education in countries around the world', *International Research in Geographical and Environmental Education*, 10, (4), 342–362.

Hill, J. and Jones, M. (2010), ' "Joined-up geography": connecting school-level and university-level geographies', *Geography*, 95, (1), 22–32.

JCQ (2009), *GCSE, Applied GCSE and Entry Level Certificate Results Summer 2009*. http://www.jcq.org.uk/attachments/published/1129/JCQ-GCSE.pdf (accessed 24 November 2009).

Johnston, R. (2009), 'On geography, geography and geographical magazines', *Geography*, 94, (3), 207–214.

Lambert, D. (1999), 'Geography and moral education in a supercomplex world: the significance of values education and some remaining dilemmas', *Ethics, Place and Environment*, 2, (10), 5–18.

—. (2009), 'Geography in education: lost in the post?' Inaugural professorial lecture. Delivered 23 June 2009, Institute of Education, University of London.

Morgan, J. (2008), 'Curriculum development in "new times" ', *Geography*, 93, (10), 17–24.

OfSTED (2008), *Geography in Schools – Changing Practice*. London: HMSO.

Rawling, E. (2001), *Changing the Subject: The Impact of National Policy on School Geography 1980–2000*. Sheffield: Geographical Association.

—. (2004), 'Introduction: school geography around the world', in A. Kent, E. Rawling and A. Robinson (eds), *Geographical Education: Expanding Horizons in a Shrinking World*. Glasgow: Scottish Association of Geography Teachers with the Commission on Geographical Education (IGU), pp. 167–169.

Unistats (2009), *UK University and College Search*. http://www.unistats.com (accessed 10 November 2009).

Part 1
Children, Young People and Geography
Mary Biddulph

Research evidence articulating young peoples' crime-orientated territorial behaviour in local communities (Kintrea et al., 2008), and the growth of childhood poverty in the United Kingdom (MacInnes et al., 2009) paints a somewhat gloomy picture of the marginalized lives of children and young people – lives either blighted by social and economic depravation that require increasing state intervention and management, or sanitized and constrained lives sheltered from the real world by anxious and protective adults. Reducing such marginalization requires a greater understanding of the social and cultural capital of children and young people in order to develop policies and practices that then actively invite them to participate in wider societal decision-making processes.

In this part we explore the means by which school geography can contribute to young peoples' capacity to participate in decision-making processes that affect them, namely their education. The geographies of children and young people is a growing area of research in the academic discipline, an understanding of which can enable educators to better connect the geographies learned in school with the daily realities of many children and young people. Each of the chapters here differently represents the relationship between young people, their geographical lives and their potential to participate in and contribute to their own educational processes.

References

Kintrea, K., Bannister, J., Pickering, J., Reid, M. and Suzuki, N. (2008), *Young People and Territoriality in British Cities*. A report by the Joseph Rowntree Foundation.

MacInnes, T., Kenway, P. and Parekh, A. (2009), *Monitoring Poverty and Social Exclusion 2009*. A report by the Joseph Rowntree Foundation.

Children's Geographies in the Primary School

1

Simon Catling

Chapter Outline

Introduction

Until the latter half of the twentieth century, geographical studies in English primary schools, as in many other countries, focused on introducing children to aspects of other children's lives, the physical and economic geographies of their own and other countries, alongside an overview of the world. In the United Kingdom this was placed in the context of Britain's connections and interests across the world, initially with its Empire and then with its Commonwealth. Studies of the geography of primary children's own locality played only a very minor part, if included at all. By the 1970s, there had been a shift towards a perspective that focused more directly on the local environment, complemented by studies of a range of landscapes and themes often linked to economic resources and activities and topics such as weather – connecting their relevance to younger children's lives (Marsden, 2001). The 1990s maintained the studies of local places, comparing and contrasting these with other localities, providing some wider sense of national context and of global awareness. Environmental change and sustainability became emphasized, together with studies of people acting on and affected by landscapes through topics such as settlement and river or coastal studies. Processes and patterns at work in the human and natural worlds completed the English primary geography curriculum required in the first decade of the twenty-first century (DfEE, 1999).

While there had been intimations of younger children's experience in and of places, urban and rural landscapes and environmental change, there had been little recognition in their geographical studies of their awareness, knowledge and understanding developed through their personal experience. Even in studies of and in their own localities, children's personal and collective geographies were rarely considered, let alone explored. The emphasis remained on the adults' sense of a local area even when initiated through activities such as mapping children's routes to school. This remained the case even in the guidance given to primary teachers into the late twentieth century (Carter, 1998).

The emergence of focused research into 'children's geographies' during the 1990s (Holloway and Valentine, 2000), building on the early work of environmental psychologists and geographers (Altman and Wohlwill, 1978; Spencer et al., 1989; Matthews, 1992), drew together and stimulated research into younger children's experiences of and in places, a focus still actively investigated (Ba, 2009). Research into children's broader world awareness and environmental knowledge and values (Palmer and Birch, 2004; Hicks, 2002) extended appreciation of their experience to taking account of their understanding of other places, environments and concerns, which continues to be explored (Spencer and Blades, 2006; Davis, 2010), extended into areas such as children's social and environmental participation and engagement with nature (Louv, 2006; Percy-Smith and Thomas, 2010). All of this is increasingly having an impact on advice about approaches to primary geography teaching (Scoffham, 2004; Martin, 2006; Catling and Willy, 2009).

Younger children's geographies

Younger children's daily lives are lived in their home localities, more specifically in their *neighbourhoods* (Ba, 2009; McKendrick, 2009). Neighbourhoods provide their home, schooling and community – key elements of their local attachment and identity. They are the sites of friendships and acquaintances, of early and later play and social activities (in gardens, playgrounds, and adapted or subverted spaces, such as around the communal garages or the stairwells to blocks of flats), and perhaps of shopping and 'hanging out' space for older children. Neighbourhoods are places of smells and textures, of temporary escape from, sometimes even for quite young children, parental or carer oversight, and of imagination – for games played alone, or with close friends. For the youngest children experience in the neighbourhood is accompanied by adults or older siblings; often it involves neighbours' homes, the shops and playgrounds, with such experiences providing enjoyment and frustration, pleasure and tedium, its *affordances* centred around people, toys, games and spaces. For older children, now from 7–8 years of age or older, there may be opportunities to visit friends close by, to go out in a small group to agreed locations and to run errands and make particular journeys without parental guidance, thus providing these children with opportunities to explore locally.

Ba's (2009) study of 10-year-old city children's explorations of their locality provides insight into the context of children's experience of places. He identifies children as supervised and independent explorers. *Supervised explorers* are monitored in a variety of ways, by being accompanied by parents, other adults and siblings or peers, or kept 'in sight' through mobile phone contact and by community oversight, such as by shopkeepers and family friends. Children are also guided to where they might go, which routes to use and the knowledge that they are being monitored. The wealthier the family the more likely this is, in part for protective reasons but also because of parental confidence in their children's abilities to deal with challenges while out. *Independent explorers* are trusted to a greater extent, to be aware of possible dangers, such as traffic or strangers, and to act sensibly in such situations. Their families know they have extensive local networks on which they can call. This sociability means that they are rarely out alone, meeting up with friends, going to their homes or to sites they like and are familiar with. As a result they have greater freedom to roam and can move freely within and extend the boundaries of their home range. Ba argues that place exploration is rule-based, concerns children's and parents'/carers' levels of confidence and develops through childhood as parents help their children get to know the social and physical spaces of the neighbourhood and locality. He sees place exploration for younger children providing experience in socializing and confidence building, contributing to their sense of self and self-esteem and developing negotiation and communication skills – alongside their knowledge and understanding of the environment and the facilities and character of their place. It supports children's sense of belonging and of being-in-the-community.

A key aspect of children's 'freedom to roam' is parental attitudes to children, particularly in the environment. A core concern is that for many adults children on the street or in the shopping centre – where not explicitly supervised by adults – are seen as 'out of place'. This social perspective views children as a 'problem' when exploring their neighbourhood or visiting public arenas (Valentine, 2004; Catling, 2003, 2005; McKendrick, 2009). The social and cultural geographies of children are not free from controversy, nor are they unaffected by the nature of the places in which they reside. Younger children express the view that they want to live in pleasant environments, have these looked after and, expressly, have accessible places for play (O'Brien, 2003). Yet children make something of the environments they have access to, acting imaginatively and innovatively, for instance in their use of wild or wasteland areas for den-building and imaginative play. The creation of particular spaces for children, such as playgrounds, presumes that children should be confined to 'their' areas – whereas a positive perspective sees children as one of the 'groups' of people in any neighbourhood, for whom the whole neighbourhood is accessible. McKendricks' (2009) challenge is that children should be involved in the development of their neighbourhoods, not to re-create them for children but to constitute the neighbourhood as available and friendly to all. Such an approach might enable Ba's supervised explorers to become increasingly independent and for this to begin at an earlier age.

The focus on children's exploration of neighbourhoods, alongside family perspectives and levels of confidence in their children, appears to downplay the wider world experience that children develop through their everyday lives. Children seem to know more of, and construct perspectives on, the wider world and the environmental concerns that they encounter than is generally appreciated (Palmer and Birch, 2004; Spencer and Blades, 2006; Barrett, 2007). Through play young children imagine and creatively enact a variety of their everyday environmental experiences (Tovey, 2007). These may draw on family and school experiences but often also involve ideas about distant places and unfamiliar social and physical environments, drawn from story books, the visits to friends' places, television programmes or, for some older children, via the internet and computer games. This, however, is a little researched area, but it points to other sources and contexts of children's geographical understandings.

Children's knowledge and understanding of both their own country and other people and places is variable, at times misconceived and partial (Barrett, 2007; Wiegand, 1992). While children's mental images of the world and its peoples are inevitably constrained, contact with children in other parts of the world can begin to overcome this (Holloway and Valentine, 2003). Email exchanges between children in the United Kingdom and New Zealand revealed to children themselves that they had somewhat limited images of each other's lives, localities and countries. This realization then provided a base from which they could build new understandings of their common life experiences and interests. Becoming better informed not only depends on knowing more about a particular individual or group but also on wider awareness of the context of that person's or group's lives in their national setting. Children's travel experience can be of value or a constraint here. Being immersed – or even spending a short stay – in places in a new country opens children's eyes to languages, lifestyles, features and activities. But travel to holiday resorts where only the weather, the pool and the holiday complex differentiates it from 'home' may offer no sense of the wider world for younger children and can fail to challenge stereotypes.

Hicks (2002) argues that younger children are aware of the issues facing their everyday environments and the wider world, be these matters of conflict or environmental concerns. This is contextualized through a view of the future. In research for the Cambridge Primary Review (Alexander, 2010), children expressed their views about environmental issues, such as care for their local area and the potential impact of climate change, and they commented that where they had opportunities to be involved in projects to create neighbourhood improvements then they were developing their sense of the value of their own and wider environments and were making a positive contribution to that future (Alexander and Hargreaves, 2007). The essence here, as they saw it, is their participation as active agents who can have an impact and make a difference, albeit in a small way (Percy-Smith and Thomas, 2010).

This account has argued that children's geographical awareness and experience, based in their everyday lives, is varied and nuanced, going beyond the local. The perspective is that there is much in children's 'ordinary experience' outside school which informs their understanding – and misunderstandings and misconceptions – of people, places and environments. This is not a new phenomenon but one which is being researched with increasing breadth and depth and which acknowledges what children have to offer (Catling and Willy, 2009).

The evolving primary curriculum

The requirements for early childhood and primary school geography in England (DfEE/QCA, 1999; DCSF, 2008, 2010; DCSF/QCDA, 2010) have and continue to evolve through practice, experience and debate (OfSTED, 2008; Catling and Willy, 2009). A number of key ideas and approaches in learning and teaching geography provide the disciplinary context of, and focus for, understanding the subject from the earliest years in the English geography curriculum.

In their earliest years children are encouraged to:

- investigate their *immediate and local environment*: what it is like; what they appreciate about it; what it is evolving into
- explore their *connections with other places*: their awareness of the world and where they live in the United Kingdom; what other places are like
- develop their *appreciation of the environment*: ways to care for and improve the environment; involvement in some decisions affecting their community or environment.

In their middle and older primary years children are encouraged to build on these initial geographical studies to investigate:

- *Places*: people's lives in their communities and localities, in their own area and in other parts of the world; the ways places change and evolve; how places are similar and yet diverse.
- *Interconnections*: between places and peoples; the interdependence of peoples and places through such activities as trade; where events occur in the world, building a knowledge of the shape and key natural and human features of the Earth; about communication through movement and digitally.
- *Natural and human processes and patterns*: the working of natural processes, such as weather and climate or rivers and floods and their effects; people's decision-making processes and their outcomes, such as shop changes or new housing estates; the patterns that result in urban areas and landscapes, such as transport and farming; how natural and human processes might interact, such as with drought and famine or with climate change.
- *Environmental impact and sustainability*: how natural processes and people's decisions and actions affect places and people's lives positively and negatively; how such matters can be appreciated differently and may be contentious; the effects in terms of unequal access to resources and resulting inequalities and poverty and wealth; the use and misuse of resources and ways to manage sustainably both for now and for future generations.

Throughout their geographical learning children should use an *enquiry approach* employing *geographical skills*, involving them in drawing on first-hand experience and secondary sources; using fieldwork, maps, photographs and a variety of other data sources, including digital sources; interpreting, analysing, evaluating and communicating findings, explanations and perspectives, and making proposals.

It is argued by Martin (2006) and others (Catling, 2003; Catling and Willy, 2009) that understanding many of these aspects of geography is underpinned by children's daily geographical experience – their *everyday geographies*. This case is premised on the argument that geography is an everyday matter for all of us, because we 'all live in the world' (Martin, 2006, p. 1). Because we are so bound up with places and communities, with our daily travel, with the connections we have, with the visits we make elsewhere and with interdependence in our daily lives, it is not unusual to pass over this 'ordinary', daily geographical engagement as too commonplace to recognize and investigate. But this is an adult, overfamiliar perspective. For children the world is new – hence their curiosity and fascination. The 'everyday' can be a wonder, as it certainly is for our youngest children – but it can also become taken for granted and its significance in our lives missed – a significance we need to understand and appreciate. What is lost concerns not just our knowledge and understanding of the daily geographies that we enact and that affect us but also our appreciation of what is around us and what else may be possible. Ba's (2009) research makes the case that not only do children have a richness of experience in their neighbourhood and local geographies, but, as McKendrick (2009) also argues, there is both more that might be possible if we engaged with children's perspectives, interest and sense of fairness by involving them to a greater extent in understanding place and environmental geographies through their geographical experiences and viewpoints. This is not to say that children's everyday geography becomes the geography curriculum but to recognize that what the curriculum may require can be significantly enhanced through connecting it with their geographies. One primary geography project provided an opportunity to do this.

Children's engagement through the Young Geographers' Project

The Young Geographers' Project, an initiative by the Geographical Association, was a 'Living Geography Project for Primary Schools' (Catling, 2008; Geographical Association, 2008). While the Project focused on helping teachers develop a new geography study unit, involving fieldwork, the local area and sustainability, it also enabled teachers to make connections between school geography and children's everyday geographies through investigations in the local neighbourhood. The rationale for this approach was that it would foster children's ownership of the project and encourage greater independence in learning, based on an enquiry approach into ways in which people affect their own locality and how they could act responsibly in their care for places. One example from the project illustrates this.

Jonathan Kersey's Year 2 class (of 6–7 year olds) focused on investigating hazards in the local environment. He decided to use a familiar story, but with a twist. Rather than Little Red Riding Hood being challenged by the Big Bad Wolf, he became her protector. In the 'True Story of Little Red Riding Hood', she is to still make her way from her home to her granny's house. But there are many hazards along the way and the Wolf's role is to help her recognize and navigate her way around them. Rather than locate the story in an imagined place, the journey takes place through the children's local neighbourhood, and, to add another dimension, it was to be filmed in role. At the heart of this study was the children's voice, their perceptions of the routes and hazards in their own environment, and their acting and filming.

An initial task was to undertake the fieldwork to identify and decide upon the route to use for the story and the sites for filming. This involved the children in considering what they knew of the local area, noting possible routes, surveying and mapping those routes for hazards, and deciding on the variety of hazards they wanted to cover and the final route to use. The children made these decisions. During filming they undertook the journey and captured the advice from the good Wolf on how to deal with the local hazards identified in their planning. What emerged for the children from this project was an increased awareness and knowledge of their own locality. The children debated their perceptions of their place and developed real clarity about the 'hazardous' locations to use in their film. Their understanding of environmental hazards improved because of their investigation in their own locality, and they developed a more informed sense of how to avoid them. Their advice included the following:

> We shouldn't cross the main London Road unless we use the pedestrian crossing. The London Road is very dangerous because there are always lots of cars.

> Don't pick up glass because you could cut yourself. The alleyway near Prospect Road has lots of dangerous broken glass.

> You should not sit at the end of a slide in case someone hurts you. There are slides in Crundwell Road Park and Pennington Park. Be careful in the parks.

> Never walk in the woods by yourself. You can have fun there but make sure you are with a grown up.

Never climb up places where it says danger on it. The electricity box is very dangerous. There is a yellow danger sign on it. It says 'Danger of death'.

These 6–7 year olds were too young to be allowed out to explore this urban area alone or with a group of friends without adult company. Nevertheless their Young Geographers neighbourhood project enabled them to draw on their local knowledge to create an engaging story about local hazards. These 'accompanied explorers' – perhaps a precategory to Ba's (2009) supervised explorers – gained from a school-based study involving their personal geographies. While their teacher felt that in the end the hazards study had focused too much on negative aspects in the local area, it seems that for the children such awareness enhanced their knowledge. Perhaps their parents/carers might allow them when older to explore as supervised explorers within rules for routes and hazards and, based on this, to become in their late primary years independent explorers.

For McKendrick (2009) there is now an essential next step: that of involving children in examining how they can participate in developing the neighbourhood as a more pleasant and enjoyable place to be – to become the type of place in which families allow their children to become supervised and independent explorers. The 'next steps' could be to take the children's map of the local hazards to their local councillor and to challenge that person to do something actively about their concerns. The children might propose their own ideas or look for alternative routes that are safe to follow, or create a map of local safe sites for play, contributing to the local community as active members and agents rather than simply being 'tolerated' younger people.

Issues in applying children's geographies in primary education

This example from the Young Geographers' Project illustrates an approach which drew on children's geographies at the local level. It offered a way in which younger children could participate in local exploration and analysis and be given an opportunity to make a contribution in their community. Yet involving children's geographies in this way is not without concern. These concerns relate to children and to teachers, as well as more broadly to the ways in which governments seemingly control the school curriculum.

The prime concern must be the extent to which children's personal geographies might inadvertently 'become' the geography curriculum. In this context children's geographies emerge as the object of the curriculum, rather than contributing to it. Such a development would disempower rather than enhance children's learning (Catling, 2005). Children's personal contribution to their geographical studies needs to make well-focused use of their geographical experience and understanding from their everyday lives to be of value for their learning, as the hazards study above illustrates. OfSTED (2008) has summarized several examples where children examined matters of change and development in their neighbourhood, involving them in considering issues and in using a variety of approaches in their enquiries. Of one study, OfSTED states that:

> Children's interest was engaged because the issue related to their immediate locality and the proposals [for a housing development] would also have an impact on their lives. (14)

This provided the opportunity for children to draw on their knowledge of the area and to consider the case for development, drawing out their own views and values as well as investigating the views of other people locally. The children offered their own ideas for improvements. Another example draws on one child's reflection about the class's local study, published as a perspective on a topic in a local paper.

> In a recent survey that our class carried out at Thatcham Broadway, we discovered that more than half of all respondents wanted pedestrianization or part-pedestrianization. Some people still wanted cars to be allowed in The Broadway. In elderly people's cases this is because they have to walk there and they can't walk far. In other cases they live too far away from the centre to walk. However, I strongly believe that Thatcham Broadway should be pedestrianized. The centre could be the most beautiful and interesting place in town. You could even build a play park on half the green for the children. You could keep the other half as a green. The elderly people would love a nice quiet place with no cars so they can relax. Children would also love to be able to not have to worry about the cars. It would also make Thatcham Broadway a healthier and safer place for everyone. (OfSTED, 2008, pp. 37–38)

This provides an example of children proposing ways to enhance their locality, illustrating McKendrick's (2009) call for children's involvement in the locality in order for it to be a place of all the people who live there. It has a strong citizenship ethos to it, which connects, too, with evolving curriculum developments for primary geography (DCSF, 2010; DCSF/QCDA, 2010). Curriculum approaches in this vein challenge the notion that children's geographies can be too personal to play a part in their learning and that in doing so children's lives and experiences are exploited. Rather, their geographical awareness and understanding seems enhanced and the children's concern to be involved locally, noted by Alexander and Hargreaves (2007), is met.

Secondly, there is some evidence that many primary teachers hold rather limited expectations of children in their geographical studies and understanding (OfSTED, 2008; Catling et al., 2007). In part this may be a factor of geography's scarce time in the primary curriculum, but it may also arise from many teachers' limited knowledge of the localities in which they teach, as well as their weak understanding of geography as a discipline. Failing to appreciate children's real potential may result in teachers inhibiting opportunities for children's geographical learning. To enhance children's understanding teachers need to be aware not just of their children's understanding of local and wider geographies but also of their own, including knowing the geography of the area in which they teach, the feel for it as a place and its interconnectedness with the wider world.

For many years the English school inspection service (DES, 1999; OfSTED, 2008) has argued that teachers' lack of confidence in their geographical understanding inhibits their teaching of the subject. If teachers lack understanding and confidence there will inevitably be a limited appreciation of what children's geographies can offer primary school geography. In just the same way, little knowledge of the children's local area means that teachers will struggle to make decisions on how to build local contexts into the geography curriculum and as a consequence will marginalize the children's local expertise in the curriculum making process. This exclusion of children's perspectives will not only apply to local area studies but also to other geographical issues that are important to children, such as climate change or the impacts of natural catastrophes on people's lives. The tendency will be to play safe and contain and limit the topics for study, working to rather than going beyond the published units of work readily accessible on the web (e.g. DfEE/QCA, 1998/2000). This approach compounds teachers' limited control not only of the curriculum but also in developing their knowledge, understanding and skills to create effective curricula within their schools and for the children they teach.

The third issue for primary geography concerning the use to be made of children's geographies lies in the construction of the geography requirements for early childhood and primary schooling. Governments promote a view of the geography about which children should learn (DfEE, 1999; DCSF, 2008, 2010; DCSF/QCDA, 2010). Geography in England is seen to help children make sense of and be informed about the world, to give them insight into community cohesion and to enable them to appreciate the need for a sustainable approach to the future – all matters of wider government policy and all 'good things'. The nature of the exercise of schooling is that children *must study* places and environmental matters to become (in the government's terms) informed citizens, but not that this should intentionally engage their geographical experiences, understanding and opportunities from outside school – *their geographies*. There is a challenging marriage to be made here. It concerns the need for governments that construct national curricula to set out the core elements in that curriculum, be this about subjects or areas of learning, which are consistent with their other espoused values for children, such as the intention that children's voices be heard and taken into account (DfES, 2003). The latter can clearly imply and involve children's geographies contributing to and enabling children to participate in their own geographical learning. It becomes incumbent on teachers to make this move if governments do not set out their obligations and commitments consistently and coherently. Yet, as noted above, this may be difficult to achieve where there is a lack of teacher confidence in their understanding of geography, their awareness of their children's geographies, and limited experience in planning and developing their own curriculum.

Conclusion

The challenge facing primary geography lies in the development of ways to engage children and teachers in everyday geographies, as well as in their own geographies, to enhance children's geographical learning in primary schools. Everyday geographies provide the contexts for exploring much in geography that is central to the subject as well as being vital in understanding the world as it is evolving. While the argument presented above has emphasized local geographies – in knowing, participating more fully in and contributing to our own neighbourhoods and communities – it can equally apply to the wider world. Studies of Fair Trade, equity and poverty or exploring the effects of the interplay of natural and human processes in matters of pollution and climate change can engage younger children in greater levels of understanding of their interdependence on the activities of others, nationally and globally.

Both children's and teachers' geographies are involved here – not only where such matters touch our lives, but because we are affected by them, as we affect others. Our curiosity about such matters needs to be engaged, fostered and developed, since such concerns relate to our interests. At the local level this can involve the development of local studies in which the teacher is the learner as much as the child, enhancing and deepening awareness and knowledge of the children's and school's locality, drawing on the children's and community's extensive and varied knowledge. Complementarily, the teacher's role is to support the development of the children's understanding of their personal geographies through insight about the geographical processes and patterns locally and more widely, in encouraging debate about topical interests and issues and through involving children in learning from each other. In the wider context, younger children's concern for the environment – about the inequalities in and approaches to improve people's lives, and about access to places and resources – can be engaged. Children should investigate, debate and evaluate their perspectives, values and ideas about the places in which they live and visit and in considering their futures.

Opportunities exist in the evolving primary geography curriculum to explore children's *everyday geographies*. In effect, development in geographical education is about how primary teachers might re-create themselves as *curriculum makers* even in the constrained circumstances of teaching a school structured or 'off-the-peg' curriculum unit, in order to make geographical studies and learning theirs and the children's own. More adventurous teachers will act as curriculum makers in the intended sense of the phrase by creating their own units of study, positively involving the children in its construction and evolution as a topic, using open-ended topical, problem or issue-based enquiries (Catling and Willy, 2009). Here children's geographies are central to the process of the curriculum, working with teachers' geographies – and realistically making use of and reconstituting the required geography curriculum content – to 'get inside' their topics. Children may foster and feel a sense of responsibility as citizens, putting forward proposals and communicating – even acting on – them more widely.

Drawing on children's geographies offers an opportunity for a 'step change' in the ways in which teaching geography occurs in many primary schools in the twenty-first century. It provides the basis for children to become active agents in and of their own geographical learning, not passive observers of the world. It offers teachers ways to engage not only with children's geographical experiences but also with their own, as a way to enhance the curriculum they are required to teach through revitalizing, reconstructing or creating it. This will enable teachers to develop their own geographical studies to foster, excite and deepen children's geographical understanding and engagement in and beyond school.

References

Alexander, R. (ed.) (2010), *Children, Their World, Their Education*. London: Routledge.

Alexander, R. and Hargreaves, L. (2007), *The Primary Review Interim Reports: Community Soundings*. Cambridge: University of Cambridge Faculty of Education. Available at www.primaryreview.org.uk

Altman, I. and Wohlwill, J. (eds) (1978), *Children and the Environment*. New York: Plenum Press.

Ba, H. (2009), *Children's Place Exploration*. Saarbrücken: VDM.

Barrett, M. (2007), *Children's Knowledge, Beliefs and Feelings about Nations and National Groups*. Hove: Psychology Press.

Carter, R. (ed.) (1998), *Handbook of Primary Geography*. Sheffield: Geographical Association.

Catling, S. (2003), 'Curriculum contested: primary geography and social justice', *Geography*, 88, (3), 164–210.

—. (2005), 'Children's personal geographies and the English primary school curriculum', *Children's Geographies*, 3, (3), 325–344.

—. (2008), *Young Geographers: A Living Geography Project for Primary Schools, 2008 – An Evaluation Report*. Sheffield: Geographical Association.

Catling, S. and Willy, T. (2009), *Teaching Primary Geography*. Exeter: Learning Matters.

Catling, S., Bowles, R., Halocha, J., Martin, F. and Rawlinson, S. (2007), 'The state of geography in English primary schools', *Geography*, 92, (2), 118–136.

Davis, J. (ed.) (2010), *Young Children and the Environment*. Cambridge: Cambridge University Press.

DCSF (2008), *The Early Years Foundation Stage: Setting the Standards for Learning, Development and Care for Children from Birth to Five*. Annesley: DCSF Publications. Available at www.teachernet. gov.uk/publications

—. (2010), *The New Primary Curriculum*. Available at www.curriculum.qcda.org.uk/new-primary-curriculum/index.aspx

DCSF/QCDA (2010), *The National Curriculum Primary Handbook*. Coventry: QCDA.

DES (1999), *Primary Education 1994–1998: A Review of Primary Schools in England*. London: The Stationary Office.

DfEE (1999), *The National Curriculum for England: Geography*. London: HMSO. Available at www.curriculum.qca.org.uk/key-stages-1-and-2/subjects/index.aspx

DfEE/QCA (1998/2000), *A Scheme of Work for Key Stages 1 and 2: Geography*. London: HMSO. Available at www.standards.dfes.gov.uk/schemes2/ks1–2geography/?view+get

DfES (2003), *Every Child Matters*. London: DfES.

Geographical Association (2008), *The Young Geographers' Project*. Available at www.geography.org.uk/ projects/younggeograpers/resources/

Hicks, D. (2002), *Lessons for the Future*. London: Routledge.

Holloway, S. and Valentine, G. (eds) (2000), *Children's Geographies*. London: Routledge.

—. (2003), *Cyberkids: Children in the Information Age*. London: RoutledgeFalmer.

Louv, R. (2006), *Last Child in the Woods: Saving Our Children from Nature-Deficit Disorder*. Chapel Hill: Algonquin.

McKendrick, J. (2009), 'Localities: a holistic frame of reference for appraising social justice in children's lives', in J. Qvortrup, W. Corsaro and M.-S. Honig (eds), *The Palgrave Handbook of Childhood Studies*. Basingstoke: Palgrave MacMillan, pp. 238–255.

Marsden, W. (2001), *The School Textbook: Geography, History and Social Studies*. London: Woburn Press.

Martin, F. (2006), *Teaching Geography in Primary Schools: Learning to Live in the World*. Cambridge: Chris Kington Publishing.

Matthews, H. (1992), *Making Sense of Place*. Hemel Hempstead: Harvester/Wheatsheaf.

O'Brien, M. (2003), 'Regenerating children's neighbourhoods: what do children want?', in P. Christensen and M. O'Brien, (eds), *Children in the City: Home, Neighbourhood and Community*. London: Routledge, pp. 142–161.

OfSTED (2008), *Geography in Schools: Changing Practice*. Available at www.ofsted.gov.uk/publications

Palmer, J. and Birch, J. (2004), *Geography in the Early Years*. London: RoutledgeFalmer.

Percy-Smith, B. and Thomas, N. (2010), *A Handbook of Children and Young People's Participation: Perspectives from Theory and Practice*. London: Routledge.

Scoffham, S. (ed.) (2004), *Primary Geography Handbook*. Sheffield: Geographical Association.

Spencer, C. and Blades, M. (eds) (2006), *Children and Their Environments*. Cambridge: Cambridge University Press.

Spencer, C., Blades, M. and Morsley, K. (1989), *The Child in the Physical Environment*. Chichester: Wiley.

Tovey, H. (2007), *Playing Outdoors: Spaces, Places, Risk and Challenge*. Maidenhead: Open University Press.

Valentine, G. (2004), *Public Space and the Culture of Childhood*. Aldershot: Ashgate.

Wiegand, P. (1992), *Places in the Primary School*. Lewes: Falmer Press.

2 Young People's Conceptions of Geography and Education

Nick Hopwood

Introduction

Why should we care about young people's conceptions of geography and education? We cannot fully address the big questions posed in this book without considering the views of school students. Does geography education contribute significantly to help young people understand the societies and environments in which they live and which they will shape in the future? Has geography education adapted successfully to the major social changes that result from the restructuring of economies, technologies and employment? Will geography and geography education offer something distinctive for both the learner and the citizen in the twenty-first century? Understanding the perspectives of those who study geography in school is a crucial component in answering these questions and thinking about the directions that geography education will take in the future. What are the issues that concern and inspire young people in relation to the world around them and the wider global contexts to which they are increasingly linked? What value do they perceive in their geography education? What are they looking for their schooling to provide in terms of understanding important and relevant issues?

The following paragraphs make a more detailed case for the need to pay attention to young people's conceptions of geography and education, beginning with a fundamental set of values regarding the status of young people and their views, exploring links between conceptions and learning, and considering the relationship between young people and the future of geography as a subject.

Taking young people and their views seriously

A central argument in the first part of this book follows a strand of research which makes children and young people the central focus of enquiry, recognizing their status as legitimate human beings and participants in society and education in their own right. Prout and James (1990) suggested the 'New Social Studies of Childhood' as a novel paradigm in the study of children and their lives. They brought together a number of ideas, many derived from work that began in the 1970s (e.g. Young, 1971; Hardman, 1973; Giddens, 1979), to form the basis of an approach that involved a clear shift in focus and emphasis. Four key principles can be identified as defining features: that children's social relationships and cultures are worthy of study in their own right; that children must be seen as active in the construction and determination of their own social lives rather than passive subjects of social structures and processes; that childhood must be understood as a social construction; and that there are a multiplicity of childhoods, influenced by many social variables including class gender and ethnicity.

Each of these principles has a bearing on the way we might seek to understand young people's conceptions of geography. Taking children's lives and cultures as worthy of study in their own right means that we explore their perceptions of geography education as valid entities in themselves, and should resist temptations to interpret them from a deficit model which sees them only of value as interim stages towards more sophisticated ideas. The role of children in actively constructing their lives and ideas means that we do not assume young people's conceptions are an automatic reflection of their experiences in geography classrooms or elsewhere. Each student has the capacity to interpret experiences in their own way and to construct their own sense of the subject and how it relates to their lives. Viewing childhood as a social construction and recognizing the multiplicity of childhoods leads us to important assumptions that young people's views of geography may vary over space and time. The dynamic economic, cultural, political and environmental geographies of particular places will shape (but not entirely define) the experience of childhood in those places, and within a particular location young people will navigate, interpret and draw meaning from their social and physical environments in different ways. This chapter thus shares much of the view articulated by Rudduck et al. (1997, p. 76):

> Young people are observant, are often capable of analytic and constructive comments, and usually respond well to the serious responsibility of helping identify aspects of schooling that strengthen or get in the way of their learning.

They regard the bracketing of young people's voices as an 'outdated view of childhood that fails to acknowledge children's capacity to reflect on issues affecting their lives' (p. 89). Any attempt to think through the future of geography education must take seriously the views of young people.

Conceptions and learning

A second reason for paying attention to young people's conceptions of geography and education is that these conceptions may exercise an important influence on their learning, as well as being potentially valued learning outcomes in themselves. Almost half a century ago Carswell (1970) argued that school geography must not only do more than simply cover a series of topics, theories and themes, but also enable pupils to see that the subject is a distinctive form of enquiry, arguments often repeated (Woodhouse, 1984; Marsden, 1997; Leat, 2000), and which are implicit in the National Curriculum for Key Stage 3 (11–14 years) (QCA, 2008). The GA's recent manifesto, *A different view* (GA, 2009), makes this point clear: 'an essential educational outcome of learning geography is to be able to apply knowledge and conceptual understanding to new settings: that is, to 'think geographically' about the changing world' (p. 30).

Bruner (1960) wrote that pupils should develop a 'deep grasp' of the subjects they study, suggesting that conceptions of subjects can support extended and more complex learning experiences. Schoenfeld (2004) argues that a deeper understanding of the nature of subjects helps students move away from learning a series of unconnected chunks towards a more coherent approach. These arguments are supported by growing evidence that pupils' beliefs about subjects and knowledge influence both processes and outcomes of their learning (Buehl and Alexander, 2005). Evidence from research based on geography classrooms lends further credence to this view (Davies et al., 2004). We should seek to better understand young people's conceptions not only because they form a legitimate part of the construction of childhood, but also because doing so might help us better understand the processes and outcomes of geographical learning.

Conceptions and the future of geography education

Learners' conceptions of geography are not only mediators of the process of learning, but may also influence young people's decisions and motivation to engage in the act of learning geography itself. This may operate within particular lessons, as students engage or disengage from particular learning activities based on particular value judgements made in relation to perceptions of how current experience relates to what they understand as a valid or relevant focus of learning in geography to be (Rickinson, 1999; Hopwood, 2007a, 2007b; Rickinson et al., 2009, ch. 6).

It may also operate in young people's subject choice decisions, which in England may determine their continuation of formal geography education beyond the age of 14. Rawling (2001) joins many others in expressing concerns that commonly held utilitarian views underpin pupils' disaffection with geography as a subject, and there is some empirical support (Adey and Biddulph, 2001) to suggest such views might be associated with the declining popularity of geography in England and Wales (Stott et al., 1997; Butt, 2002; OfSTED, 2008). A decade ago Rawling (2000) argued that the 'biggest issues facing school geography in England in 2000 are now concerned with status' (p. 211). More recently the subject has suffered negative public exposure in an OfSTED report (2008) which described substandard provision in primary schools, and perceptions of geography as 'boring' in secondary school (Key Stage 3). Alarmingly this report was interpreted in the media as suggesting geography to be the 'worst taught subject in 2004–5' (Marley, 2008).

As was pointed out by commentators from within the geography education community at the time, there are also many positive indicators and exciting changes (the new GCSE first piloted in 2003, the Action Plan for Geography, curricular review at Key Stage 3). This said, it is clear that there is little room for complacency: as the options available to school pupils diversify, geography will have to capture the energies and interests of young people. A secure future for geography in school education rests, then, at least in part, on understanding what young people need from and value in their education, and the role they see for geography in this.

What do we know about young people's conceptions of geography?

Geography compares poorly to many other subjects in terms of the attention paid by researchers to pupils' experiences and views (Lord, 2003). Over the past decade a number of studies have addressed this gap, although there is clearly need for further work of this kind, as discussed in the concluding part. Table 2.1 provides summary details of these studies. In this chapter, reference is made to studies of young people of secondary school age, although studies of those in primary school (e.g. Catling, 2001) are acknowledged. The discussion below identifies major themes across this research, citing specific studies only where findings are particular to that context. It addresses general perceptions of content, explores issues relating to values, and finally focuses on futures.

What do young people think geography is about?

The studies outlined in Table 2.1 provide a sense of what young people think geography is about. Prominent themes relate to notions of geography as about the world, other places (especially countries), other cultures, landscapes and physical features, people-environment relationships, and natural hazards (especially earthquakes and volcanoes) in particular. Strong associations between the subject and map work are also apparent. While these themes may resonate with many readers' sense of the subject or memories of their own studies, a number of issues are notable for their absence. What are we to make of a lack of reference to childhood and local environments? It was apparent from the Young People's Geographies Project (see Chapter 3) that students were clearly enthused and excited by the prospect of studying geography in relation to their own lives and those of other young people. However it was also clear that this kind of geography was quite unfamiliar to and unexpected by many of the young people involved.

Table 2.1 Overview of recent studies of young people's conceptions of geography

Reference	Methods	Sample	Further details
Dowgill (1998)	Interviews and learning diaries completed by pupils	Two geography classes over 3 years of Key Stage 3 (11–14 years)	Focuses on conceptions and experiences of geography and learning geography; phenomenographic approach to analysis
Adey and Biddulph (2001)/ Biddulph and Adey (2003, 2004)	Written survey, followed by interviews	Initial survey of 1,400 Year 9 pupils from 10 schools across England; subsample interviewed in Year 11; interviews with 6 Year 8 pupils from each of 12 schools across England	Focuses on conceptions and experiences of school geography and history, and subject choice; mainly quantitative frequency analysis
Lam and Lai (2003)	One-off interviews	12 students aged 11–14 from 6 secondary schools in Hong Kong	Pupils presented with series of situations and asked to comment whether and how they are related to geography; qualitative grounded coding analysis, some frequency counts
Norman and Harrison (2004)	Written survey	~400 Year 9 (13–14 years) pupils in Brighton and Hove area (Southern England)	Likes and dislikes in geography, associated keywords, uses of the subject; frequency count analysis
Hopwood (2004)/ Hopwood et al. (2005)	Survey, poster drawing, interviews, classroom observation	2 Year 9 classes in 1 English secondary school	Conceptions, definitions of geography, nature of geographical knowledge, nature of subject conceptions; mixture of quantitative and holistic qualitative analysis
Hopwood (2007a, 2007b, 2008, 2009)	Repeat interviews, classroom observation, photography, concept mapping	6 Year 9 pupils, 2 each from 3 English secondary schools	Details of subject conceptions, relevance and value of geography, links between conceptions and classroom experiences; grounded and thematic qualitative analysis
Ipsos MORI/GA (2009)	Interviews	598 interviews with 11–14 year olds across England	Issues children think are important to them (local area, globally), what they learn at school in relation to these issues, role of geography; frequency counts and analysis by class, location, age

In 2009 Ipsos MORI undertook a poll on behalf of the Geographical Association (Ipsos MORI/GA, 2009; see Table 2.1). This is distinct from many of the other studies because it was not focused on geography education *per se*, but on the issues which young people think are important. When asked about issues affecting the area which they live, the most common response was crime and anti-social behaviour (61 per cent), followed by the economy and jobs (37 per cent), with environment and climate change ranking third (14 per cent). When asked what they thought the important issues affecting the world are, the results were as follows: crime and anti-social behaviour (45 per cent), war and terrorism (44 per cent), economy and jobs (41 per cent), environment and climate change (34 per cent) and poverty and hunger (32 per cent). However none of these themes was mentioned as having been learnt or discussed at school by the majority of respondents: most students' experiences of learning at school do not resonate with the issues they think the most important.

The same survey revealed that where students do feel these kinds of issues have been discussed, they are most likely to name geography as the context for having done so, and as a subject in which they would expect to learn about these issues. OfSTED's (2008) report suggested that the global dimension remains underdeveloped in geography education in the majority of schools, with inadequate support given to students in understanding links between themselves and global citizenship, human rights and sustainable development. The MORI poll found that 93 per cent of young people aged 11 to 14 think it is at least fairly important to learn about issues affecting people's lives in different parts of the world, with nearly half thinking this very important. However, over half thought that there is not enough time spent on learning about the wider world in school.

Given the number of reform initiatives undertaken over the past few years, the situation may not be as dire as the OfSTED report suggests. However it is clear that while students are looking to geography as a source of learning about the issues which are most important to them, the subject has historically failed and to a certain extent still fails them in this regard.

How do young people conceive the relationship between geography education and values?

Most of the studies also generated evidence regarding pupils' views as to the nature of geographical knowledge, for example, whether the subject is based on facts or involves considering opinions, whether they are right and wrong answers in geography, and whether a particular value stance is associated with the subject. Some of the students responding to Norman and Harrison's (2004) survey considered geography to be a 'very green subject' (p. 14), a view mirrored by several students in Hopwood's (2004) work, by one of the six young people (Lisa) in Hopwood's (2007a, 2008) study, and a minority of students in Dowgill's (1998) research.

These findings are particularly worthy of attention given ongoing debates among the geography education community about the role of values in geographic education (see Morgan, 2003; Morgan and Lambert, 2005; Hopwood, 2008). Some argue the need to challenge an apparently widespread view that the purpose of geography is to promote an environmental ethic (Lidstone and Gerber, 1998), concerned about greenwashing (Harrison, 2002) or indoctrination (Marsden, 1997). Others favour a more committed approach (Fien, 1996). What the studies cited above show is that the green, moralistic, or even indoctrinatory nature of geography education or otherwise is not simply determined at a curricular level, nor by particular teachers and their practices in the classroom. Consistent with the principles of the new social studies of childhood, they point to an active role played by young people in constructing their own sense of the subject.

Young people, geography and the[ir] future

Geography education, young people and the future intersect in at least three ways. One relates to the ways in which young people think geography involves learning about the future, another to young people's views on what geography education contributes to their own futures, and a third concerns the role of young people in shaping the future of geography education. Each of these will now be discussed in turn.

The future in geography education

That geography education should help students think and learn about the future is a common argument expressed in research literature, curriculum documents and professional- or practice-oriented texts. For example, Hicks (1998) argues the importance of a futures dimension in teaching and learning about sustainable development in geography, and 'Futures' was one of five concepts underpinning the pilot GCSE geography launched in 2003 (Westaway and Rawling, 2003). The GA's *Global Dimension* project also aims, among other things, to help teachers provide opportunities for pupils to envision possible, probable and alternative futures in relation to sustainable development.

Issues relating to learning about the future have not generally been addressed explicitly in studies of young people's conceptions of geography. However there is an implicit sense that students are describing the subject as being about the world as it is or how it came to be, more than how it might be. There are some suggestions of future-oriented thinking in terms of predicting climate change or natural disasters, but in general the emphasis does not reflect the strength of the futures theme in adult-framed discussions. Some exceptions to this are evident, for example, small number of students in Dowgill's (1998) study who expressed an ' idealistic conception' focused on present and future impacts of people and nature with a view to changing behaviour and securing a particular kind of future. This has parallels with a reconstructionist or radical ideology (Rawling, 2001) in which geography education is seen as an agent for future change.

In Hopwood's more recent study (Hopwood, 2007b, 2009; Rickinson et al., 2009) a particularly interesting case emerged with respect to one of the participating pupils, Bart. He felt strongly that school geography does not involve studying or thinking about the future, believing that the future is simply too unpredictable to enable any kind of firm knowledge. His sense of geography is not one of imagining possibilities, but seeking certainty of understanding. He found classroom activities based on the future to be irrelevant to the subject, disengaging from particular tasks or reframing them to be about the past or present. Bart's classmate Lisa described many aspects of school geography as being about what might happen, embracing uncertainty is something which can itself be a focus of geographical study.

Sara described geography as a subject that can be applied to help people and which thus plays an active role in creating alternative futures, for example, helping to reduce poverty or alleviate long-term risk from natural hazards. Ryan had different views again. He thought school geography makes valuable contributions to making the world a better place by educating people so that they can then make beneficial contributions themselves through research or particular kinds of employment. In his view geography education is intimately related to global development through the potential for people to understand things differently and use this understanding as a basis for changing the world. Ryan and Sara's concepts of the future are based less on notions of uncertainty and more on the idea of the future as being malleable or changeable.

As with key content areas, and issues concerning values in the subject, current research tells us that young people's conceptions of the relationship between geography and the future are not a straightforward reflection of views espoused by adults: they are actively constructed by young people themselves. The different views highlighted among the six students studied by Hopwood reinforce the principle outlined earlier that suggests we treat childhood as a multiple rather than singular phenomenon.

Geography education and young people's futures

The uses of school geography referred to across several of the studies listed in Table 2.1 included working in the travel tourism industry or being a meteorologist, repeating findings from Rickinson et al.'s (2009) collaborative analysis. Young people thus often conceive school geography in ways that are resonant with Rawling's (2001) description of utilitarian or vocationalist ideologies. Such ideas focus on the subject playing a role in future employment based on factual information or skills. In Hopwood's (2007b, 2009) research some different ideas emerged. Lisa, for example, felt that geography helped her learn how to lead an environmentally friendly life, offering applications of geographical knowledge that she could use in her life from the present through to the future. Ryan felt that geography education not only benefited the world generally (as described above) but also that it played a crucial role in the development of his own future. He photographed his geography teacher in order to emphasize the point that she was helping him to develop skills and abilities that he would use when he was older, in work.

We may recall David Bell's comments, given prominent status in OfSTED's (2008) report:

> It is important that the citizens of tomorrow understand the management of risk, appreciate diversity, are aware of environmental issues, promote sustainability and respect human rights and social inclusion. If the aspiration of schools is to create pupils who are active and well rounded citizens, there is no more relevant subject than geography. (p. 7)

Some studies suggest that young people view geography education as teaching them to respect other opinions, seek to understand alternative points of view, and think through decisions and actions with a view to social equity and justice (Biddulph and Adey, 2004; Hopwood, 2008). Interestingly while pupils seemed to see these issues as part of their learning of geography, they rarely articulated a sense that this was about the production of a future global citizenry – for young people these issues are much more grounded in the present.

Young people and the future of geography education (research)

If similar studies were to be repeated in five years' time, which themes would remain strong? Which might become less apparent? Which would we want to see making an appearance? These questions certainly require the thoughtful attention of geography educators, academic researchers and curriculum makers. However we must face up to the fact that conceptions of geography education cannot be straightforwardly (re)shaped by simply changing what is taught or how. Young people lie at the heart of geography's future and must play a role in shaping it (as in joint processes of curriculum reform of the kind exemplified in the Young People's Geographies Project).

It is all too easy for debate about the nature and preferred future of geography education to ignore the crucial role played by young people. Statements by ministers, curriculum texts and even explicit comments made by teachers to students are not mechanically reproduced in the minds of young people. As Rickinson et al. (2009, ch. 6) point out, seductive notions such as 'relevance' often turn out to be slippery and complex, especially when one replaces adult assumptions with evidence of how young people experience and construct their worlds. The next step in discussions of the relationship between geography as a school subject, values and young people surely rests on better understanding the processes through which perceptions of the subject are constructed among learners and the impact that these perceptions have on learning, young people's values, their behaviour towards each other and their actions in their local and global contexts.

Hopwood (2007b) explores reasons why teachers may or may not seek to influence their students' conceptions of geography, mindful (as the new social studies of childhood tells us) that this influence is finite and that young people have their own active role to play in constructing their own views, lives and futures. That discussion merely pinpoints the starting place for a much-needed debate among the geography education community around the ways that it conceives the outcomes of geography education, its control over them and the role of young people in shaping their own geographical learning.

The MORI poll (Ipsos MORI/GA, 2009) is distinctive among the studies discussed here in the explicit attention it pays to variation in young people's views according to age, socio-economic status and geographical location. In this respect it is the only one which takes seriously the principle that childhood should be understood as a variable of social analysis that cannot be divorced from class, ethnicity, gender, and so on. These issues clearly require further empirical attention. Research on young people's conceptions of geography should not be seen as an obscure outpost within the field of geography education, subservient to core enquiry focused on teaching, learning or curriculum development. It is about all of these. And all of these issues require a deeper understanding of young people, their views, the influence conceptions have on learning, and the role that young people might potentially play in reshaping geography education and indeed future geographies of the world.

Acknowledgements

The author wishes to thank Graham Corney, Ann Childs, Anna Pendry and Geoffrey Walford for their support during his research, which was funded by the Economic and Social Research Council. He also owes a great deal to the ongoing support of the GEReCo group.

References

Adey, K. and Biddulph, M. (2001), 'The influence of pupil perceptions on subject choice at 14+ in geography and history', *Educational Studies*, 27, 439–450.

Biddulph, M. and Adey, K. (2003), 'Perceptions v. reality: pupils' experiences of learning history and geography at Key Stage 4', *The Curriculum Journal*, 14, 291–303.

—. (2004), 'Pupil perceptions of effective teaching and subject relevance in history and geography at key stage 3', *Research in Education*, 71, 1–8.

Bruner, J. (1960), *The Process of Education*. Cambridge, MA: Harvard University Press.

Buehl, M. M. and Alexander, P. A. (2005), 'Motivation and performance differences in students' domain-specific epistemological belief profiles', *American Educational Research Journal*, 42, 697–726.

Butt, G. (2002), *Reflective Teaching of Geography 11–18*. London: Continuum.

Carswell, R. (1970), 'Evaluation of affective learning in geographical education', in D. Kurfman (ed.), *Evaluation in Geographic Education*. Belmont, CA: Fearon Publishers, pp. 109–127.

Catling, S. (2001), 'English primary schoolchildren's definitions of geography', *International Research in Geographical and Environmental Education*, 10, 363–378.

Davies, P., Durbin, C., Clarke, J. and Dale, J. (2004), 'Developing students' conceptions of quality in geography', *The Curriculum Journal*, 15, 19–34.

Dowgill, P. (1998), 'Pupils' conceptions of learning geography under the National Curriculum'. Unpublished Ph.D. thesis, University of London, London.

Fien, J. (1996), 'Teaching to care: a case for commitment to teaching environmental values', in R. Gerber and J. Lidstone (eds), *Developments and Directions in Geographical Education*. Clevedon: Channel View Publications, pp. 77–92.

GA (2009), *A Different View: A Manifesto from the Geographical Association*. Sheffield: Geographical Association.

Giddens, A. (1979), *The Central Problems of Sociological Method*. London: Macmillan Press.

Hardman, C. (1973), 'Can there be an anthropology of children?' *Journal of the Anthropological Society of Oxford*, 4, 85–89.

Harrison, D. (2002), 'Children "being brainwashed" by new green geography lessons', *Sunday Telegraph*, 24 November.

Hicks, D. (1998), 'A geography for the future', *Teaching Geography*, 23, 168–173.

Hopwood, N. (2004), 'Pupils' conceptions of geography: towards an improved understanding', *International Research in Geographical and Environmental Education*, 13, 348–361.

—. (2007a), 'Environmental education: pupils' perspectives on classroom experience', *Environmental Education Research*, 13, 453–465.

—. (2007b), 'Pupils' conceptions of geography: issues for debate', in J. Halocha and A. Powell (eds), *Conceptualising Geographical Education*. London: International Geographical Union Commission for Geographical Education/Institute of Education, pp. 49–65.

—. (2008), 'Values in geographic education: the challenge of attending to learners' perspectives', *Oxford Review of Education*, 34, 589–608.

—. (2009), 'UK high school pupils' conceptions of geography: research findings and methodological implications', *International Research in Geographical and Environmental Education*, 18, 185–197.

Hopwood, N., Courtley-Green, C. and Chambers, T. (2005), 'Year 9 students' conceptions of geography', *Teaching Geography*, 30, 91–93.

Ipsos MORI/GA (2009), *World Issues Survey*. Available at http://www.geography.org.uk/aboutus/adifferentview/worldissuessurvey/ (accessed 3 September 2009).

Lam, C.-C. and Lai, E. (2003), '"What is geography?" In the eyes of junior secondary students in Hong Kong', *International Research in Geographical and Environmental Education*, 12, 199–218.

Leat, D. (2000), 'The importance of "big concepts" and skills in learning geography', in C. Fisher and T. Binns (eds), *Issues in Teaching Geography*. London: Routledge/Falmer, pp. 137–151.

Lidstone, J. and Gerber, R. (1998), 'Theoretical underpinnings of geographical and environmental education research: hiding our light under various bushels', *International Research in Geographical and Environmental Education*, 7, 87–89.

Lord, P. (2003), *Pupils' Experiences and Perspectives of the National Curriculum: Updating the Research Review 2002–2003*. London: QCA.

Marley, D. (2008), 'Geography is too out of this world', *Times Educational Supplement*, 18 January.

Marsden, B. (1997), 'On taking the geography out of geographical education: some historical pointers', *Geography*, 82, 241–252.

Morgan, J. (2003), 'Comment', *Geography*, 88, 151.

Morgan, J. and Lambert, D. (2005), *Geography: Teaching School Subjects 11–19*. London: Routledge.

Norman, M. and Harrison, L. (2004), 'Year 9 students' perceptions of school geography', *Teaching Geography*, 29, 11–15.

OfSTED (2008), *Geography in Schools: Changing Practice*. London: OfSTED.

Prout, A. and James, A. (1990), 'A new paradigm for the sociology of childhood? Provenance, promise and problems', in A. James and A. Prout (eds), *Constructing and Reconstructing Childhood: Contemporary Issues in the Sociological Study of Childhood*. London: Falmer, pp. 7–33.

QCA (2008), *The National Curriculum KS3: Geography*. QCA. Available at www.curriculum.qca.org. uk/ (accessed June 2009).

Rawling, E. (2000), 'Ideology, politics and curriculum change: reflections on school geography 2000', *Geography*, 85, 209–220.

—. (2001), *Changing the Subject: The Impact of National Policy on School Geography 1980–2000*. Sheffield: Geographical Association.

Rickinson, M. (1999), 'People-environment issues in the geography classroom: towards an understanding of students' experiences', *International Research in Geographical and Environmental Education*, 8, 120–139.

Rickinson, M., Lundholm, C. and Hopwood, N. (2009), *Environmental Learning: Insights from Research into the Student Experience*. London: Springer Press.

Rudduck, J., Day, J. and Wallace, C. (1997), 'Students' perspectives on school improvement', in A. Hargreaves (ed.), *Rethinking Educational Change with Heart and Mind: 1997 ASCD Yearbook*. Alexandria, VA: Association for Supervision and Curriculum Development, pp. 73–91.

Schoenfeld, A. H. (2004), 'Multiple learning communities: students, teachers, instructional designers, and researchers', *Journal of Curriculum Studies*, 36, 237–255.

Stott, T., Howard, R. and Linnett, R. (1997), 'What influences students' choice of geography at GCSE?' *Teaching Geography*, 22, 192–193.

Westaway, J. and Rawling, E. (2003), 'A new look for GCSE geography?' *Teaching Geography*, 28, 60–63.

Woodhouse, M. (1984), 'Geographers: to be or not to be?' *Geographical Education*, 4, 238–247.

Young, M. F. D. (ed.) (1971), *Knowledge and Control: New Directions for the Sociology of Education*. London: Routledge and Kegan Paul.

Young People's Geographies: Implications for Secondary School Geography

3

Mary Biddulph

Changes in the subject: 'Young People's Geographies'

Young people's geographies, youth geographies and children's geographies constitute significant fields of research conducted by academic geographers trying to unravel the complex geographical lives of young people. Geographers have, since the 1970s been working to develop a more informed understanding of the particularities of the geographical lives of young people and how these connect, or otherwise, to changing global context (Aitken, 2001). However, these geographical lives are largely neglected geographies in the UK's school curriculum, a curriculum that in the past 20 years has been subject to increasing regulation and centralization (Lambert and Morgan, 2010) and one where the concept of 'curriculum' has been interpreted along technological and industrial lines. In the United Kingdom currently the school curriculum is forcibly represented as 'curriculum as product' whereby the curriculum is constructed beyond the remit of the classroom, is structured around lists of behavioural objectives and success is judged in term of allegedly measurable outcomes (Smith, 1996, 2000). The curriculum is in effect 'teacher-proofed' as teachers assume the role of technicians who 'deliver' a preordained curriculum, and students assume somewhat passive roles as 'receivers' whose views, perspectives and life experiences are largely ignored (ibid.).

That these lives and experiences should inform the school curriculum is subject to debate. Writers such as Standish (2006) and Whelan (2007) argue that 'such an approach to curriculum development is fundamentally anti-intellectual and reduces not only the content of what is taught, but also young people's interest in it' (Firth and Biddulph, 2009b, p. 32). However, the notion of actively engaging young people in the processes that shape their educational experiences would seem to have some merit. If, in a fast changing world interconnected lives are subject to the ongoing forces of rapid globalization – and if we see education as having a role to play in enabling young people to develop the critical insights and understandings necessary to support not just their role as young citizens in the present, but also their participation as global citizens in the future – then it would seem sensible and desirable to develop this participatory capacity via their learning experiences in school.

This chapter opens up discussions around the notion of young people's *participation*, with a specific focus on the school geography curriculum. The aim is to begin to consider the means by which young peoples' lived experiences can contribute to participatory practices within school geography and through these to develop the confidence and motivation to participate in and contribute to wider societal debates as they grow up. This exploration of participation is structured around three key themes: young people's engagement through discursive practices, young people's geographies and what these mean, and finally, practical participatory processes which facilitate young people's access to curriculum making in school geography. How these themes interconnect to enable young people to better locate themselves (their identities, their concerns, their aspirations) within their own geographical learning is of central importance.

The discussion is informed by the work of a curriculum development project, titled 'Young People's Geographies' (YPG). The project was conceptualized as an opportunity to provide more radical spaces for dialogue between students, their teachers and recent developments in the subject discipline. The metaphor for participation in the project by both teachers and students was 'conversation': whereby teachers, through conversation, would collaborate with their students, drawing on their own lived geographies, to develop school geography together.

Engagement and the geography curriculum: tokenism or democratic opportunities?

Listening to young people's perspectives is now much more embedded in UK government-sponsored policy and development since the publication (1989), and subsequent ratification in the United Kingdom (1994), of the United Nations Convention on the Rights of the Child. Articles 12 and 13, in particular, require that children have the right to express their views freely in matters affecting them in ways most appropriate to them, including their education and schooling.

Following the 1989 Children Act (DfES, 1989) there have been multiple policy initiatives aimed at implementing the spirit and intentions of the United Nation's articles. These include The Education Act of 2002 (DfES, 2002) requiring schools and local authorities to consult with students about decisions affecting them; the publication in 2003 of the UK government's Green Paper 'Every Child Matters' (DfES, 2003) calling for children to have a say in policy development as it relates to their needs; The Children's Act of 2004 (DfES, 2004) creating a 'Children's Commissioner' for England, and the inclusion in the School Inspection Framework of compulsory consultation with students about their school experiences (OfSTED, 2005).

These developments indicate the degree to which the UK government and children's agencies in the United Kingdom are increasingly keen to hear young people's perspectives. Bragg (2007) however, argues that the more radical rights-based agenda established in the Articles is frequently utilized for other ends when political policy is at play and that in a policy context consultation with young people is frequently utilized to serve other agendas, such as institutional betterment and accountability (p. 14). This is a view echoed by others. Heart (1997), Matthews et al. (2000) and Lundy (2007), agree that consultation processes with young people are often tokenistic and inappropriately linked to agendas such as school improvement rather than 'existing as a public good in and of itself' (Thomson and Gunter, 2006, p. 842).

Fielding and Rudduck (2002) suggest that in schools a more genuine engagement of young people, that take seriously their concerns, perspectives and opinions can have a significant impact on policy developments and institutional change. This is especially the case when encapsulated in a school ethos which clearly acknowledges and values not just some students' 'voices' but the full participation of all students in the life of the school. They expand this idea of engagement and link it not just to the 'here and now' of school life, but to the establishment of ideals and principles by which young people can live in the future; if, as a society, we are serious about a democratic future then, they contend, schools need to afford young people the experience of living democratically now: 'it's not enough to teach about democracy; you have to enact it in the daily exchanges of life in school' (p. 2).

While students' voice and consulting with students is high on the accountability and policy agendas it seems ironic that their perspectives on a key area of their daily school experience – the curriculum – are rarely considered. Yet students have a great deal to say about their curriculum experiences in geography and in other subjects (see Hopwood's chapter and Biddulph and Adey, 2003; Biddulph and Adey, 2004) and they evidently possess thoughtful and informed opinions about the curriculum. However, students seldom have any opportunity to actively and creatively contribute to curriculum making processes:

> While the curriculum supposedly exists to serve the needs of learners, their preferences, if sought at all, are marginalised and their voices mostly silent in curriculum making. (Brooker and MacDonald, 1999, p. 84)

Developments at a disciplinary level may help us to consider how young peoples' geographies can provide opportunities for young people to participate in making the curriculum and in doing so support both the future development of more relevant school geography as well as more democratic exchanges between students and their teachers.

Young people's geographies: what are they?

Research into young people's geographies focuses on how young people's perceptions, experiences and life opportunities are formed by their social, cultural and spatial existences:

> Study of the geographies of children and young people range widely in subject matter, methodology and philosophical approach . . . Much of the work relates to

> families, communities, places, spaces, environments and institutions and the ways those contexts mould young lives. Attention is given to the diverse experiences of young people at various scales, to the way age intersects with other important identities such as gender, disability and ethnicity, and to young people as social agents in their own right, with their own lives, needs and desires. It recognises that young people do not passively accept adult productions of domestic, institutional, urban and rural space and the ways in which such adult definitions and structures are resisted and subverted. (Firth and Biddulph, 2009a, p. 15)

The impact of globalization and its social, economic and cultural consequences is an ongoing research theme in young people's geographies. Dolby and Rizvi (2008) dig deep into the global cultural, social and spatial shifts that are influencing and being influenced by young people's lives, while Gillis (2008) suggests that:

> In the past thirty years the processes associated with globalisation have produced more diversity than similarity. We now live in an era when modernity takes many forms and childhood comes in many varieties. Instead of declining, child labour has increased in many underdeveloped countries; . . . ever-larger generations of unschooled street children engage in crime and violence; child prostitution is on the rise and child soldiers have become common place in Africa and Asia. (p. 322)

What Gilles articulates here is the macro-scale impact of globalization on young people's lives in the global South. However, this conception of division and diversity is also echoed on a more local scale by others such as Nayak (2003a, 2003b, 2004), Skelton and Valentine (1998), Aitken (2001) and Jeffrey and Dyson (2008) all of whom articulate the role globalization processes play in shaping young people's daily socio-cultural existences. Writing about Kabir, a Scottish, Muslim university student, Hopkins (2008) captures the ongoing connections between one young man's everyday practices and the global forces that shape them:

> Kabir's engagement with Scottishness and global issues are connected with his religious identity. But his personal identities and political futures are rooted in the lived and material cultures that are positioned close by: his sense of self and community are critically shaped by the scales 'closest in'. (p. 79)

Such accounts successfully bring into focus the very personal geographies of young people and how these geographies are shaped by the subtle interplay of complex local-global forces. They also suggest the importance of understanding young people as members of, and contributors to, wider networks and to appreciate that they are subject to many layers of influences – such as their families, their communities (Punch, 2007) and other structures and institutions. The implication here is that it is impossible and undesirable to divorce young people and their geographical lives from the lives of adults and organizations that directly and indirectly exert influence over them.

The multiple geographies described above highlight shifts at a disciplinary level to take greater account of the hitherto marginalized voices/lives of young people. This process of 'account taking' can also lead to a more informed understanding of other kinds of geographies such as political geographies, social geographies or economic geographies, as young people become integral to subject discourses. The question however is: 'If young people's geographies have something to say to the wider discipline then what do they have to say to school geography?' The next section explores the potential for a more rigorous relationship between young people's geographies and young people's participation in making the geography curriculum.

Participatory processes: a framework for curriculum conversations

The ambitions of the Young People's Geographies Project was to create the metaphorical space in which to establish a new culture of curriculum dialogue between teachers and students and to knit together an aspect of the subject discipline (young people's geographies) with dialogic pedagogies (process) to bring about a more collaborative form of curriculum making (engagement). Fielding (2009) explores space as a means of engendering a greater desire in young people to participate, arguing that failure to create and activate public spaces in schools will leave young people without either the skills or the motivation to be publicly active in their future adult lives.

Curriculum conversations and YPG

The creation of just such an active 'public' space in the YPG project was centred on eight key principles (see Figure 3.1) which collectively shaped a framework for open dialogue. The principles create the metaphorical space referred to above, for conversation, and in doing so explicitly challenge the prevailing notion of disciplinary knowledge in school geography; the framework shifts the emphasis from preordained knowledge authorized by adults to young people's own knowledge, what Thomson (2002) calls their '*virtual school bags*' (p. 7).

These eight key principles serve to provide a counter balance to the kinds of knowledges currently valued by the geography curriculum. Within the context of student participation and engagement this counterbalance is necessary, for as Thomson and Hall (2008) argue, not only do schools fail to take account of young people's virtual school bags but too often '*school only draws on the contents of some young people's school bags, those whose resources match those required in the game of education*' (p. 89). What is called for is not just the need to recognize and use students owned knowledge:

> Rather, the object is to also change what counts as important knowledge so that the dominant forms of knowledge are decentred and more inclusive models of knowing – and being – are recognised and taught to all. (p. 89)

The principles explicitly seek to recognize and value all contributions to the curriculum making process and for students, with their teachers, to share, in democratic ways, both their own and their owned knowledges as well as disciplinary knowledge via creative processes.

Students' lived geographies: using their own experiences, ideas and issues and the ability of students with their teachers to turn these into a focus for curricula

Conversation: using conversation between teacher-student, student-student and teacher-teacher as a basis for curricula possibilities and knowledge building

Ideas diversity and improvement: the importance of ideas to knowledge building, recognizing the diversity of ideas that can be contributed by students and teachers and that ideas are improvable

Disciplinary knowledge: its use as a resource for curriculum development and knowledge building

Taking responsibility for the advancement of knowledge and enquiry (epistemic agency): students have agency and share responsibility for contributing regularly to advance their work

Knowledge building, community knowledge and collective responsibility: ideas provided by individuals should contribute to the collective goal and are of value to others

Democratizing knowledge: all students contribute to discussion and development of knowledge without overdominating and valuing others' contribution

Embedded and transformative assessment: the ability of students to review and evaluate progress being made within the investigation/enquiry
(Firth and Biddulph, 2009a, 2009b)

Figure 3.1 Eight key principles for student participation in curriculum making

However, it cannot be assumed that students will have the language or the dispositions with which to talk about the curriculum (Rudduck and Flutter, 2000); curriculum conversations need to happen on students' terms in order to avoid tokenism and to help them develop the necessary participatory understanding. In Heart's (1997) ladder of participation, conversation between adults and children is an implied part of the engagement process, likewise Scardamalia and Bereiter's (2003) principles explicitly refer to 'conversation' in the knowledge creation process. 'Conversation' is a useful metaphor for describing a process of participation, as conversation '*enables individuals to genuinely share, argue, reflect, reconsider and deliberate*' (Lambert, 1997, p. 6; emphasis added) and it implies a more equal exchange of ideas and perspectives. It is also a means through which young people can engage, at their own level. Conversation implies more open-ended exchanges where individuals have the opportunity to explore their own and other peoples ideas in order to develop the capacity to understand others and to deal creatively with the unpredictable (Fielding, 2009); as a model for both how to operate now and to develop conversational skills in young people this seems highly desirable.

Project experience demonstrates that teachers operationalize the eight principles in ways suitable to the context of their schools and students. The examples that follow demonstrate how the principles can provide an inclusive framework, one that is subject to modification by students and teachers.

Vignette 1

In one participating school the new head of department drew on the Philosophy for Children (P4C) approach with his Year 9 students (13 years old). Via this conversational methodology students were encouraged to generate their own geographical questions to pursue. After some negotiation, between the teacher and the students and between the students themselves, the class agreed that the focus for their work would be the school catchment area and different perceptions/images of the places students came from. This geography emerged from concerns the students had about the stereotypical impressions they themselves had of certain areas within the school's catchment. Having established an overarching theme subgroups opted to investigate particular matters of concern to them. One group conducted interviews with other students around school on catchment area perceptions trying to establish sources of perceptions as well as counteract them. Another made a 'geography video' based upon their investigations into the location and types of graffiti in certain places and consider the implications of this for young people's social use of spaces. Students worked in small groups using a range of appropriate technologies to support their learning.

Vignette 2

Three schools in the same city collaborated on the theme of 'My Place'. This theme emerged from informal conversations with small groups of students which were then shared and agreed with larger groups. Students in each school investigated places of inclusion and exclusion in their own school environment using photographic evidence they collected for themselves. They then collated a series of collages to capture their viewpoints which were then presented to headteachers/principals. The collaboration across schools supported the refinement of project ideas and approaches between teachers, but it also encouraged some, limited conversations between students across schools.

Other kinds of geographies emerged in other participating schools as a consequence of curriculum conversations between students and their teachers. Some students used emotional mapping techniques to capture areas of their locality in which they felt both safe and included, or where they felt were dangerous and excluding. Another included an investigation into the sources of raw material for students' iPods and the implications of exploiting these sources for the people who lived in distant locations (see Cook et al., 2007a, 2007b).

The way the project has been conceived to give both students and teachers a voice would have something to offer a range of contexts. The energy and creativity that has been released by doing this has been simply amazing to witness (Hopwood, 2007, p. 13)

As these examples suggest students *with* their teachers can contribute to a more collaborative and creative process of curriculum making, while young people and their lived geographies can actively be part of this process. Rudduck and Flutter (2000) contend that 'students do not have much to say about the curriculum' (p. 76), but appropriate participatory frameworks underpinned by a participatory ethos mean that students can reveal what they understand about their own geographies and they can also be creative in how they choose to make sense of these. It would seem that creating conversation spaces has the potential to engage the enthusiasm and commitment of young people to participate in matters of concern to them.

Curriculum conversations: some dilemmas for teachers and students

If young people are to be enabled and encouraged to participate in school-based decision-making then the work of the YPG project suggests that the traditional role of geography teachers and students also has to change, but this is not without its difficulties:

> The open-ended nature of the project itself, and particular activities within it, presented challenges for many students and also some teachers. (Hopwood, 2007, p. 5; emphasis added)

Participating teachers '*reported some difficulties in persuading students that they might have a say in the curriculum decisions. They were constrained not only by traditional teacher roles but limitations in appropriate language to engage in such discussions*' (Davidson, 2009, p. 4).

In one school the geography teacher admitted her own initial reservations in allowing students real freedom in deciding what and how to learn:

> The involvement of students in planning YPG was my main dilemma when starting out as I had to give up control in the classroom and pass it on to thirty-two Y8 (age 12) students who have about a million ideas each regarding what they wanted to study. (Participating teacher in Firth et al., 2010; emphasis added)

The negotiation process in this school also revealed that when confronted with an open agenda students tend to revert to a stereotypical conception of the discipline – 'the study of different countries around the world'. In some respects there is nothing wrong with this, but it highlights the important role that teachers also have to play in any curriculum negotiation process. In this school it was only after sharing ideas and negotiating barriers that a collective agreement was reached; the students elected to draw on research from a local university on the carbon footprints of different foods and recipes. The to-ing and fro-ing of conversation coupled with research in the discipline led to the construction of types of geographies that neither the students nor the teachers had previously considered.

Some teachers handed over a significant degree of responsibility to students, seeing their own role more as a facilitator rather than the 'fount of knowledge'. This kind of pedagogical shift does not however permit an 'anything goes' approach to geographical learning. Here the role of subject expertise and understanding is extremely important, a role that the students themselves recognize:

> We had the actual idea, the teacher helped make it more educational. (Participating student in Hopwood, 2007; emphasis added)

> *We couldn't just say anything, it had to be related to geography; we needed*
> *someone to guide us and that's what the teacher did and that made it better.*
> (Participating student in Hopwood, 2007; emphasis added)

Students are very clear that they needed their geography teachers, as both subject experts to guide and challenge them to think *about* the subject and *with* the subject, and as expert teachers who understand how to enable young people to access new and complex ideas.

Curriculum conversations: some curriculum dilemmas

In addition to changing roles teachers also need to think differently about how to construct the curriculum. A positivist framework for curriculum planning is all pervasive in UK schools at present (Roberts, 2010). Driven by powerful accountability and outcome agendas exemplified by demanding inspection regimes and the publication of examination league tables, such a framework has no real space for students to contribute to the process of curriculum making or to hone their dispositions for future societal participation. Under such a technical model the notion of engaging students in taking responsibility for what and how they learn can be potentially compromised. As one YPG teacher stated:

> *You can only give them a certain amount of choice obviously. I have got a head*
> *of department and people on my back to make sure I always have learning*
> *intentions.* (Participating teacher in Davidson, 2009, p. 6)

Such an approach to curriculum results in students being taught a particular view of the world without recourse to question how that view was constructed, who constructed it and what was their motivation (Whitty, 1985). YPG requires a different view of curriculum as an educational construct. It is diametrically opposed to the traditional transition models of the curriculum that reflect and '*accord with the values/beliefs of dominant groups*' (Whitty, 1985, p. 8; emphasis added) and is in favour of inclusive curricula that value difference and engage students in what Greene (in Flinders and Thornton, 2004, p. 121) describes as 'an interior journey' that is more relevant to students' lives.

The idea of the curriculum as an interior journey links with the process model of curriculum making whereby the curriculum is an active process of constant interactions between student, teacher and knowledge. Conversation is at the heart of the process model and outcomes are linked to both thinking and action (Smith, 1996, 2000). This idea of 'action' implies that curricula experiences do not simply serve to structure a series of learning events, but that they provide students with opportunities to construct and reconstruct knowledge and develop insights, and dispositions to *do* something with learning; to question prevailing world views (Roberts, 2010).

In some YPG schools the teacher-student conversations provided more of a platform of how to reconstitute the existing curriculum. The 'interior journey' of the students was controlled by the teacher, as the positivist outcome-driven model of curriculum proved difficult to relinquish. As one teacher commented:

> I think it is still teacher led, but not in the sort of rigid conventional sense where teachers come up with all the ideas, do all the preparation and students just do what they're told to do. (Hopwood, 2007, p. 12; emphasis added)

Some teachers saw the project as a vehicle for engaging students in more relevant geographies and many informally reported significant increases in student motivation during project-type lessons where students were overwhelmingly enthusiastic about what they were doing. The difficulty here is that relevance and motivation does not necessarily equate with more significant or more sophisticated conceptual development and so as well as engaging students in the curriculum planning process geography teachers have to exercise significant subject expertise if they are to help students connect their own geographies with other facets of the discipline:

> It's not just motivation, but it helps them engage with the content . . . We have done different cases of things in the world and you come back at the end with debrief and plenaries and help people make links back to more straightforward geography. It gives them a vehicle to see things a bit differently. A lot of kids struggle to understand how the different bits of the subject interrelate, but this can give them insight into how it is different bits of geography relate and link into each other. (Hopwood, 2007, p. 8)

Making such connections with young people has the potential to develop a more informed and complex understanding of the world in which they live.

Conclusions

Laura Berman (2009), writing in the *Guardian* newspaper, recently concluded that '*it matters what's on the school curriculum in the sense that it's a signal about the values of the whole society*' (emphasis added). An exclusive and

excluding curriculum that only values certain kinds of knowledge and experience signals to many young people how we, as a society, value them now – as
individuals, as members of diverse communities and as contributors to wider
society. It could be deemed educationally careless to ignore the social and
cultural capital of this significant group whose spatial lives are shaped by
powerful local-global forces; ignoring these geographies runs the risk of alien-
ating significant proportions of young people and of leaving school geography
out of kilter with their needs and interests. Young people's geographies, as
a research paradigm, can tell us a great deal about the lives of young people
in order to support the development of a more relevant and inclusive school
curriculum, but accessing these geographies can only happen with the consent
and participation of young people themselves.

As the work in the YPG project demonstrates, helping young people make
sense of and critically consider their own geographies has the potential to help
them see the connections between the life decisions and choices they make,
the perceptions and misconceptions that they have of 'others' and the potential
they have to influence their own learning. This discussion suggests that such
a connection can be achieved via appropriate dialogic pedagogies which provide both young people and their teachers with the opportunity to collaborate
in the process of curriculum making. The YPG project clearly communicates
the willingness of young people to talk to and with their teachers about their
curriculum experiences and interests they have and the capacity to take seriously their curriculum responsibilities. Combining participatory practices and
disciplinary thinking can and does, despite its challenges, result in geographical learning that young people can have some ownership of; young people
become engaged in the education process, not as passive recipients of centrally
authorized often disjointed ideas, but as individuals with perspectives, experiences and aspirations that can be used creatively to create a challenging and
meaningful school geography curriculum.

And so it *does* matter what is on the curriculum, but it also matters how the
curriculum is constructed. If the school geography curriculum is to fulfil its
potential of contributing something that is educationally worthwhile to the
lives of all young people then the complex realities which shape and influence
young people and the effects these have on what they say, how they say it,
where they say it and to whom they are willing to talk might be the place to
start (Bragg, 2001). Research evidence strongly suggests that unless they are
afforded participatory opportunities then young people are less likely to exercise their participatory rights when they become adults. If we are serious about
the power of democratic living then as a society we can ill afford not to develop

participatory dispositions in young people, both through their school experiences and in other ways.

References

Aitken, S. C. (2001), *Geographies of Young People: Morally Contested Spaces of Identity*. London: Routledge.

Berman, L. (2009), 'Let's talk about sex', *Guardian Newspaper*, 9 December.

Biddulph, M. and Adey, K. (2003), 'Perceptions v. reality: pupils' experiences of learning history and geography at key stage 4', *The Curriculum Journal*, 14, 291–303.

—. (2004), 'Pupil perceptions of effective teaching and subject relevance in history and geography at key stage 3', *Research in Education*, 71, 1–8.

Bragg, S. (2001), 'Taking a joke: learning from the voices we don't want to hear', *Forum*, 43, (2), 70–73.

—. (2007), *Consulting Young People: A Review of the Literature*. A Report for Creative Partnerships. Arts Council England.

Brooker, R. and McDonald, D. (1999), 'Did we hear you: issues of student voice in a curriculum innovation', *Journal of Curriculum Studies*, 31, (1), 83–97.

Cook, I., Evans, J., Griffiths, H., Morris, R. and Wrathmell, S. (2007a), It's more than just what it is': defetishising commodities, expanding fields, mobilising change . . .', *Geoforum*, 38, (6), 1113–1126.

Cook, I., Evans, J., Griffiths, H., Mayblin, L., Payne, B. and Roberts, D. (2007b), 'Made in . . . ? Appreciating the everyday geographies of connected lives', *Teaching Geography*, Summer, 80–83.

Davidson. G. (2009), *Young People's Geographies Project: Evaluation Report 2008/9*. Sheffield: Geographical Association. Available at http://www.youngpeoplesgeographies.co.uk/

Department for Education and Skills (1989), *The Children's Act*. London: HMSO.

—. (2002), *The Education Act*. London: Office for Public Sector Information (OPSI).

—. (2003), *Every Child Matters: Government Green Paper*. Published by The Stationary Office (TSO). Crown copyright.

—. (2004), *The Children's Act*. London: Office for Public Sector Information (OPSI).

Dolby, N. and Rizvi. F. (2008), *Youth Moves: Identities and Education in Global Perspectives*. London: Routledge.

Fielding, M. (2009), 'Communal space, radical education and the demands of republican democracy: reclaiming and renewing our radical traditions'. Unpublished presentation given to Institute of Education, University of London seminar.

Fielding, M. and Ruddock, J. (2002), 'The transformative potential of student voice: confronting the power issues'. Contribution to the symposium: Student Consultation, Community and Democratic Tradition. Paper presented at the Annual Conference of the British Educational research Association, University of Exeter, England, 12–14 September 2002.

Firth, R. and Biddulph, M. (2009a), 'Whose life is it anyway?' in D. Mitchell (ed.) *Living Geography*. Cambridge: Chris Kington Publishing.

—. (2009b), 'Young People's Geographies', *Teaching Geography*, 34, (1), 32–34.

Firth, R., Biddulph, M., Riley, H., Gaunt, I. and Buxton, C. (2010), 'How can young people take an active role in the geography curriculum?' *Teaching Geography*, 35, (2), 49.

Flinders, D. and Thornton, S. (2004), *The Curriculum Studies Reader*, 2nd edition. Routledge. New York.

Gillis, J. (2008), 'Epilogue', in M. Gutman and N. Connick-Smith (eds), *History, Space and the Material Culture of Children*. USA: Rutgers University Press.

Heart, R. (1997), *Children's Participation: The Theory and Practice of Involving Young Citizens in Community Development and Environmental Care*. London: Earthscan.

Hopkins, P. (2008), 'Young, male, Scottish and Muslim: a portrait of Kabir', in C. Jeffrey and J. Dyson (eds), *Telling Young Lives: Portraits of Global Youth*. Philadelphia, PA: Temple.

Hopwood, N. (2007), *Young People's Geographies Evaluators Report*. Sheffield: Geographical Association. Available at http://www.youngpeoplesgeographies.co.uk/

Jeffrey, C. and Dyson, J. (eds) (2008), *Telling Young Lives: Portraits of Global Youth*. Philadelphia, PA: Temple.

Lambert, D. (1997), 'Geography education and citizenship: identity and intercultural communication', in J. Bale and F. Slater (eds), *Reporting Research in Geography Education: Monograph No.5*. Institute of Education, University of London.

Lambert, D. and Morgan, J. (2010), *Teaching Geography 11–18: A Conceptual Approach*. England: Open University Press.

Lundy, L. (2007), 'Voice is not enough: conceptualising Article 12 of the United Nations Convention on the Rights of the Child', *British Education Research Journal*, 33, (6), 927–942.

Matthews, H., Limb, M. and Taylor, M. (2000), 'The street as thirdspace', in S. Holloway and G. Valentine (eds), *Children's Geographies: Playing, Living, Learning*. London: Routledge.

Nayak, A. (2003a), '"Last of the Real Geordies?" White masculinities and the subcultural response to de-industrialisation', *Environment and Planning D: Society and Space*, 21, 7–25.

—. (2003b), 'Through children's eyes: childhood, place and fear of crime', *Geoforum*, 34, (3), 303–315.

—. (2004), *Race, Place and Globalisation*. New York: BERG.

OfSTED (2005), *The Common Inspection Framework for Education and Training 2005*. OfSTED. Crown Copyright.

Philosophy 4 Children. Available at http://www.philosophy4children.co.uk/ http://www.p4c.com/ (accessed 28 December 2009).

Punch, S. (2007), '"I felt they were ganging up on me": interviewing siblings at home', *Children's Geographies*, 5, (3), 219–234.

Roberts, M. (2010), 'Geographical enquiry', *Teaching Geography*, 35, (1), 6–9.

Rudduck, J. and Flutter, J. (2000), 'Pupil participation and pupil perspective: "carving a new order of experience"', *Cambridge Journal of Education*, 30, (1), 75–89.

Scardamalia, M. and Bereiter, C. (2003), 'Knowledge building environments: extending the limits of the possible in education and knowledge work', in A. DiStefano, K. Rudestam and R. Silverman (eds), *Encyclopedia of Distributed Learning*. Thousand Oaks, CA: Sage.

Skelton, T. and Valentine, G. (1998), *Cool Places: Geographies of Youth Culture*. London: Routledge.

Smith, M. K. (1996, 2000), 'Curriculum theory and practice', *The Encyclopaedia of Informal Education*. Available at www.infed.org/biblio/b-curric.htm (accessed 15 March 2010).

Standish, A. (2006), 'Shrunken world of global ethics. Opinion', *Times Educational Supplement*, 21 April.

Thomson, P. (2002), *Schooling the Rustbelt Kids. Making the Difference in Changing Times*. Sydney: Allen & Unwin; United Kingdom: Trentham Books.

Thomson, P. and Gunter, H. (2006), 'From "consulting pupils" to "pupils as researchers": a situated case narrative', *British Education Research Journal*, 32, (6), 839–856.

Thomson, P. and Hall, C. (2008), 'Opportunities missed and/or thwarted? "Funds of knowledge" meet the English national curriculum', *Curriculum Journal*, 19, (2), 87–103.

Whelan, R. (ed.) (2007), *The Corruption of the Curriculum*. Trowbridge: Cromwell Press.

Whitty, G. (1985), *Sociology and School Knowledge: Curriculum Theory, Research and Politics*. London: Methuen.

Discussion to Part 1

Pat Thomson

Curriculum is contentious. Questions of knowledge – what is taught to whom, why and to what ends – continue to vex both educators and the general public. This is both inevitable and also desirable. What one generation passes on to another, via the institution of schooling, has both individual and social, short- and long-term effects. In times when we understand the world to be fragile and vulnerable, and human endeavours to be fallible and risky, curriculum debates have stakes much higher than the test/examination results of successive cohorts of students.

With hearts and minds fixed firmly on a school curriculum that contributes to a more equitable, just and sustainable world, the authors whose work is represented in this first part of *Geography, Education and the Future* seek to challenge and unsettle some current dominant classroom assumptions. They query what counts as significant knowledge and how it is produced and reproduced in schools and they offer alternatives grounded in practice and in theory.

These authors are not alone in this kind of endeavour. Across the field of education there are discernible trends in proposals for curriculum change. We might see these shifts in laminations and layers of disciplinary traditions and conventions as constituting living geographies of new/old pedagogy/ies.

Contemporary pedagogical geography/ies share some significant working assumptions, namely:

1. *'Children and childhood' are not terms to be taken for granted*
Childhood is understood to be a social construction heavily shaped in space/time in different cultural contexts (Aries, 1962; Qvortrup et al., 1994). The 'power-geometries' (Massey, 1993) of childhood are understood as not simply diverse, but also unequal within and across localities, regions and nations. Social patterning by gender, race and ethnicity, dis/ability and sexuality map

onto individual family trajectories; some are highly mobile, while others are fixed in place.

2. *Children and young people are seen as knowledgeable about their own lives*

Rather than being simply vulnerable 'becomings' children are 'beings' in their own right. They are seen as having particular knowledges and views about their daily lives and their future and of being capable of expressing these views. They are 'expert witnesses' to their own lives. Children and young people are also understood to have rights to basic human services such as schooling, as well as to a range of cultural experiences; they also have the right to have a say in things which are of concern to them (Franklin, 1986; John, 2003).

3. *Children do not come to school as 'empty vessels'*

Children bring with them a range of life experiences, 'funds of knowledge' (Gonzales et al., 2005), concerns (Beane, 1997) and networks. Contemporary childhoods are often saturated in digital and youth cultures (Sefton-Green, 1998), and can be much more worldly wise than many adults often wish to acknowledge (Rose, 1984).

These assumptions underpin a view of curriculum which seeks to have teachers ask 'Who are the children that I teach?' rather than take a deficit view, such as that often endorsed in policy, which sees particular children and young people as always wanting, feckless, deviant and/or incapable (Valencia, 1997).

The authors propose that the starting-point for teachers is that prior, worthwhile and important knowledge is not just in a prescribed syllabus or curriculum framework, but is also to be found in the collective experiences of all students. Furthermore, because learning occurs not just in the classroom and is not always teacher directed, it is imperative that teachers work in partnership with their students to co-construct approaches which work with inchoate insights and experiences to make them explicit, subject to critical interrogation and systematically connected with other extant bodies of knowledge.

While this kind of activity can be challenging for some teachers who have been taught that they are technicians delivering a curriculum designed by others, these understandings do offer genuine opportunities to add to a repertoire of pedagogical practice. They do not imply that teachers simply replace one orthodoxy with another nor that there is only one way to teach.

The authors in this volume have gone further than simply espouse these perspectives. They are working actively to extend their own knowledges and to support teachers to find ways to recognize, research and value the holistic life-worlds of children and young people. They are working for experiential pedagogy/ies which not only connect children to the mandated curriculum and make it meaningful, engaging and enjoyable, but which also change the nature of the curriculum itself. They understand this to be an exercise which is never complete and always subject to critical discussion.

References

Aries, P. (1962), *Centuries of Childhood*. New York: Vintage Books.

Beane, J. (1997), *Curriculum Integration. Designing the Core of Democratic Education*. New York: Teachers College Press.

Franklin, B. (1986), *The Rights of the Child*. Oxford: Blackwell.

Gonzales, N., Moll, L. and Amanti, C. (2005), *Funds of Knowledge*. Mahwah, NJ: Lawrence Erlbaum Associates.

John, M. (2003), *Children's Rights and Power. Charging Up for a New Century*. London: Jessica Kingsley.

Massey, D. (1993), 'Power-geometry and a progressive sense of place', in J. Bird, B. Curtis, T. Putnam, G. Robertson and L. Tickner (eds), *Mapping the Futures. Local Cultures, Global Change*. London: Routledge.

Qvortrup, J., Bardy, M., Sigritta, G. and Wintersberger, E. (eds). (1994), *Childhood Matters: Social Theory, Practice and Policy*. Aldershot: Avebury.

Rose, J. (1984), *The Case of Peter Pan and the Impossibility of Children's Fiction*. London: Macmillan.

Sefton-Green, J. (ed.) (1998), *Digital Diversions. Youth Culture in the Age of Multimedia*. London: UCL Press.

Valencia, R. (ed.) (1997), *The Evolution of Deficit Thinking. Educational Thought and Practice*. London: Falmer.

Part 2
Place, Space and Change
John Morgan

The chapters in this part of *Geography, Education, and the Future* take their cue from the 'spatial turn' in the social sciences and humanities. The 'spatial turn' is based on the understanding that the Western academy has tended to privilege time over space, and history over geography. However, from the mid-1980s it became increasingly common for social scientists, historians, literary critics and philosophers to 'theorize' about the significance of space for understanding the world. Landmark texts include Frederic Jameson's *Postmodernism, or the Cultural Logic of Late Capitalism*, Ed Soja's *Postmodern Geographies: The Reassertion of Space in Critical Social Theory*, Derek Gregory's *Geographical Imaginations* and Doreen Massey's *For Space*. The widespread use of geographical metaphors and images found its way into discussions of pedagogy and education, with its notions of 'centres', 'margins' and 'border crossings'.

While the focus in this work has tended to be on space – with its attendant tropes of mobility, movement and flow – there is an important sense in which it is now recognized that any education for the future will need to pay attention to the particularities and significance of 'place', and the contributions to this book usefully set out some of the ground on which the development of a 'pedagogy of place' will occur. Eleanor Rawling's chapter provides an accessible and challenging introduction to some of the ideas associated with the field of 'ecocriticism'. While geographers have long recognized the importance and value of poetry in developing the ever-elusive 'sense of place', Eleanor shows how an ecocritical approach (associated in her chapter by the work of Jonathan Bate and Terry Gifford) provides a more challenging set of concepts and ideas for geographers to work with. There are strong resonances with Alun Morgan's chapter, which explores the tensions between 'place-based pedagogy' and 'geography education'. The paradox that Alun sets out to explore is why these two 'discourses' about place and education have tended to operate in separate realms. He creatively explores the common ground between the two discourses, providing an agenda for future development. A careful reading of the chapters in this part yields the insight that there is not a single and final definition of 'place' – there are very different approaches, definitions and traditions of thought. Rather than seeing this 'disunity' as a problem, I suggest that this should be viewed as an indication of a growing maturity in the study of geographical education. My chapter in this part draws upon the notion of the 'socio-spatial' dialectic and provides an account of the changing nature of the UK economic and cultural space. It attempts to explore how any discussion of place is shaped by the economic context, and, in a serious but playful ways, asks geography educators to imagine alternative places and spaces.

Reading and Writing Place: A Role for Geographical Education in the Twenty-First Century?

Eleanor Rawling

4

We need myths that help us venerate the earth as sacred once again, instead of merely using it as a 'resource'. This is crucial because unless there is some kind of spiritual revolution that is able to keep abreast of our technological genius, we will not save our planet.

Armstrong, 2005, p. 143

Introduction

Geographical education has always been concerned with knowledge of the earth, through studying its features, its landscapes, its people and its places. My contention is that school geography, as currently taught, encourages young people to focus primarily on descriptive and analytical approaches to the visual and material features of places – the observed landscape, the challenges which the physical/natural world provides, economic and social changes – and to undervalue the poetic, the emotional and the spiritual dimensions of 'being in place'. If we have occasionally directed our attention to art, music, literature, it is only with the intention of using a picture, a piece of music or a poem as an extra resource to heighten description, to add information or to analyse past narratives and power relations, that is, to help us describe and explain places. While greater uses of literary and poetic approaches may be powerful aids in this respect, more significant for this chapter is the possibility of giving pupils a place experience, enhancing their awareness of what it means to 'be in place' and, perhaps, reminding them of their connection with, and power to 'save', the planet.

This is not something to be left to other school subjects – arguably it is the core domain of geography (writing about the earth). Recent moves in cultural geography are re-emphasizing personal engagement with the world. As Wylie (2007) explains, rather than studying landscape and places only as if we are detached spectators, there is value in considering 'the interconnectedness of self, body, knowledge and place'. This focus on 'being in' and 'engaging with' the world, results in a revaluation of the resources and practices appropriate for academic study – for instance, literature, painting, gardening and walking are mentioned by Wylie. What is more, popular nature writing and the growth of outdoor challenges and activities are also opening up new ways of being connected with the world, from which geographical education could benefit. In this chapter, I want to consider the particular value of using literary and poetic writing about the earth as sources and as inspiration in school geography education. If, as Jonathan Bate (2000, p. 282) suggests the role of the poet is 'to remind the next few generations "that it is we who have the power to determine whether the earth will sing or be silent"' surely one role of the geographer (and the geographic educationalist) is to recognize this dimension of humanness alongside our more rational and objective attributes. Reading and writing place may be one way to help pupils to reconnect with, as well as to understand, the world.

Studying place: in academia and in school

In his book *Place; a Short Introduction*, Cresswell (2004) provides a genealogy of place, explaining that although place has always been a central idea in human geography, approaches to studying and understanding it have been extremely varied. Place 'is not simply something to be observed, researched and written about, but is itself part of the way we see, research and write' (p. 15). The oldest approach is that of regional geography in which the purpose of study was to recognize and describe discrete portions of the earth's surface (regions) each of which has its own physical and human characteristics. By skilfully synthesizing the diverse elements, the geographer was able to draw out a 'sense of place' for each of the distinctive places studied, that is, with identifying the 'sense of many places'. This approach was dominant all through the first half of the twentieth century and was implicit in school geography. Since the late 1950s the subject has experienced successive waves of change and development, including the spatial revolution of the 1960s and 1970s when a science of space was promoted and place was relegated to a minor role. Humanistic and phenomenological geographers revived an interest in place – albeit in a more philosophical vein – in the 1970s and 1980s. For example, Yi Fu Tuan (1974)) and Relph (1976) both built on the work of the philosopher Martin Heidegger and explored notions of being an insider or outsider of places. Cresswell also refers to a wide range of critical and analytical approaches which flourished in the 1980s and 1990s under such headings as radical, Marxist, post-colonial and feminist geographies and were primarily aimed at uncovering the social, economic and political processes of place formation and the underlying power relations implicit in place. David Harvey's claim that 'the only interesting question that can be asked is: by what social process is place constructed' (1996, p. 261) reflects the main focus of attention for many of these geographers in the 1990s and suggests that a 'sense of process' was seen as more important than a sense of place. To some extent, recent work in material cultural studies and actor-network theory (e.g. Whatmore, 2002) follow on with this non-subjective focus on the processes of becoming. Nevertheless, phenomenological approaches have also continued to develop rapidly, opening up whole new areas of study, including the 'non-representational approaches' to landscape study, links with anthropology and archaeology and the 'performative turn' as seen in the work of Tilley (2004), Wylie (2007) and Lorimer (2005). As Lorimer explains, in these studies 'the focus falls on how life takes shape and gains expression in shared experiences, everyday routines, fleeting encounters, embodied movements' and so the acts of responding – as in speaking, writing, painting, creating – are understood to be in and of the world rather than taking place outside it. Table 4.1 summarizes Cresswell's three approaches to place and this framework will be used as the basis for considering the way that place has appeared in the national school geography curriculum.

Table 4.1 Approaches to Studying Place (based on Cresswell's approaches, 2004)

Approaches to Studying Place (Cresswell)	How Place is Understood	How to Characterize this?	Representation in National Curriculum	Contribution to Geographical Education
Descriptive Geographers aim to identify and describe each particular and unique place and to draw out the salient characteristics. e.g. regional geographers, common sense idea of geography	Places are discrete areas of land with their own characteristics and ways of life.	A sense of *places*	Strong representation in original National Curriculum (NC) 1991, but gradually decreasing emphasis through the revisions. 2007 NC – not required but possible via 'place investigations'	Describing, synthesizing Drawing together Overlap with history
Social Constructionist Geographers are interested in particular places as instances of more general underlying social processes. e.g. radical, post-colonial, feminist geographers	Places are reflections of the processes and power relations that formed them.	A sense of *process*	Poorly represented in first NC 1991, but more strongly promoted in subsequent revisions via enquiry/themes. 2007 NC – greater emphasis on interdependence and processes allows more socially critical approaches	Analysing Deconstructing Critically evaluating Generalizing Overlap with social, economic, political sciences
Phenomenological Geographers are interested in how place is an essential part of being human and how this is revealed. e.g. humanistic and phenomenological geographers	Place is a fundamental way of 'being in the world'.	A sense of *being in-place*	Hinted at but not promoted in all early versions of NC. 2007 NC refers to 'sense of wonder about places' and to 'developing geographical imagination'. Left to teacher to develop.	Responding Appreciating, being aware Sensing/feeling emotions Being creative Overlap with literature and the arts

The first version of the Geography National Curriculum (GNC) for 5–16 year olds (Interim Report of the GWG, 1989) contained a strange amalgam of regional and thematic approaches. Four out of the eight original attainment targets were regional in character, three were thematic and one was methodological. By the time the requirements became statutory (1991) the regional element had been reduced to one attainment target, although the programmes of study still required a major emphasis on regional and descriptive place study. Successive versions of the GNC have sought to reduce the weight and prescriptive detail of the curriculum and to make possible a greater variety of approaches to the subject, to reflect at least some of the changes under way in academic geography. The 1995 version referred to places, themes and skills but seemed to suggest that the study of places comprised predominantly description and simple explanation, and that challenging issues about people, environment and society remained the domain of thematic studies. The open format of places, themes and skills did allow scope for teachers to explore the processes behind the formation of particular places (what Cresswell would call Social Constructionist approaches) if they were aware of these possibilities, and some school texts did promote this more analytical view of place study (e.g. Lambert, 1995). However, the best-selling texts of the early National Curriculum period tended to be those that 'delivered' facts about themes in the same way that regional texts had presented facts about places (e.g. the Waugh *Key Geography* series). The 1999 revision moved school geography towards a greater awareness of the underlying concepts or big ideas and of different approaches to geography through identifying four aspects of places, processes, environmental change and sustainable development, and geographical enquiry and skills. The intention was to signal that place was an idea as well as a bounded entity and that, ideally, school pupils should be given access to different approaches to place study, including awareness of *the distinctive character of places*. The 2007 revision made explicit a selection of big ideas or key concepts of the subject (including place) and completed the process of reducing the required content so effectively that teachers are now required to select all their own content and to construct their curricula around key concepts and key skills. For 'place', the first of the seven key concepts identified, the rubric requires:

- understanding the physical and human characteristics of real places
- developing geographical imagination of places.

These two statements about place hint at the three ways of approaching place referred to in Table 4.1. The first statement might include description and critical analysis, and the second might give an opening for image, emotion and meaning. However, given that there is little further guidance it is unclear what teachers will make of these opportunities and, particularly, of the need to develop 'geographical imagination of places'.

In all these changes, there has never been clarity about the role and diversity of place studies, so that for many teachers and pupils, place remains merely a convenient container for factual details about different parts of the world. In 1991, I noted that the National Curriculum was likely to encourage a great deal of learning about specific places, but little deeper understanding of why place was important to people (Rawling, 1991). In 2008, Cresswell repeated this concern, arguing that place as an idea has hardly penetrated school geography, even at Advanced Level where a more philosophical approach might promote 'a degree of self-reflection about the relationship between humanity and the planet Earth that lies at the heart of the discipline' (p. 139).

The tensions of place and landscape study

In his book *Landscape*, John Wylie shows how the development of landscape studies has followed a similar trajectory to that of place in general. An initial emphasis on detached observation, description and explanation (characterized by the expert observer approach of Carl Sauer in the United States and W. G. Hoskins in Britain) has been followed by a period in the 1980s in which the focus, though still detached, has been on ways of seeing and representing the world. It was at this point that analysis turned to visual symbols and other representations such as photography, art, poetry and literature (e.g. Cosgrove, 1984). In the 1990s, the gaze became more critical, analysing the ways in which landscapes of all kinds can reveal power relations and inequalities, for instance, in the context of discourses about colonialism, imperialism and national identity.

Wylie is part of a movement to reclaim a more phenomenological approach to landscape in which the focus is not on representation but on seeing self and landscape as intertwined, and on foregrounding the ways in which the individual relates to the world around them. This emphasis on the individual's involvement traces back to the philosopher, Martin Heidegger and to his concept of 'dasein' – dwelling in, or being in, the world. Although humanistic geographers opened up these ideas in the 1970s, a new generation of cultural geographers is now examining afresh the non-representational (or as it has been called the 'more-than-representational' to make the point that this is not seen as 'instead of' but 'as well as' socially critical representational studies). Studies underway aim to consider our direct personal participation in landscapes and places, or what Wylie (2005) calls these 'embodied acts of landscaping'. Lorimer, for example, has looked at the undertaking of field work (2003) and deerstalking (2000) in the Scottish Highlands and is studying pedestrian geographies (or the way in which practices of walking and hiking are part of knowing the landscape) (Lorimer and Lund, 2003). Other researchers are looking at polar exploration (Wylie, 2002), walking on the South West Coast Path (Wylie, 2005) dwelling and landscape in Somerset (Cloke and Jones, 2001), and our spiritual relationship with the planet (Abrams, 1996; Holloway, 2003). Such studies tend to involve rural or wild places, although there is a strand of writing and research which continues the psychogeographers' interest in the experiences of streets and built environments (Smith, 1996, 2000; Parsons, 2000).

Wylie argues that these newer approaches help to illuminate the tensions which have been implicit in earlier forms of study and that this will both enrich geography and inspire a new agenda for research. I would suggest that such approaches can also enhance education through geography and apply equally to place study. The tensions are those between distance and proximity (is the landscape being seen from afar or is it being experienced closely from within?); observing and inhabiting (is the landscape a scene we are looking at or is it a world we are living in?); eye and land (do we see the landscape or does the landscape speak through us?); culture and nature (are we, as humans a part of nature or are we totally separate from it?) All these tensions are to do with detachment or involvement and all raise valid questions for young people to explore.

The last of the tensions identified by Wylie, nature/culture, is one that is at the heart of many debates in the social sciences, not only in geography but also in archaeology and anthropology. Traditionally nature and culture have been seen as separate realms but then where does one draw the line? Early deterministic geographies seemed to imply that all cultural practices were a response to the original (whatever they were) natural conditions of climate, geology, soil, relief and plant life. More recently cultural geographers have focused on the way in which nature itself is culturally constructed through the ways we have used, written about and represented nature (e.g. Cosgrove and Daniels, 1988). Whereas in the first case, the natural environment was dominant, in this second approach the danger is that nature may be reduced to either a set of passive resources or a mere backcloth against which the lives and activities of people are played out. This is where issues for education are raised. School geography has moved on from environmental determinism. It has begun to take on more socially critical and constructionist forms of study, asking questions about inequalities in places, representations of power, and the diversity of images of place and identity. What it has not done is to make young people reflect on the way their lives are intertwined with that of the places and landscapes they inhabit, to introduce them to the more subjective and personal responses of others, or as Jonathan Bate asserts, to remind them at this crucial moment in earth history, of their own power to make the earth 'sing or be silent'.

In this respect, there is one more tension that needs exploring – and that is the relationship between literature and literary studies on the one hand and geography on the other. The date of publication of Rachel Carson's *Silent Spring* (1962) is often seen as the moment at which concern with the environment translated into overt literary expression, not in a purely descriptive and celebratory way as in the past but in a way that recognized our potential for damage and destruction. The early warnings of scientists like James Lovelock (1982, 1988) that the earth would adjust to unprecedented anthropogenic change – by ridding itself of its human inhabitants, if necessary – were quickly swelled by many other scientific voices, intergovernmental panels and eventually social and economic commentators. The literary world has responded with a huge and growing interest in the environment, ecology, landscape and place, with novels, poetry collections and ecocritical commentaries providing what Boyd Tonkin (*The Independent* 27 Nov. 2009) calls 'a tide of green ink'. This tide includes, for example, reassessments of the original 'green writers', the Romantic Poets; new interest in the poetry of Ted Hughes and Seamus Heaney; an outpouring of dystopian environmental novels such as Cormac McCarthy's *The Road* and Margaret Atwood's *Flood*, and the increasing urgency of place-based and environmental poets such as Alice Oswald, Owen Sheers, Gillian Clarke and Michael Longley. There are many new collections of the so-called green or environmental poetry, aimed at alerting readers to environmental crises, disappearing species or problems of pollution or climate change. The terms ecocritical and ecocriticism have been coined to describe this increasingly hard-edged and earth-focused approach to literature and to critical commentaries (e.g. Buell, 1995; Garrard, 2004). While such material has its place in teaching and learning, there is a danger in presenting the human/nature relationship as always problematic. As Ian MacEwan pointed out in a recent interview, readers do not like 'preachiness', although they do seem to be enjoying the many environmental disaster novels and films currently being produced.

There is also a tide of new popular nature writing. Authors like Robert Macfarlane (*The Wild Places*), Richard Mabey (*Beechcombings*), Mark Cocker (*Crow Country*) and Roger Deakin (*Wildwood*) are addressing our concerns in a way that combines an easy popular style and personal anecdotes with a passionate concern for environment, place and wildlife. David Matless (2009), a cultural geographer, recently reviewed these books together, commenting:

> The books work the boundaries of the 'popular' and 'scholarly', and usefully remind an academic readership that complex reflections on the nature of nature have occupied writings beyond the academy for many years.

In the literary and cultural journals, and even in the popular press, the assumption seems to be that it is through literature and poetry that the populace will explore and reflect on our relationship with the world around us. In schools, apart from in a few enlightened examples (Matthewman, 2008; Matthewman and Morgan, forthcoming), the vast majority of English and Geography departments carry on studying place and environmental themes in semi-ignorance of each other. In fact, there may be a perception that geography is best dealing with the harder edged science of the environment and that we should leave the softer imaginative and creative explorations to literature and the arts. In my view this would be a mistake. As Karen Armstrong suggests emotional, spiritual and technological developments will need to progress together and if geography is to continue to offer a holistic view of present and future, then it will need to provide young people with insights from all these perspectives.

The developments in geography described above seem to provide a foundation from which to move outward. In 1988, Pocock examined the relationship between literature and geography, explaining that literature is not just an illustrative source but can also be a tool allowing us 'to articulate qualities of life-world or place which might otherwise remain half hidden' (p. 96). Nevertheless, since that time, we seem to have concentrated almost exclusively on literature as a source of illustration or a reminder of environmental guilt, leaving the task of engaging senses, feelings and emotions to other disciplines. A refocus on the latter would be to the benefit of literature and geography, and would provide potential enrichment for geography education.

Reading and writing place

So how should geography educators rethink the way they deal with place and landscape? I suggest that there are a number of broad strategies that we can adopt and these are all based on the assumption that imaginative and creative responses to place are as important to twenty-first-century geography education as the descriptive, explanatory and scientific approaches. Note that the 2007 Geography National Curriculum already moves us in this direction with its statement about 'developing geographical imagination'. The list of strategies would include making room in geographical study for:

- reading imaginative and emotional responses to place and landscape, as in novels, poetry, nature writing and travel writing
- expressing personal responses to place, landscape and environment in creative and imaginative ways, for example, geography as creative writing
- drawing on young people's own experiences of place in everyday contexts as well as in travel or field expeditions
- using ways of being in the world as starting-points for response and exploration, for example, cycling, walking, sailing, canoeing, windsurfing or gardening, sight-seeing, painting
- developing fieldwork strategies that include occasions for reflection, wonder and creativity
- using literary material (poems, literary extracts, spoken word, dramatization) as tools to stimulate exploration and inspiration
- undertaking cross-disciplinary approaches to place and landscape with English (and Art and Music) departments in schools.

It is easy to suggest the kinds of writing and the places/landscapes that would lend themselves to this more humanistic approach. There are the well-known authors of classic novels and poetry usually associated with particular places, for example, Thomas Hardy and Dorset; Wordsworth and the Lake District; George Mackay Brown and the Orkneys. In an essay titled 'The Place of Writing' (1989, reprinted 2002), Seamus Heaney explains that 'the usual assumption when we speak of writers and place is that the writer stands in some directly expressive or interpretative relationship to the milieu. He or she becomes a voice of the spirit of the region. The writing is infused with the atmosphere, physical and emotional of a certain landscape or seascape, and while the writer's immediate purpose may not have any direct bearing upon the regional or national background, the background is sensed as a distinctive element in the work' (2002, p. 232). This kind of writing is easily understood by the geographer; after all it is expressing what geographers have always called a sense of place, defined as something which is already immanent in the place but waiting for the writer or geographer to recognize it and express it. Thus Heaney says of Hardy's Dorset 'Hardy country, in other words, predated Hardy. It awaited its expression' (2002, p. 232).

While this kind of writing is a good introduction to literature and place, we need also to look to other kinds of writing which excavate the human/nature relationship more deeply and provide more of an individual dialogue between person and place, allowing expressions of emotions like awe, joy, sadness, bitterness, despair. It is often poets who can succinctly express this kind of 'being in-place' experience. Wordsworth and his fellow Romantics were presenting this relationship two centuries ago but since then John Clare, Gerard Manley Hopkins, Edward Thomas, Ivor Gurney, Seamus Heaney and Ted Hughes have all explored intense place and natural world relationships. Hopkins and Gurney, in particular, in poems about walking, observing the weather, the seasons or the wildlife, expressed the pure rush of joy and wonder permeating their own relationships with the countryside. Hopkins spoke of 'inscape' – the distinct individuality or self expressed by and in places, and recognized their special quality for him personally 'the dearest freshness deep down things' (God's Grandeur). Gurney explained that he found 'a store of poetry, an accumulation of pictures' in the Gloucestershire countryside around him – 'dead leaves, Minsterworth orchards, Cranham, Crickley and Framilode reach – they do not merely mean intensely to me; they are me' ('Letter, 1915', Thornton, 1991). Even where there is bitterness, these poets do not preach or hector but present what Tonkin calls 'a nagging ache about the fate of beloved places and creatures'. In *Remembrances*, John Clare regrets that the old meadows rich in wildlife are 'all banished like the sun where that cloud is passing now' and in *Yesterday Lost*, Ivor Gurney watches the sun rising over the Cotswold Edge and speaks of 'a sense of mornings, once seen, forever gone'.

Currently, there are many poets such as John Ashbery, Owen Sheers, Kathleen Jamie, John Burnside, Alice Oswald (to mention but a few) who are illuminating places and landscapes in personal and responsive ways. It is not just the experience of being in specific, named locations that these writers create but also the way in which kinds of place and landscape are sensed and imagined – what its like to be there, in a woodland or forest; on moorland, downland or cliff-top; beside a river or estuary – and how far the relationship with such places is a fundamental part of human identity and existence. Owen Sheers writing in *Geography* (2008) explains that poems can excavate what he calls 'the layered associations of their environments', revealing the internal geographies of memory, history and language. His own poem 'History' begins:

> Don't try to learn this place
> in the pages of history
> but go, instead, up to
> the disused quarry

where the water lies still
and black as oil
and the only chiselling
is that of the blackbird's song

drilling its notes
into the hillside's soil.

(*Skirrid Hill*, 2005, p. 35)

Reading the River Severn

If we focus on one river – the River Severn in Gloucestershire (Figure 4.1) – and its places and landscapes, we can explore the geographical imagination that is evoked. The Gloucestershire poet Ivor Gurney (1890–1937) is best known for his poetry of the First World War and for his song compositions as a musician. However, his poetry of the Severn Meadows and Cotswold Hills is now being more critically explored, revealing, not only his sharp observational powers and a walker's closeness to the land, but also a deep sense of belonging to these Gloucestershire places (Rawling, forthcoming). Gurney expressed the character and distinctiveness of the River Severn and its surrounding meadows in a way that painted a lasting sense picture of this place. In one poem, he described the changing character of the river in winter and summer, evoking the 'brown thick flood' and the 'low meadows flooding deep' in winter, compared with June's picture of 'a tide of blue' 'flecked always with gold' and the 'crew of seagulls snowy white' ('Near Midsummer', *War's Embers*, 1987 edition, p. 69). Other poems referred to elver fishing, sailing on the Severn and the changing weather conditions. He knew the Severn as a real place. But his writing goes beyond the immediate descriptive and picturesque to express his deeper sense of intimacy with this place. This is sometimes a matter of content, as in Passionate Earth where Gurney expresses the way in which the Severn meadows evoke music and spiritual renewal. For him, composing music and writing poetry both sprang from the same natural sources of inspiration in the Gloucestershire landscape.

Where the new-turned ploughland runs to clean
Edges of sudden grass-land, lovely, green-
Music, music clings, music exhales,
And inmost fragrance of a thousand tales.

('Passionate Earth', *War's Embers*,
1987 edition, p. 94)

Figure 4.1 The River Severn at Framilode Reach (photograph; Eleanor Rawling)

Or in the unpublished poem, First Framilode (1925 Gloucester archives), when Gurney explains his fascination with the little riverside settlement of Framilode, 'a blowy Severn tided place under azure sky'. Gurney explains that he recognizes both the drama and adventure (what he calls 'the boy') and the beauty and 'sea breathed romance' ('the girl') aroused by this watery landscape and that the mix of these features brings to mind other writers – R. L. Stevenson, Walt Whitman, Shakespeare.

In other cases it is a matter of the style and syntax. For example, in Early Spring Dawn (Kavanagh, 2004, p. 148), written about walking on the Severn Meadows, he writes 'Gone out the level sheets of mists and see, the West/row of elms black on the meadow edge.' The missing words (**in** the West **is a** row of elms **that are** black) accentuate the line end breath even though the punctuation makes no such pause. It is an involuntary gasp, like the pause of an observer who is in awe at the sight of blackened trees on the horizon as the dawn breaks. This kind of 'stream of place consciousness' is typical of Ivor Gurney, so that we feel ourselves in the place with the poet. Eventually the Severn Meadows became a part of his identity, the place of memory and longing when he served in the trenches in the First World War. Musing on the violence and trauma visited on soldiers by the war experience, he referred (in Strange Service) back to his Severn meadows as a touchstone of fragile sanity. Before the war, he had felt safe and content, walking besides the river, observing the low riverside hills, the orchards and the river 'muddy and strongly flowing'. During the war, he can still draw on these memories but, just as the reflection of the sky in the water surface ('rushy sky-pools') is continually disturbed by moving air, so his memories are 'fragile mirrors easily broken' (*Severn and Somme*, 1987 edition, p. 26).

More poignantly, remembering a friend who was missing and assumed dead, Gurney writes of the Severn valley orchards, of the rough winds tossing the branches, of the leaves strewn on the pastures and of the memories of sailing his boat with his friend. The Severn and its landscapes have become the 'good place', the memory that should be preserved despite the horrors of the 'bad places' of war ('To His Love', *War's Embers*, 1987 edition, p. 76).

Gurney suffered a mental breakdown in 1922 and a poem of that period (Autumn in *Collected Poems*, 2004, p. 244) regrets his inability to call upon his beloved places to save him.

> 'Could you not, with your untouched power, save me from this breaking / Tyranny: not Severn have safed me?'

Gurney was confined for the last 15 years of his life in an asylum with his memories of the places of Gloucestershire as his only lifeline back to his previous existence. Although he could still conjure up images of the Severn meadows and the Cotswold Hills, his poetry reveals that his joy and creativity suffered without the direct experience of being in-place and, as he saw it, the place was left without a voice. In a poem titled Moments (*Collected Poems*, 2004, p. 65), he talks of the joys of high autumn going 'beyond his pen' and of 'snow lying inexprest in the deep lane'. The reader realizes that it is not a detached beauty that the poet is missing – after all he can still imagine it. What he cannot do is experience the reality of being there and as he explained in another poem, 'the walking into clarity' essential to the creative process. Although there have been major changes in the twentieth and twenty-first centuries, in terms of managing and living with the river, it is interesting to note that several modern poets have continued to find the Severn mysterious and fascinating. In 2009, Alice Oswald wrote *A Sleepwalk on the Severn*, a long prose poem that wanders the Severn estuary watching the different phases of the moon and the reactions and activities of those who inhabit it. Oswald is acutely aware of the transitory nature of the estuary environment (or the 'beautiful uncountry' as she calls it). The very first words of the poem describe the pale light of the moon glancing on stone and mud, and she writes of the 'many moodswung creatures' that have settled here (Oswald, 2009, p. 3 Prologue). Her poem changes rhythm, style and voice as the changing sensory moods of the Severn are evoked, through the experiences of bird-watcher, fishermen and watchers of the Severn Bore.

In *The Water Table* Philip Gross's book, winner of the T. S. Elliot Prize 2009, the poet conveys the same notion of the river and its estuary as transitory and ever changing. A set of ten poems called Betweenlands I–X summarize the intense mystery of the river environment. Geographic truths are illuminated by poetic imagination – the estuary is like 'a battered pewter hearing trumpet amplifying distance'; the catchment is 'a sort of self', described as 'a notional line within which nothing is alien to the river'. In Severn Song, he paints a picture of the ever-changing colours and textures of the river –

The Severn was brown and the Severn was blue –
not this-then-that, not either-or,
no mixture. Two things can be true.

The Severn was water, the Severn was mud
Whose eddies stood and did not fill,
The kind of water that's thicker than blood.
The river was flowing, the river was still,

The tide-rip the sound of dry fluttering wings
With waves that did not break or fall.

(*The Water Table*, 2009, p. 64)

In another poem about the Severn estuary (Elderly Iceberg off the Esplanade), he hints at images of more threatening change. An elderly iceberg 'jumped ship from the loosening Arctic' and was wandering up the Bristol Channel before it became 'trapped in a tide pool, half a mile out / on the silt you can't trust your weight to'. An augur of the future, Gross explains 'it wasn't the last / Just a message from the lastness'. The environmental concern is generated even more effectively because it is phrased in terms of love and awe for the river and its landscapes.

The hope must be that those who read poetry such as that written by Gurney, Oswald and Gross, may be moved to take action to sustain the earth's changing places and environments, not because the science says so or the latest regulation requires it but because they have realized the importance of place to human existence.

The post-pastoral: a blueprint for geographical education?

Consider the term 'pastoral'. Originally referring to a form of writing derived from Greek and Roman poetry about the life of shepherds and rural folk, pastoral has come to mean any writing about the countryside as opposed to the town. In this sense, novels and commentaries on country life, such as James Herriot's life of a country vet, are pastoral as, at face value, is the poetry of Wordsworth, Edward Thomas and John Clare. However, not only has recent research shown how these poets are much more than pastoral in the descriptive, idyllic sense, but the use of pastoral has expanded to cover a bewildering variety of forms recognized by modern critics, 'ranging from any rural to any form of retreat to any form of simplification or idealization'. To many commentators, pastoral has become a pejorative term identifying a tendency to idealize the natural world at the expense of a more pragmatic recognition of pressing ecological issues (i.e. in opposition to the term ecocritical). Terry Gifford, in his book *Pastoral* (1999) argues that it may be time to move away from introspective debates and to recognize that much literature now reaches beyond ecocritical and beyond 'the closed circuit of pastoral and anti-pastoral' to achieve 'a vision of an integrated natural world that includes the human'. He coins the term 'post-pastoral' for this, as I read it, suggesting that in addition to the hard analytical edge of ecocriticism, we still need the retreat to nature offered by the pastoral but within a more mature frame of recognizing ourselves as part of a fragile planet. He cites Laurence Buell (1995) as being part of this movement and suggests that even in writers such as Wordsworth, Hopkins and Hughes, we can already detect these elements. Gifford suggests the following six criteria that would characterize post-pastoral and I believe that these could beneficially characterize geographical education about place:

1. Recognition of the creative and the destructive character of the earth. These two are always in balance in a continuous momentum encompassing birth and death, growth and decay, ecstasy and dissolution. Recognition of the cycles of life and death are present, for example, in the writings of Ted Hughes, D. H. Lawrence, but are also a natural part of geographical study – cycles of erosion, of seasonal change, of global climate, of plant succession and animal adaptation.

2. Human nature is best understood in relation to external nature. Modern urban life has tended to cut us off from this important relationship and education has favoured scientific detachment, but writers such as Ruskin and Wordsworth believed that we abandoned this link at our own peril. Ruskin argued that the love of nature was 'an invariable sign of goodness of heart and justness of moral

perception' while modern writers like Gary Snyder, Alice Oswald and Adrienne Rich suggest that interactions with the natural world are still crucial to our moods and actions.

3. Nature can be seen as culture, culture can be seen as nature. Through the arts and literature we can think ourselves back into the natural world. In Ted Hughes book *Remains of Elmet* (1979) the abandoned farms and mills are as much a part of the natural order as the moorlands. Richard Mabey's book *Nature Cure* reminds us that the Chiltern Beechwoods, a beloved natural environment, is actually intensely man-made, a part of culture.

4. With consciousness comes conscience. Understanding and emotional connection is a first step towards caring and commitment. Conversely, requiring young people to care when they feel no deep-seated connection to or understanding of the natural world must surely be doomed to failure, as the Karen Armstrong quote at he beginning of this chapter recognizes.

5. Exploitation of the natural world embodies the same mind-set as exploitation of other parts of humanity because of gender, race and ethnicity. The implications are that, as ecofeminists have realized, dealing with environmental exploitation and social exploitation need to take place together. This is often best explored through poetry or fiction. Again this is very appropriate for school education in which the national curriculum now requires us to explore cultural understanding, diversity and interdependence alongside environmental interaction and sustainable development.

6. Post-pastoral is seen as encompassing a spirit of awe and wonder in relation to the natural world. This is more than just a superficial enjoyment; it encompasses a deep-down sense of fascination, recognition and respect for the immanence of place. This is something that we may be in danger of losing in school geography by focusing predominantly on environmental concerns and catastrophes. It is possibly the most important point for geography education.

Jonathan Bate's book, *The Song of the Earth* implies, even in its title, that 'learning about' must always include hearing the music of the earth and feeling the awe and wonder if future generations are to have the will to change the human relationship with the planet for the better.

References

Abrams, D. (1996), *The Spell of the Sensuous*. London: Vintage.

Armstrong, K. (2005), *A Short History of Myth*. Edinburgh: Canongate Books.

Atwood, M. (2009), *The Year of the Flood*. London: Bloomsbury.

Bate, J. (2000), *The Song of the Earth*. London: Picador.

Buell, L. (1995), *The Environmental Imagination: Thoreau, Nature Writing and the Formation of American Culture*. Cambridge MA: Harvard University Press.

Carson, R. (1962), *Silent Spring*. London: Penguin.

Cloke, P. and Jones, O. (2001), 'Dwelling place and landscape: an orchard in Somerset', *Environment and Planning A33*, 649–666.

Cocker, M. (2007), *Crow Country; A Meditation on Birds, Landscape and Nature*. London: Jonathan Cape.

Cosgrove, D. (1984), *Social Formation and Symbolic Landscape*. London: Croom Helm.

Cosgrove, D. and Daniels, S. (eds) (1988), *The Iconography of Landscape*. Cambridge: Cambridge University Press.

Cresswell, T. (2004), *Place: A Short Introduction*. Oxford: Blackwell.

—. (2008), 'Place; encountering geography as philosophy', *Geography*, 93, (3), 132–139.

Deakin, R. (2007), *Wildwood: A Journey through Trees*. London: Hamish Hamilton.

Garrard, G. (2004), *Ecocriticism*. London: Routledge.

Gifford, T. (1999), *Pastoral*. London: Routledge.

Gross, P. (2009), *The Water Table*. Northumberland: Bloodaxe.

Gurney, I. (1917), *Severn and Somme*. London: Sidgwick and Jackson.

—. (1919), *War's Embers*. London: Sidgwick and Jackson.

Harvey, D. (1996), *Justice, Nature and the Geography of Difference*. Oxford: Blackwell.

Heaney, S. (2002), 'The place of writing', in *Finders Keepers; Selected Prose 1971–2001*. London: Faber and Faber, pp. 232–245.

Holloway, J. (2003), 'Make-Believe; spiritual practice, embodiment and sacred space', *Environment and Planning*, A35, (11), 1961–1974.

Hughes, T. (1979), *Remains of Elmet: A Pennine Sequence*. London: Faber and Faber.

Kavanagh, P. (2004), *Ivor Gurney: Collected Poems*. Manchester: Carcanet.

Lambert, D. (1995), 'Jigsaw pieces', *Cambridge Geography Project KS3*. Cambridge: Cambridge University Press.

Lorimer, H. (2000), 'Guns, game and the grandee; the cultural politics of deer-stalking in the Scottish Highlands', *Ecumene*, 7, (4), 431–459.

—. (2003), 'The geographical fieldwork as active archive', *Cultural Geographies*, 10, 278–308.

—. (2005), 'Cultural geography; the busyness of being "more-than-representational"', *Progress in Human Geography*, 29, (1), 83–94.

Lorimer, H. and Lund, K. (2003), 'Performing facts: finding a way through Scotland's Mountains', in B. Szerszynski, W. Heim and C. Waterton (eds), *Nature Performed: Environment, Culture and Performance*. London: Blackwells.

Lovelock, J. (1982), *A New Look at Life on Earth*. Oxford: Oxford University Press.

—. (1988), *The Ages of Gaia*. New York: W. W. Norton.

Mabey, R. (2005), *Nature Cure*. London: Chatto and Windus.

—. (2007), *Beechcombings; the Narrative of Trees*. London: Chatto and Windus.

McCarthy, C. (2006), *The Road*. London: Picador.

MacFarlane, R. (2007), *The Wild Places*. London: Granta Books.

Matless, D. (2009), 'Nature voices, review article', *Journal of Historical Geography*, 35, 178–188.

Matthewman, S. R. E. (2008), 'But what about the fish? Teaching Ted Hughes' Pike with environmental bite', *English in Education*, 41 (3), 66–77.

Matthewman, S. R. E. & Morgan, J. W. (2006), 'English and geography: common ground? From Planet Earth to Pigs', *Changing English*, 13, (3), 259–272.

Oswald, A. (2009), *A Sleepwalk on the Severn*. London: Faber and Faber.

Parsons, D. (2000), *Streetwalking the Metropolis*. Oxford: Oxford University Press.

Pocock, D. (1988), 'Geography and literature', *Progress in Human Geography*, 12, (1), 87.

Rawling, E. (1991), 'Places I'll remember . . .', *Geography*, 76, (4), 289–291.

—. (forthcoming), *Ivor Gurney's Gloucestershire; Exploring Poetry and Place*. Stroud, Glos: History Press.

Relph, E. (1976), *Place and Placelessness*. London: Pion.

Sheers, O. (2005), 'History', in *Skirrid Hill*. Bridgend Wales: Seren Books.

—. (2008), 'Poetry and Place; some personal reflections, in Poetry and Place; a special feature', *Geography; An International Journal*, 93, (3), 172–175.

Smith, S. J. (2000), 'Graffiti', in S. Pile and N. Thrift (eds), *City A–Z*. London: Routledge.

Thornton, R. K. R. (ed.) (1991), *Ivor Gurney: The Collected Letters*. Northumberland: The Mid Northumberland Arts Group and Carcanet Press.

Tilley, C. (2004), *The Materiality of Stone, Explorations in Landscape Phenomenology*. Oxford: Berg.

Tonkin, B. (2009), 'A Tide of Green Ink', *The Independent (Arts, Music, Films, Television Review)*, 27 November.

Tuan, Yi-Fu (1974), *Topophilia*. Englewood Cliffs, NJ: Prentice Hall.

Whatmore, S. (2002), *Hybrid Geographies; Natures, Cultures, Spaces*. London: Sage, p. 225.

Wylie, J. W. (2002), 'Becoming-icy; Scott and Amundsen's polar voyages', *Cultural Geographies*, 9, (3), 249–265.

—. (2005), 'A single day's walking; narrating self and landscape on the South West Coast Path', *Transactions of IBG*, NS30, 234–247.

—. (2007), *Landscape*. Abingdon: Routledge.

5 Place-Based Education versus Geography Education?

Alun Morgan

Introduction

As this chapter discusses, 'place' was historically an important theme in educational practice which fell out of favour over during the latter half of the twentieth century. Now a consensus appears to be re-emerging as to the importance of 'place' as a crucial dimension of education. It seems to be the case that this rediscovery of place in education can take one of two distinct yet not mutually exclusive forms: as an intellectual inquiry into 'place' as an abstract multidimensional analytical concept vis-à-vis 'places' (singular or plural) as holistic milieux for experiential learning of one type or another. Either perspective then gives rise to important and sometimes divergent educational and pedagogical implications some of which are explored in this chapter. Geography education in recent years has tended to stress 'place' as a complex and multidimensional abstract concept informed by developments within the academic discipline of geography (and cognate disciplines) which can be 'applied' at a range of scales and to a range of locations. In this new understanding place is seen as a relational concept with both material and imaginative – real and ideal – attributes. Furthermore, it is an understanding in which places are seen to have agentic properties in their own right both 'at a place' and across spatial scales. This represents a significant advance from previous decades when place was at best all too often treated unproblematically as a bounded and neutral backdrop for the particular geographical themes under consideration, or at worst had completely slipped from the educational scene.

However, such a contemporary conceptually oriented approach to 'place' has still yet to inform practice in certain sections of the geography education community which still too often treats place prereflectively. This is largely because the greater part of this community has yet to engage with these complex intellectual developments. Even when embraced, these new perspectives on place are all too easily treated merely as abstract intellectual conceptions to be learned within the hermetically sealed confines of the classroom or institutional gates. For very many educationalists 'schooling' of this nature divorces learning from real places (as opposed to neat case studies in textbooks or film clips) making its relevance questionable. More worryingly, such 'schooling' tends to restrict learning to the 'cognitive' domain (even if ostensibly exploring humanistic dimensions of geography) crucially arresting the potential for personal, social, emotional, moral and even spiritual development that only experiential engagement with real and meaningful places (such as the 'home locality') can engender.

It is in response to such dissatisfaction with prevailing mainstream schooling practice that 'Place-Based Education' (PBE)[1] has emerged as an international educational 'movement' in recent decades (Sobel, 2004; Gruenewald and Smith, 2008b; Smith and Sobel, 2010). From such a perspective mainstream mass education is decried as delivering a standardized and universalizing 'one size fits all' package insensitive to the contingencies and needs of particular localities. Learners are seen to be 'fenced off' from the real world where they learn centrally sanctioned universal and decontextualized knowledge which ultimately serves the prevailing globalized economic market. This all too often leads to a lack of relevance and the disengagement of many learners. Conversely, successful learners in such a system are encouraged to join the 'brain drain' away from, and to the detriment of, their home locality and community.

The purpose of PBE becomes, then, to 'situate' learning firmly in the learners' own 'place' or home locality and is oriented towards the good of the local community and/or environment.

PBE educators are likely to advocate a more holistic understanding of learners as intellectual, emotional, moral, spiritual and social creatures and seek to address this in their work. Typically, PBE advocates 'hands-on', collaborative, participatory and project-based inquiry approaches exploring locally relevant 'real-world' issues with a view to understanding and taking action and thereby contributing to the improvement of the home locality. Furthermore, they will almost certainly advocate cross-curricular approaches to teaching and learning variously employing multi-, inter- and even transdisciplinary strategies.[2] These represent quite radical departures from most mainstream visions of education. In these respects, PBE is often closely allied to, and inspired by, more socially transformative forms of Environmental Education (EE), Education for Sustainable Development (ESD) and, indeed, geography education. While such a radical vision of education remains somewhat marginal the increasing emphasis on Citizenship and ESD around the world means that PBE potentially has a great deal to contribute to mainstream practice.

PBE does, then, represent an interesting contrast to mainstream geography education as practiced in the United Kingdom and other contexts. This chapter will consequently explore theoretical and practical commonalities and divergences between these two 'geographically oriented' approaches to learning. Actually, many attributes of PBE are advocated by those in the geography education community, whether they are aware of this fact or not, as this chapter reveals. Rather than calling for the championing of one educational vision – geography education versus PBE; or school-based conceptual versus community-based experiential engagement with 'place' – over the other, this chapter seeks to explore the extent to which they are antagonistic or complementary. It concludes that they can, from a certain progressive ideological persuasion, be complementary and calls for a mutual dialogue and rapprochement between them.

Geographical versus cross-curricular approaches to place in education

First, a significant tension needs to be addressed. In mainstream schooling students are likely to overtly and intentionally encounter 'place' either through the particular subject or discipline of geography, or through cross-curricular formulations. The former is largely the case in the UK context where geography crucially occupies a place in the National Curriculum, albeit a somewhat subordinated one as a 'foundation' subject relative to the 'core' disciplines of science, English and mathematics. This is partly the consequence of the championing of a disciplinary approach to curriculum design generally, and the discipline of geography in particular, within the education community and by policy makers (Walford, 1997, Rawling, 2001a, 2001b). This is not so in many other English-speaking contexts such as Australia, New Zealand, Canada and the United States where for many decades geographical themes, knowledge and skills acquisition have tended to be subsumed within cross-curricular formulations such as 'social studies'[3] or 'integrated humanities'. Similarly, much of the innovative work in PBE is being undertaken by educators with non-geographical backgrounds and/or who are against what is often referred to, rather pejoratively, as a 'cookie-cutter' approach to curriculum design based around disciplines (Elder cited in Lane-Zucker, 2005, p. iii).

Perhaps unsurprisingly, critics of such cross-curricular or interdisciplinary approaches as the relatively mainstream 'social studies' or more marginal and critical PBE are often avowed subject specialists who decry the lack of disciplinary rigour and identity (Morgan and Lambert, 2005; Lambert, 2009; Lambert and Morgan, 2010). Other geography educators are critical of the apparent championing of instrumentalist and often contentious moral agendas such as 'education *for . . .*': social justice, peace, happiness, sustainable development, and so on towards which PBE usually aspires (Standish (2007, 2009) presents a particularly extreme version of this argument). From the other perspective, advocates of social studies, integrated humanities and PBE might accuse subject specialists of: 'disciplinary chauvinism' (the belief that theirs is the only legitimate approach to the teaching of place); taking a reductive approach to learning and the world in which crucial dimensions of either are neglected (such as the affective domain, artistic expression, the natural world, etc.); and of adopting a 'naive realist' view of disciplinary knowledge and education which see the prevailing wisdom of existing disciplinary divisions as essential and value free (for a range of pro-interdisciplinary approaches to place see, for example, Kincheloe and Pinar, 1991; Gruenewald, 2003; Hutchinson, 2004; Sobel, 2004; Ardoin, 2006; Curthoys, 2007; Gruenewald and Smith, 2008a; Smith and Sobel, 2010). However, there are a significant number of geography educators broadly in sympathy with these charges against their subject specialism as commonly conceived and practiced who are keen to explore the links between their subject and other disciplines. Equally, rather than advocating a conceptually 'free floating' approach to education in which 'anything goes', many from the 'cross-curricular' camp seek to draw, as appropriate, on disciplinary expertise. Consequently, adequate opportunity for dialogue exists 'for those with ears to hear'.

The concept of 'place' in mainstream (geography) education – the United States and United Kingdom

As might be expected, 'place' has represented a key or core concept in school geography along with others such as 'scale', 'environment', 'landscape' and 'human-environment interaction' for much of its history. In the United States the influence of education philosophers such as Rousseau, Pestalozzi and, more particularly, Dewey have given rise to a long-standing focus among so-called progressive educators on active enquiry learning in the local community for the purposes of advancing democracy and civics education (Hutchinson, 2004). However, this has largely depended upon the particular motivation of individual teachers or school cultures and is by no means universal practice. In recent decades significant concern has been raised nationally about 'geographic illiteracy' in the population at large and particularly among K-12[4] students leading to 'a rediscovery of the importance of geography in education in the United States' (Rediscovering Geography Committee of the National Research Council, 1997, p. 1).[5]

'Place' has represented a constant theme in these developments in the United States. For example, 'place' was identified as one of five themes of geography[6] by the Joint Committee on Geographic Education (Lanegran and Natoli, 1984). Ten years later, the influential Geography for Life: National Geography Standards (Geography Education Standards Project, 1994) identified six essential elements of geography including specifically 'Places and Regions'.[7] The geography education community in the United States is, it seems, currently largely exercised by the notion of '21st Century Skills' in terms of 'Thinking Spatially' which is somewhat narrowly interpreted as positivistic skills in Geographical Information Science (GIS) (see, for example, CSTS/CG/NRC, 2005).[8] However, the proposals of the influential 'Partnership for 21st Century Skills' (P21) are framed in a more expansive way. P21 recognizes nine 'core subjects' including geography; and five '21st century interdisciplinary themes' which crucially include: global awareness; civic literacy; and environmental literacy. Notably, P21 has produced, in cooperation with the National Council for Geographic Education (NCGE), a 'map' to illustrate the intersections between geography and their vision of 21st Century Skills (P21 and NCGE, 2008).[9]

Of course the situation is complicated in the United States by the fact that geography does not often feature as a discrete curriculum subject. There is no uniform national education system with decision about curriculum structure being devolved to School Boards and Districts at the sub-State level. In many cases learning about geographic themes is subsumed within Social Studies (Mintrop, 2004) which seeks 'the integrated study of the social sciences and humanities to promote civic competence' (NCSS, no date). The NCSS has developed a 10-theme framework (ibid.) which include the following specifically 'geographical' thematic strands: 'People, Places, and Environment' and 'Global Connections' with most other themes permitting significant exploration of geographical themes.[10]

The situation in the schools sector in the United Kingdom is clearer as geography has been a recognized foundation subject in National Curriculum (NC) since its inception in 1991 (DES, 1991). Long before this 'place' and particularly 'region' were key aspects of the subject in its formative years as a school and, indeed, university subject in response to the 'regionalism paradigm' prevailing in the discipline during the first half of the twentieth century (Walford, 2001). However, with hindsight this represented little more than the 'capes and bays' approach to geography in which gazetteer of places, often selected in relation to perceived Imperial needs, was presented for rote learning (Walford, 2001). There was some focus on actual engagement with the local environment or locality in the early decades of the twentieth century in terms of fieldwork thanks to innovative educators such as Fairgrieve who 'advocated that children should explore their own local surroundings and that geography should form strong links with other subjects' (Walford, 2001, p. 98). Overt links between such work was sometimes made with 'civics' education (Evans et al., 1949) although too often, this was seen as appropriate mostly for lower ability learners (see ibid.). With the advent of the quantitative revolution in academic geography from the 1950s the emphasis on place and region became subordinated to spatial analysis at both university and school levels (Walford, 2001). There were some educators who continued to champion the use of the locality and/or an overt focus on 'place study' although this was typically seen as being most applicable to learning in earlier phases of schooling (see, for example, Pluckrose, 1971, 1989; Wiegand, 1992) and/or as part of 'integrated' studies movement (e.g. Prosser, 1982).

The introduction of the National Curriculum for England and Wales 1991 actually represented to an extent a 'restoration and rehabilitation of place and area studies which, in previous decades, had fallen out of favour as organizing frameworks in many schools' (Walford, 1997, p. 18). In this first Geography National Curriculum (GNC) 'Knowledge and Understanding of Places' became one of the five Attainment Targets (ATs)[11] and the geography 'cube' comprising three 'facets' – geographical skills, themes and areas (i.e. 'places') – was presented as an heuristic device to convey the integrity of the subject (DES, 1991). The post-Dearing GNC taught from 1995 significantly reduced content and the Programme of Study was now structured in terms of three dimensions: geographical skills, knowledge and understanding of *places* and thematic studies.

The election of the New Labour Government in 1997 led to a third iteration of the whole NC and GNC in particular with a so-called New Agenda of Citizenship, Personal, Social and Health Education (PSHE) and Education for Sustainable Development (ESD) being a major innovation (Grimwade et al., 2000, Morgan, 2006). The GNC2000 was structured into four key aspects: 'geographical enquiry and skills'; 'knowledge and understanding of *places*'; 'knowledge and understanding of patterns and processes'; and 'knowledge and understanding of environmental change and sustainable development' with the expectation that all four dimensions were to be delivered in a coherent and interdependent fashion. The most recent curriculum innovation within the schools sector in the United Kingdom have been the Secondary Curriculum Review (QCA, 2007) and the Primary Review (at the time of writing just reaching completion). The former has reoriented the GNC around seven 'key concepts', the first of which is 'place' (QCA, 2007)[12] while the latter has been organized around interdisciplinary 'areas of learning' with geography now being subsumed within 'Historical, geographical and social understanding'. This is intended to help 'children make sense of our place in the world and is central to their development as informed, active and responsible citizens' (QCDA, 2010a).[13]

Clearly then, in one form or another, 'place' has represented a key concept in school-level geography (or cognate disciplines) in the United States and United Kingdom. However, despite this apparent overt focus on 'place' as a central organizing concept or framework in school curricular it is true to say that

> there has long been a focus on the subject content which students are to grabble with, as opposed to developing an initial understanding of the core concepts of the subject; these are included but often in a passive and implicit way. As a consequence the core concepts of the subject have often been ignored and students are not given an opportunity to consider them explicitly. (Wood, 2009, p. 8)

Wood is specifically discussing the situation in the United Kingdom but provides a description which is probably applicable generally. He recognizes, however, that this situation has been changing in more recent years. This re-evaluation and problematizing of the concept of 'place' in school geography is a consequence of a number of interrelated factors: a broad societal concern with issues constellating around environment, development and globalization and the need for a 'geographically literate' society; developments in the Academy; and threats to geography in the schools sector from falling rolls and allegedly uninspiring and irrelevant teaching (OfSTED, 2008). This has stimulated a host of 'soul searching' within the geography education community which has led to a number of responses.

Recent critical responses

Place is becoming an increasingly important feature in discourses from human geography, sociology, cultural studies, anthropology, psychology and applied disciplines such as architecture and planning. Indeed, it is not unusual to speak of the social sciences as having undergone a 'spatial turn' in recent decades. A range of perspectives emerging from the Academy are presenting a view of place which demands convergence between positivist, humanist and critical/structural philosophical approaches (Walmsley and Lewis, 1993). Such a convergence, which is in line with a post-modern sensibility, debunks the notion that any one approach, perspective or discipline is capable of explaining the real world or prescribing solutions to its supposed ills. Unfortunately, space precludes a detailed discussion of these place-related developments in higher education.[14] Suffice to say, this 'spatial turn' has given rise to a reconceptualization of space and place which are now seen as multidimensional and relational concepts. Some have tried to tease out the constituent facets of place from which this plurality emerges. For example, Lukerman presents six constituent values of place: 'location; "ensemble" (integration of "nature" and "culture"); uniqueness, though within an interconnected framework; localized focusing power; emergence (within an historico-cultural sequence of change); and meaning (to human agents)' (cited in Johnston et al., 1986, p. 346). Each of these characteristics has provided a specific focus for place-related studies. For example, 'location' is a key theme of spatial science while 'ensemble' is the concern of those particularly interested in human-environment transactions, and humanistic geographers have focused particularly on 'meaning'.

Another crucial dimension of this new conceptualization of place is an awareness of the relationships between places. Such a view has both descriptive and, more significantly, normative implications. It supposedly 'avoids the implications of boundedness, homogeneity and exclusion' (Johnston et al., 2000, p. 583) so much a feature of prevailing understandings of place. Instead it favours a view of a place 'which is extroverted, which includes a consciousness of its links with the wider world, which integrates in a positive way the global and the local' (Massey, 1991, p. 244). Massey describes such a perspective as a 'progressive sense of place' (1993a) or a *global sense of place* (1991) which is characterized by an 'appreciation, and an understanding of the importance, of the uniqueness, of place while insisting always on that other side of the coin, the necessary interdependence of any place with others' (Massey, 1993b, p. 146). Thus 'places' are increasingly seen as multifaceted phenomena which can be partially understood from any number of perspectives (philosophical, scientific, sociological, psychological) but their 'totality and contextuality' can only be appreciated holistically through the synthesis of these perspectives at a range of scales.

'School-based' geography education has a history and tradition significantly informed by the developments in the mainstream academic discipline in the Anglophone world (Walford, 2001) although a disjuncture between school and academic geography has been in evidence in recent decades in response to accountability agendas operating in both school and higher education phases, and the advent of the National Curriculum (Brown and Smith, 2000). Many have called for a rapprochement (see, for example, Stannard, 2003) with teacher educators being recognized as a key mediating group (Brown and Smith, 2000). There have been various recent attempts to integrate these theoretical developments in higher education geography into school geography. Such efforts have included the GeoVisions Project which was initially instigated by the Birmingham Development Education Centre[15] (DEC) and then taken forward by the Geographical Association (GA). Indeed, the GA has represented a key driver in these developments within the United Kingdom as evidenced by some publications in the GA's *Theory into Practice* series notably Morgan and Lambert (2003), Brooks and Morgan (2006) and Rawding (2007). The OCR[16] 'Pilot Geography GCSE' represents a specific attempt to integrate these developments into a 14–16 age group examination course (Wood, 2009). In addition, there has been an educational response to the emerging academic subfield of 'children's geographies' (Holloway and Valentine, 2000; Aitken, 2001; Matthews, 2003), for example, the GA's work on 'Young People's Geographies' (Firth and Biddulph, 2009).

The emerging experience of place-based education

Having detailed some pertinent themes in relation to the discipline of geography and mainstream schooling, we now turn specifically to the emerging field of PBE. Of course, learning set firmly within the concrete realities of particular places should be seen as nothing new in the sense that has been the educational practice (albeit informally) of communities across the globe for the greater part of human history. Equally, there have been significant voices calling for just such an education since at least Rousseau in the eighteenth century. However, given the hegemony exercised globally over the past century by Western – that is Enlightenment inspired, educational theorizing and practice – PBE does indeed represent a potentially radical and innovative educational movement in the contemporary world. In many respects the PBE movement can be seen as the educational community's response to 'new localism' and other 'post-modern' movements which attempt to step away from the universalizing project of Modernity. As such it represents 'the educational counterpart of a broader movements toward reclaiming the significance of the local in the global age' (Gruenewald and Smith, 2008a, p. xiii). Figure 5.1 presents a selection of definitions of PBE.

These definitions all imply that PBE is 'not simply a way to integrate the curriculum around a study of place, but a means of inspiring stewardship and an authentic renewal and revitalization of civic life' (Lane-Zucker, 2005, p. iii). Thus PBE as normally formulated carries an overtly instrumentalist agenda related to the interface between the moral development of the learner, civic participation, environmental sustainability and social justice. It is consequently closely allied to, or an umbrella term for, a host of other 'progressive' or 'transformative' educational approaches.[17]

Some PBE educators have engaged with the same academic discussions about 'place' noted above. However, PBE can more readily be recognized as having emerged from the Environmental Education movement and, as such, has drawn particularly on work within the field of Environmental Psychology and Conservation Psychology (Clayton and Myers, 2009). An important concept shared by both environmental psychologists and human geographers such as Relph (1974), Tuan (1974, 1976, 1977) and Buttimer (1980, 1993) is 'sense of place' which may be defined as the constellation of attitudes a resident or community has with regards its place of residence. A 'sense of place' can be negative or positive, or more likely a complex combination of the two.

Place-based education (PBE) immerses students in local heritage, cultures, landscapes, opportunities and experiences, using these as a foundation for the study of language arts, mathematics, social studies, science and other subjects across the curriculum. PBE emphasizes learning through participation in service projects for the local school and/or community.

(Center for Place-Based Learning and
Community Engagement, no date)

'Place-based' education is learning that is rooted in what is local – the unique history, environment, culture, economy, literature, and art of a particular place. The community provides the context for learning, student work focuses on community needs and interests, and community members serve as resources and partners in teaching and learning. Place-based educators have discovered that this local focus has the power to engage students academically, pairing real-world relevance with intellectual rigor, while promoting genuine citizenship and preparing people to respect and live well in any community they choose.

(Rural School and Community Trust, 2003)

Place-based education is the process of using the local community and environment as a starting point to teach concepts in language arts, mathematics, social studies, science, and other subjects across the curriculum. Emphasizing hands-on, real-world learning experiences, this approach to education increases academic achievement, helps students develop stronger ties to their community, enhances students' appreciation for the natural world, and creates a heightened commitment to serving as active, contributing citizens. Community vitality and environmental quality are improved through the active engagement of local citizens, community organizations, and environmental resources in the life of the school.

(Sobel, 2004, p. 7)

Figure 5.1 A selection of definitions of place-based education

This is highly significant because one is more likely to behave in a way which is environmentally and socially responsible within a place one evaluates positively. Furthermore, place identification represents an important ingredient of individual, social and cultural identity (Low and Altman, 1992, p. 10) and it is 'through personal attachment to geographically locatable places, [that] a person acquires a sense of belonging and purpose which gives meaning to his or her life' (Proshansky et al., 1995, p. 90). Where individuals have a 'strong, local sense of home and are emotionally attached to their local area' (Hummon, 1992, p. 263), the sense of place is described as 'rootedness' (ibid.) or 'Place Attachment' (Altman and Low, 1992).

A major focus of PBE is, then, on engendering 'place attachment' or *topophilia* (Tuan, 1974) with the actual home locality, the assumption being that '[i]n general, people who evaluate an attitude object favourably tend to engage in behaviours that foster or support it, and people who evaluate an attitude object unfavourably tend to engage in behaviours that hinder or oppose it' (Eagley and Chaiken, 1993, p. 12). The geographer Wright (1966) coined the term *geopiety* to describe a particularly strong and virtuous form of place attachment which has been further developed by Tuan (1976) which could be seen as one of the goals of PBE. Orr discusses how such a relationship between positive attitudes and behaviour may lead to the enhanced sustainability of a place. He makes the distinction between a 'resident' and an 'inhabitant'.

> A resident is a temporary occupant, putting down few roots and investing little, knowing little, and perhaps caring little for the immediate locale beyond its ability to gratify . . . The inhabitant, in contrast, 'dwells' . . . in an intimate, organic, and mutually nurturing relationship with a place . . . Historically, inhabitants are less likely to vandalize [*sic*] their's or others' places. They also tend to make good neighbors [*sic*] and honest citizens. They are, in short, the bedrock of the stable community and neighbourhood that . . . [is] regarded as the essential ingredient of democracy. (Orr, 1991, p. 130)

It would seem that place attachment develops through positive experiences (and the memory thereof) associated with a place. Three distinctive foci for the development of these experiences are discernible in the environmental psychology literature. Thus, for 'environmental sociologists' the overriding factor is social interaction with 'neighbours' engaged in collaborative tasks which enhances the 'social capital' of the community. Alternatively, individual-nature exchanges in natural settings are seen to be particularly powerful, with wilderness settings considered most efficacious and social interactions a distraction in terms of developing personal growth (e.g. Kaplan and Talbot, 1983; Ulrich, 1983). A third alternative concerns transactions with the built environment in terms of 'architectural phenomenology' (Seamon, 2000), urban-focused 'eco-phenomenology' (e.g. Bognar, 2000; Jager, 2000) and psychogeography (Sadler, 1999; Coverley, 2006). Increasingly, environmental psychologists and educators (and by implication PBE) are much more likely to acknowledge non-Western, indigenous or even 'spiritual' 'ways of knowing' as a way to engage with place (Van Damme and Neluvhalani, 2004; Barnhardt, 2008).

PBE is seen by its proponents as a win-win situation which simultaneously raises academic achievement, enhances social capital and improves environmental quality (Sobel, 2004; Smith and Sobel, 2010). This is also borne out by evaluative research such as undertaken by the 'Place-Based Education Evaluation Collaborative' (PEEC) (see, for example, Lieberman and Hoody, 1998; Powers, 2004; PEEC, 2007; Duffin et al., 2008). Such an educational project works against a narrow accountability agenda based on narrow metrics such as is associated with the No Child Left Behind in the United States. Indeed, Gruenewald (2005) points out that a particular institutional barrier to the integration of PBE in mainstream education is an accountability agenda. Consequently, innovative and expansive methods of assessment need to be developed.

There are, of course, tensions within the PBE education movement. According to Gruenewald (2003), there has been an unfortunate tendency for two mutually compatible, yet divergent, traditions within PBE to have emerged. On the one hand there are those working broadly within what Huckle and Sterling (1996) would term 'liberal/holistic' approaches which emphasize the holistic potential of the concept in terms of integrating various false dichotomies such as self-other, inner-outer, intellectual-affective, human-'more-than-human', and so on but which can be criticized for tending to adopt an exclusively ecological and rural emphasis and for being socially and politically naïve. On the other hand are those working from a 'critical pedagogy' approach emphasizing socio-political power relations and structural forces but which can be criticized for an implicit anthropocentrism and often urban bias. Gruenewald (2003) has therefore called for a merging of these traditions to give rise to a 'critical pedagogy of place' to provide an important corrective to both positions. Such a perspective appears to be gaining widespread currency and acceptance within the PBE community.

Another potential tension is the extent to which PBE should focus on the home locality to the exclusion of all else. For many this runs the risk of encouraging parochialism, a loss of solidarity with other places and peoples, and even xenophobia which is inimical to the practice and achievement of global sustainability. Consequently, many exponents of PBE now stress the need to develop a globally oriented understanding of place along the lines of Massey's Global Sense of Place and specifically aim to develop 'Global citizens' through their overt focus on the home locality (see, for example, Thomashow, 1999, 2002; Szerszynski, 2006; Gruenewald and Smith, 2008b).

Geography education and place-based education – incompatible or complementary?

The foregoing sections have dealt with geography education and PBE discretely. This final section now attempts to draw them together. Crucially, it raises the question of whether a hypothetical 'place-based geography education' (PBGE) is an oxymoron, a tautology or an achievable aspiration? For some PBGE would be an oxymoron in that *good* education is the antithesis of PBE. Perhaps the chief proponent of such a view within the geography education community is Standish (2007, 2009) who champions a traditional 'disciplinist' position. To him, anything which is critical of the traditional discipline, by which he appears to mean geography as a positivistic science firmly within a Western Enlightenment pedigree, is a dangerous and ideologically driven project leading to indoctrinatory practice and/or a dumbing down of education. His position effectively disavows as irrelevant or ideologically suspect any developments in the discipline since the 1970s, that is, humanistic, welfare, radical and post-modern 'turns' as well as any post-modern/post-structuralist debates about the 'politics of knowledge'.

A subtly different yet comparable argument is advanced by Bowers (2008) who denies the possibility of PBE and allied 'critical pedagogies' of being worthy of the term 'education' since, for him, they 'close down' choices rather than equipping learners with the full range of experience from which they are free to choose develop their own perspective. Such critiques as Standish's and Bowers' are easily dismissed as being based on a narrow and naive (whether deliberate or otherwise) reading of either prevailing disciplinary knowledge such as geography; or the indoctrinatory power of processes prevailing in mainstream society such as advertising which 'critical pedagogy' attempts to combat. They also present a very one-sided, skewed and anachronistic understanding of the 'opposition' (such as 'critical pedagogues') in order to advance their arguments (Greenwood, 2008).[18]

A more mainstream perspective is more likely to see PBGE as a tautology by recognizing a near identity between geography education and PBE in terms of both focus (geography education is inherently 'place-based'; PBE is inherently 'geographical') and underlying ideology and pedagogy. If any ideology could be identified as the prevailing one within education generally and geography education specifically it is likely to be 'liberal humanism' (Halstead, 1996). This is most clearly reflected in those forms of geography education which are concerned with developing learners' freedom and autonomous rationality within an overarching value system of respect and equality (Lambert, 2003). Such approaches are likely to be relatively 'learner-centred' and acknowledge young people's lived experience and expertise as a starting-point for learning. Such a 'constructivist' perspective is also likely to favour enquiry approaches to knowledge construction (Roberts, 2003) and to promote innovative approaches to fieldwork which acknowledge the affective, values and experiential dimensions (Job, 1999; Job et al., 1999; Caton, 2006).

Such a 'liberal' approach is also likely to acknowledge the contribution of (geography) education to wider 'personal and social development' (PSD), the promotion of democracy within a pluralist context, environmental and global perspectives (Inman et al., 2003). These are all aspirations which most geography educators and PBE educators are likely to share although the extent to which this will be pursued at the expense of disciplinary integrity will vary between educators. Thus, the importance of inducting learner's into the discipline itself, its 'grammar' and 'vocabulary', remains crucial for very many who subscribe to a more overtly subject-oriented 'geography education' position (see particularly Lambert, 1999, 2003, 2009). Those who are more critical of the 'cookie-cutter' approach to constructing the curriculum and/or pupil engagement with the world will be more likely to favour a cross-curricular or interdisciplinary approach to achieving the same liberal ends.

However, the phrase PBE subtly hides the more radical and transformative ambitions of the emerging educational movement in evidence in much of the recent literature. For example, the range of case studies presented in a recent PBE anthology (Gruenewald and Smith, 2008b) are all, to a greater or lesser extent, concerned with issues of 'environmental justice' and take 'place' in locations that might be characterized as marginalized such as socially and/or economically deprived, ethnically diverse, indigenous and rural communities across a range of settings such as urban, tribal and rural. Rather than comparable with mainstream practice, this ideological position makes PBE more akin to 'critical instrumentalist' (Scott, 2008) versions of geography education which extend the 'liberalist humanist' goals to advocate societal transformation. Such a radical perspective has been in evidence in geography education particularly since the 1970s albeit as a somewhat marginal strand. From this time until the early 1990s the British context marked a particular 'hot bed' of activity in terms of progressive approaches to education in the United Kingdom with projects such as the World Studies Project, World Studies 8–13 and Centre for Global Education.

Early notable examples include Colin Ward's 'Streetwork' (Ward and Fyson, 1973), the work of the Town and Country Planning Association and its associated Bulletin of Environmental Education. The type of vision for geography education advanced by Huckle (1983, 1985, 1997, 2001a, 2001b) and, to a lesser extent, the Schools Council Geography projects[19] also represented quite radical and transformative visions for geography education which have much in common with contemporary visions for PBE. From such a perspective geography and PBE educators see their moral role as 'Teaching Geography for a Better World' (Fien and Gerber, 1988). Such transformative positions are likely to advocate a form of enquiry into real-world issues of environmental or social injustice which is action-oriented in which participatory research methodologies should form the principal (or at least a major) pedagogical approach (see, for example, Hague et al., 2003; Kindon et al., 2007; Fortmann, 2008; Wilmsen et al., 2008).

Conclusion

It is in this more radical and transformatory vision that the educational projects, whether within geographical or place-based camps, coincide most strongly. However, as has been suggested at the outset of this chapter, rather than operating independently towards the same transformative learning goals, each has much to contribute to the other. PBE will, almost by definition, provide the basis for the development of what Geertz termed 'thick' description of the lived experience within the home locality. Further, it will be particularly focused on the development of a situated and context-sensitive 'thick, particularistic morality' (Smith, 2000, 2004; Sullivan, 2007) which represents a necessary response to contemporary issues within the globalized world. However, the merely 'thick' and particularistic could, as noted earlier, give rise to parochial and, ultimately xenophobic responses. What is needed to counter these dangers is a dialogue with a 'thin', universalist morality which can be provided by the concepts associated with the contemporary discipline of geography (ibid.). Together, this dialogue between 'thick' (place-based) and 'thin' (disciplined) morally informed 'knowledges' will give rise to a perspective which acknowledges the situatedness, contingency, particularity and diversity of life, and will be suspicious and critical of any essentializing and universalizing 'truth claims' while *at the same time* accepting '[t]he natural fact of human similarity [thereby permitting] . . . the identification of common human needs' (Smith, 2004, p. 203). From such a perspective opens the possibility of an intellectually rigorous moral geography (Smith, 2000, 2004) within which to make ethical judgements at a local *through to* global scale, a situation precluded in the relativizing climate of much post-modern discourse which emphasizes particularity and diversity at the expense of commonality and solidarity.

This chapter therefore concludes by advocating a transformative approach to learning which advances an experiential and committed engagement with place which is, in turn, informed by recent intellectual developments within the discipline in order to work towards a 'better world' both locally and globally (for which PBGE might serve as shorthand). This represents a position which has traditionally been quite marginalized. However, it is a position which seems to be gaining support from a range of other directions. For example, key non-governmental organizations are increasingly advocating a more 'place-based' orientation to learning such as the UK's Commission for Architecture and the Built Environment (CABE) and specifically their 'Engaging Places' initiative.[20] The GA's own 'Building Sustainable Communities' initiative[21] and their efforts to develop local communities of practice to undertake locally relevant 'curriculum making' are also welcome developments. Finally, the increasing emphasis on the potential synergies (but also dangers) between geography education and Citizenship (see, for example, Lambert and Machon, 2001) and the recent UK Curriculum reviews[22] provide such 'spaces of hope'.

This is a vision for education in which 'place' is understood to be a multidimensional concept (i.e. comprises *both* environmental/ecological *and* social dimensions in complex interaction). Consequently, learning needs to be holistic and emphasis needs to be placed on human-environment interaction. As well, 'place' needs to be understood as multiscalar: ranging across a variety of scales from small (e.g. campus, estate, neighbourhood) through medium (Borough) to city- and region-wide. Ultimately, all these scales can be understood to 'nest' within larger scales from the national, international and continental and ultimately to the global. Equally, it is a vision in which learning is rooted in, but not confined to, the learners' own 'place' or home locality. Thus consideration of the links between the 'home locality' and the wider world is an important dimension. The goal is to develop both 'place attachment' and a 'Global Sense of Place' which will allow solidarity with other places and peoples at a range of scales around the world. PBE *and* progressive forms of geography education will, indeed, prove complementary in such an endeavour.

Notes

1 For the purposes of convenience this chapter will only use the term 'Place-Based Education' (PBE) in preference to alternatives such as Place-Based Learning (PBL) or 'pedagogies of place'. This is not to imply any prejudice against such alternative terms which are considered to be broadly synonymous.

2 For the purposes of this chapter the distinction is as follows: multidisciplinarity employs a range of insights from a diversity of different disciplines but in a non-integrative fashion (i.e. the disciplinary contributions remain discrete); interdisciplinarity attempts to cross-disciplinary divides, blend disciplinary approaches and integrate disciplinary insights; and transdisciplinarity attempts to transcend traditional disciplines to create a new holistic and integrative understanding of the phenomena under consideration which addresses the 'blind spots' of disciplinary and inter-disciplinary study.

3 Such a 'meta-subject' represents an amalgam of approaches drawn from social science disciplines such as history, economics, sociology and citizenship or civics as well as geography (Mintrop, 2004).

4 The period of free schooling from Kindergarten through to 12th Grade (generally the final year of Secondary or High School).

5 Geography was identified by both the Bush Sr and Clinton Administrations as a core subject for American schools, on a par with science and mathematics perhaps most notably in terms of the 1994 'Goals 2000: The Educate America Act' Rediscovering Geography Committee of the National Research Council, 1997. Such concern also led to the setting up of the 'Rediscovering Geography Committee' of the National Research Council which had a remit to 'identify ways to make the discipline more relevant to science, education, and decision making' (ibid.). Rediscovering Geography Committee of the National Research Council, 1997; and the creation of the voluntary yet influential 'Geography for Life: The National Geography Content Standards' (National Geography Standards/Geography Education Standards Project, 1994).

6 Along with location, human-environment interaction, movement and region.

7 The other 'essential elements' being: 'The World in Spatial Terms', 'Physical Systems', 'Human Systems', 'Environment and Society' and 'The Uses of Geography'.

8 Committee on the Support for the Thinking Spatially: The Incorporation of Geographic Information Science across the K-12 Curriculum, Committee on Geography, and National Research Council.

9 At the time of writing available at http://www.21stcenturyskills.org/documents/21stcskillsmap_geog.pdf (accessed 3 January 2010).

10 The full list of thematic strands is Culture; Time, Continuity, and Change; People, Places, and Environment; Individual Development and Identity; Individuals, Groups, and Institutions; Power, Authority, and Governance; Production, Distribution, and Consumption; Science, Technology, and Society; Global Connections; Civic Ideals and Practices.

11 The other ATs being Geographical Skills, Human Geography, Physical Geography and Environmental Geography.

12 The full list of Key Concepts are Place, Space, Scale, Interdependence, Physical and human processes, Environmental interaction and sustainable development, Cultural understanding and diversity.

13 The most relevant items of 'Essential Knowledge' are 'b) how and why places and environments develop, how they can be sustained and how they may change in the future' and 'd) how people, communities and places are connected and can be interdependent at a range of scales' (QCDA, 2010b).

14 The reader is encouraged to refer to any number of accessible synopses see, for example, Holloway and Hubbard, 2001; Cresswell, 2004; Hubbard et al., 2004.

15 Subsequently known as 'Teachers in Development Education' (TIDE) and most recently as TIDE-Global.

16 Oxford, Cambridge and RSA Examinations Board.

17 Such as (Using the) Environment as an Integrating Concept (EIC) (Lieberman and Hoody, 1998); Streetwork (Ward and Fyson, 1973); Action Research and Community Problem Solving (Stapp et al., 1996); Community-Based Participatory Research; Community-Based Environmental Management or Natural Resource Management (Wilmsen et al., 2008); Service Learning (Ward, 1999; Annette, 2000); Community Knowledge/Street Science (Corburn, 2005); and Bioregional Education (Traina and Darley-Hill, 1995).

18 The author was formally known as Gruenewald.

19 Including Avery Hill Project/Geography for the Young School Leaver (GYSL); Geography 16–19.

20 At the time of writing available from http://www.cabe.org.uk/education/engaging-places

21 At the time of writing available from http://www.geography.org.uk/projects/buildingsustainableco mmunities/#top

22 For example, the Secondary Curriculum review aims to develop (among other things) 'responsible citizens' through the cross-curricular dimensions of 'community participation' and 'Global Dimension and Sustainable Development'. The 'framework for personal learning and thinking skills' (PLTS) specifically states that effective participators 'actively engage with issues that affect them and those around them. They play a full part in the life of their school, college, workplace or wider community by taking responsible action to bring improvements for others as well as themselves' (QCDA, 2009).

References

Aitken, S. C. (2001), *The Geographies of Young People: The Morally Contested Places of Identity*. London: Routledge.

Altman, I. and Low, S. M. (eds) (1992), *Place Attachment*. New York: Plenum Press.

Annette, J. (2000), 'Education for citizenship, civic participation and experiential and service learning', in D. Lawton, J. Cairns and R. Gardner (eds), *Education for Citizenship*. London: Continuum.

Ardoin, N. M. (2006), 'Toward an interdisciplinary understanding of place: lessons for environmental education', *Canadian Journal of Environmental Education*, 11, 112–126.

Barnhardt, R. (2008), 'Creating a place for indigenous knowledge in education: the Alaska Native Knowledge Network', in D. A. Gruenewald and G. A. Smith (eds), *Place-Based Education in the Global Age: Local Diversity*. Abingdon, Oxon: Lawrence Erlbaum Associates.

Bognar, B. (2000), 'A phenomenological approach to architecture and its teaching in the design studio', in D. Seamon and R. Mugerauer (eds), *Dwelling, Place and Environment: Towards a Phenomenology of Person and World*. Malabar, FL: Krieger Publishing Company.

Bowers, C. A. (2008), 'Why a critical pedagogy of place is an oxymoron', *Environmental Education Research*, 14, 325–335.

Brooks, C. and Morgan, A. (2006), *Theory into Practice: Cases and Places*. Sheffield: Geographical Association.

Brown, S. and Smith, M. (2000), 'The secondary/tertiary interface', in A. Kent (ed.), *Reflective Practice in Geography Teaching*. London: Paul Chapman.

Buttimer, A. (1980), 'Home, reach, and the sense of place', in A. Buttimer and D. Seamon (eds), *The Human Experience of Space and Place*. New York: St. Martin's Press.

—. (1993), *Geography and the Human Spirit*. Baltimore, MD: The John Hopkins University Press.

Caton, D. (2006), *Theory into Practice: New Approaches to Fieldwork*. Sheffield: Geographical Association.

Center for Place-Based Learning and Community Engagement (no date), *What is Place-Based Education?* (The Promise of Place website).

Clayton, S. and Myers, G. (2009), *Conservation Psychology: Understanding and Promoting Human Care for Nature*. Oxford: Wiley-Blackwell.

Corburn, J. (2005), *Street Science: Community Knowledge and Environmental Health*. Cambridge, MA: MIT Press.

Coverley, M. (2006), *Psychogeography*. Harpenden: Pocket Essentials.

Cresswell, T. (2004), *Place: A Short Introduction*. Oxford: Blackwell Publishing.

CSTS/CG/NRC (2005), *Learning to Think Spatially: GIS as a Support System in the K-12 Curriculum*. Washington, DC: National Academies Press.

Curthoys, L. P. (2007), 'Finding a place of one's own: reflections on teaching in and with place', *Canadian Journal of Environmental Education*, 12, 68–79.

DES (1991), *Geography in the National Curriculum*. London: HMSO.

Duffin, M., Murphy, M. and Johnson, B. (2008), *Quantifying a Relationship between Place-Based Learning and Environmental Quality: Final Report*. Woodstock, VT: NPS Conservation Study Institute in cooperation with the Environmental Protection Agency and Shelburne Farms.

Eagley, A. H. and Chaiken, S. C. (1993), *The Psychology of Attitudes*. Fort Worth, TX: Harcourt, Brace, & Jovanovich.

Evans, F., Searson, V. F. and Williams, G. H. (1949), *Local Studies for Schools: A Practical Approach to Civics*. London: George Philip & Son.

Fien, J. and Gerber, R. (eds) (1988), *Teaching Geography for a Better World*. Edinburgh: Oliver & Boyd.

Firth, R. and Biddulph, M. (2009), 'Young People's Geographies', *Teaching Geography*, 32–34.

Fortmann, L. (ed.) (2008), *Participatory Research in Conservation and Rural Livelihoods*. Oxford: ZSL/ Wiley-Blackwell.

Geography Education Standards Project (1994), *Geography for Life: National Geography Standards*. Washington, DC: National Geographic Society Committee on Research and Exploration.

Greenwood, D. A. (2008), 'A critical pedagogy of place: from gridlock to parallax', *Environmental Education Research*, 14, 336–348.

Grimwade, K., Reid, A. and Thompson, L. (2000), *Geography and the New Agenda*. Sheffield: Geographical Association.

Gruenewald, D. A. (2003), 'The best of both worlds: a critical pedagogy of place', *Educational Researcher*, 32, 3–12.

—. (2005), 'Accountability and collaboration: institutional barriers and strategic pathways for place-based education', *Ethics, Place and Environment*, 8, 261–283.

Gruenewald, D. A. and Smith, G. A. (eds) (2008a), 'Introduction: making room for the local', in D. A. Gruenewald and G. A. Smith (eds), *Place-Based Education in the Global Age: Local Diversity*. Abingdon, Oxon: Lawrence Erlbaum Associates.

—. (eds) (2008b), *Place-Based Education in the Global Age: Local Diversity*. Abingdon, Oxon: Lawrence Erlbaum Associates.

Hague, C., Higgins, M., Jenkins, P., Kirk, K., Prior, A., Smith, H., Ellwood, S., Hague, E., Papadopoulos, A., Grimes, W. and Platt, C. (2003), *Participatory Planning for Sustainable Communities: International Experience in Mediation, Negotiation and Engagement in Making Plans*. London: Office of the British Deputy Prime Minister.

Halstead, J. M. (1996), 'Liberal values and liberal education', in J. M. Halstead and M. J. Taylor (eds), *Values in Education and Education in Values*. London: Falmer Press.

Holloway, L. and Hubbard, P. (2001), *People and Place: The Extraordinary Geographies of Everyday Life*. Harlow: Pearson Education.

Holloway, S. L. and Valentine, G. (eds) (2000), *Children's Geographies: Playing, Living, Learning*. London: Routledge.

Hubbard, P., Kitchin, R. and Valentine, G. (eds) (2004), *Key Thinkers on Space and Place*. London: Sage.

Huckle, J. (ed.) (1983), *Geographical Education: Reflection and Action*. Oxford: Oxford University Press.

—. (1985), 'Geography and schooling', in R. Johnston (ed.), *The Future of Geography*. London: Methuen.

—. (1997), 'Towards a critical school geography', in D. Tilbury and M. Williams (eds), *Teaching and Learning in Geography*. London: Routledge.

—. (2001a), 'Reconstructing nature: towards a geographical education for sustainable development', *Geography*, 87, (1), 64–72.

—. (2001b), 'Towards ecological citizenship', in D. Lambert and P. Machon (eds), *Citizenship through Secondary Geography*. London: RoutledgeFalmer.

Huckle, J. and Sterling, S. (eds) (1996), *Education for Sustainability*. London: Earthscan.

Hummon, D. M. (1992), 'Community attachment', in I. Altman and S. M. Low (eds), *Place Attachment*. New York and London: Plenum Press.

Hutchinson, D. (2004), *A Natural History of Place in Education*. New York: Teachers College Press.

Inman, S., Buck, M. and Tandy, M. (eds) (2003), *Enhancing Personal, Social and Health Education: Challenging Practices, Changing Worlds*. London: RoutledgeFalmer.

Jager, B. (2000), 'Body, house and city: the intertwinings of embodiment, inhabitation and civilization', in D. Seamon and R. Mugerauer (eds), *Dwelling, Place and Environment: Towards a Phenomenology of Person and World*. Malabar, FL: Krieger Publishing Company.

Job, D. (1999), *New Directions in Geographical Fieldwork*. Cambridge: Cambridge University Press.

Job, D., Day, C. and Smyth, T. (1999), *Beyond the Bikesheds – Fresh approaches to Fieldwork*. Sheffield: Geographical Association.

Johnston, R. J., Gregory, D. and Smith, D. M. (1986), *The Dictionary of Human Geography*. Oxford: Blackwell Reference.

Johnston, R. J., Gregory, D., Pratt, G. and Watts, M. (eds) (2000), *The Dictionary of Human Geography*, 4th edition. Oxford: Blackwell.

Kaplan, S. and Talbot, J. F. (1983), 'Psychological benefits of a wilderness experience', in I. Altman and J. F. Wohlwill (eds), *Behaviour and the Natural Environment*. New York: Plenum Press.

Kincheloe, J. L. and Pinar, W. F. (eds) (1991), *Curriculum as Social Psychoanalysis: The Significance of Place*. Albany: SUNY Press.

Kindon, S., Pain, R. and Kesby, M. (eds) (2007), *Participatory Action Research Approaches and Methods: Connecting People, Participation and Place*. Abingdon, Oxon: Routledge.

Lambert, D. (1999), 'Geography and moral education in a supercomplex world: the significance of values education and some remaining dilemmas', *Ethics, Place and Environment*, 2, 5–18.

—. (2003), 'Geography', in J. White (ed.), *Rethinking the School Curriculum: Values, Aims and Purposes*. London: RoutledgeFalmer.

—. (2009), *Geography in Education: Lost in the Post?* London: Institute of Education.

Lambert, D. and Machon, P. (eds) (2001), *Citizenship through Secondary Geography*. London: RoutledgeFalmer.

Lambert, D. and Morgan, J. (2010), *Teaching Geography 11–18: A Conceptual Approach*. Milton Keynes: Open University Press.

Lane-Zucker, L. (2005), 'Foreword', in D. Sobel (ed.), *Place-Based Education: Connecting Classrooms and Community*, 2nd edition. Great Barrington, MA: Orion Society.

Lanegran, D. A. and Natoli, S. (1984), *Guidelines for Geographic Education, Elementary, and Secondary Schools*. Washington, DC: AAG.

Lieberman, G. A. and Hoody, L. L. (1998), *Closing the Achievement Gap: Using the Environment as an Integrating Context for Learning*. San Diego, CA: State Education and Environment Roundtable.

Low, S. and Altman, I. (1992), 'Place attachment: a conceptual enquiry', in I. Altman and S. M. Low (eds), *Place Attachment*. London/New York: Plenum Press.

Massey, D. (1991), 'A global sense of place', in S. Daniels and R. Lee (eds), *Exploring Human Geography: A Reader*. London: Arnold.

—. (1993a), 'Power-geometry and a progressive sense of place', in J. Bird, B. Curtis, T. Putnam, G. Robertson and L. Tickner (eds), *Mapping the Futures: Local Cultures, Global Change*. London: Routledge.

—. (1993b), 'Questions of locality', *Geography*, 78, 142–149.

Matthews, H. (2003), 'Inaugural editorial: coming of age for children's geographies', *Children's Geographies*, 1, 3–5.

Mintrop, H. (2004), 'Fostering constructivist communities of learners in the amalgamated multidiscipline of social studies', *Journal of Curriculum Studies*, 36, 141–158.

Morgan, A. (2006), 'Sustainable development and global citizenship: the "New Agenda" for geographical education in England and Wales', in J. Chi-Kin Lee and M. Williams (eds), *Environmental and Geographic Education for Sustainability: Cultural Contexts*. New York: Nova.

Morgan, J. and Lambert, D. (2003), *Theory into Practice: Place, 'Race' and Teaching Geography*. Sheffield: Geographical Association.

—. (2005), *Teaching School Subjects: Geography*. London: RoutledgeFalmer.

National Geography Standards/Geography Education Standards Project (1994), *Geography for Life: The National Geography Standards*. Washington, DC: National Geographic Society Committee on Research and Exploration.

NCSS (no date), *About National Council for the Social Studies*. Baltimore, MA: NCSS.

OfSTED (2008), *Geography in Schools: Changing Practice*. London: OfSTED.

Orr, D. W. (1991), *Ecological Literacy: Education and the Transition to a Postmodern World*. Albany, NY: SUNY Press.

P21 and NCGE (2008), *Geography 21st Century Skills Map*. Tucson, AZ: Partnership for 21st Century Skills.

PEEC (2007), *The Benefits of Place-Based Education: A Report*. Place-Based Education Evaluation Collaborative.

Pluckrose, H. (1971), *Let's Use the Locality: A Handbook for Teachers*. London: Mills & Boon.

—. (1989), *Seen Locally*. London: Routledge.

Powers, A. L. (2004), 'An evaluation of four place-based education programs', *The Journal of Environmental Education*, 35, 17–32.

Proshansky, H. M., Fabian, A. K. and Kaminoff, R. (1995), 'Place-identity: physical world socialization of the self', in L. Groat (ed.), *Giving Places Meaning*. San Diego: Academic Press.

Prosser, P. (1982), *The World on Your Doorstep: The Teacher, the Environment, and Integrated Studies*. Maidenhead: McGraw-Hill.

QCA (2007), *The Secondary Curriculum Review*. London: QCA.

QCDA (2009), *Personal, Learning and Thinking Skills*. London: QCDA.

—. (2010a), *Historical, Geographical and Social Understanding*. London: QCDA.

—. (2010b), *Historical, Geographical and Social Understanding – Programme of Learning*. London: QCDA.

Rawding, C. (2007), *Theory into Practice: Understanding Place as a Process*. Sheffield: Geographical Association.

Rawling, E. M. (2001a), *Changing the Subject: The Impact of National Policy on School Geography 1980–2000*. Sheffield: Geographical Association.

—. (2001b), 'The politics and practicalities of curriculum change 1991–2000: issues arising from a study of school geography in England', *British Journal of Educational Studies*, 49, 137–158.

Rediscovering Geography Committee of the National Research Council (1997), *Rediscovering Geography: New Relevance for Science and Society*. Washington, DC: National Academy Press.

Relph, E. (1974), *Place and Placelessness*. London: Pion.

Roberts, M. (2003), *Learning through Enquiry: Making Sense of Geography in the Key Stage 3 Classroom*. Sheffield: Geographical Association.

Rural School and Community Trust (2003), *Documenting and Assessing Place-Based Learning: Example Portfolios*. Henderson, NC: Rural School and Community Trust.

Sadler, S. (1999), *The Situationist City*. Cambridge, MA: MIT Press.

Scott, D. (2008), *Critical Essays on Major Curriculum Theorists*. Abingdon, Oxon: Routledge.

Seamon, D. (2000), 'Phenomenology, place, environment, and architecture: a review of the literature', *Environmental & Architectural Phenomenology Newsletter*. Available at http://www.phenomenologyonline.com/articles/seamon1.html

Smith, D. M. (2000), *Moral Geographies: Ethics in a World of Difference*. Edinburgh: Edinburgh University Press.

—. (2004), 'Morality, ethics and social justice', in P. Cloke, P. Crang and M. Goodwin (eds), *Envisioning Human Geographies*. London: Edward Arnold.

Smith, G. A. and Sobel, D. (2010), *Place- and Community-Based Education in Schools*. Abingdon, Oxon: Routledge.

Sobel, D. (2004), *Place-Based Education: Connecting Classrooms & Communities*. Great Barrington, MA: Orion Society, Nature Literacy Series, No. 4.

Standish, A. (2007), 'Geography used to be about maps', in R. Whelan (ed.), *The Corruption of the Curriculum*. London: Civitas.

—. (2009), *Global Perspectives in the Geography Curriculum: Reviewing the Moral Case for Geography*. Abingdon, Oxon: Routledge.

Stannard, K. (2003), 'Earth to academia: on the need to reconnect university and school geography', *Area*, 35, 316–322.

Stapp, W. B., Wals, A. E. J. and Stankorb, S. L. (1996), *Environmental Education for Empowerment: Action Research and Community Problem Solving*. Dubuque, IA: Kendall/Hunt Publishing Company.

Sullivan, W. M. (2007), 'Ethical universalism and particularism: a comparison of outlooks', in W. M. Sullivan and W. Kymlicka (eds), *The Globalization of Ethics: Religious and Secular Perspectives*. Cambridge: Cambridge University Press.

Szerszynski, B. (2006), 'Local landscape and global belonging: toward a situated citizenship of the environment', in A. Dobson and D. Bell (eds), *Environmental Citizenship*. Cambridge, MA: MIT Press.

Thomashow, M. (1999), 'Towards a cosmopolitan bioregionalism', in M. V. McGinnis (ed.), *Bioregionalism*. London: Routledge.

—. (2002), *Bringing the Biosphere Home: Learning to Perceive Global Environmental Change*. Cambridge, MA: MIT Press.

Traina, F. and Darley-Hill, S. (eds) (1995), *Perspectives in Bioregional Education*. Troy, OH: NAAEE.

Tuan, Yi-Fu (1974), *Topophilia: A Study in Environmental Perception, Attitudes and Values*. New York: Columbia University Press.

—. (1976), 'Geopiety: a theme in man's attachment to nature and to place', in D. Lowenthal and M. J. Bowden (eds), *Geographies of the Mind: Essays in Historical Geosophy in Honor of John Kirtland Wright*. New York: Oxford University Press.

—. (1977), *Space and Place: The Perspective of Experience*. Minneapolis, MN: University of Minnesota Press.

Ulrich, R. S. (1983), 'Aesthetic and affective response to natural environment', in I. Altman and J. F. Wohlwill (eds), *Behaviour and the Natural Environment*. New York: Plenum Press.

Van Damme, L. S. M. and Neluvhalani, E. F. (2004), 'Indigenous knowledge in environmental education processes: perspectives on a growing research arena', *Environmental Education Research*, 10, 352–370.

Walford, R. (1997), 'The great debate and 1988', in D. Tilbury and M. Williams (eds), *Teaching and Learning in Geography*. London: Routledge.

—. (2001), *Geography in British Schools: 1850–2000*. London: Woburn Press.

Walmsley, D. J. and Lewis, G. J. (1993), *People and Environment: Behavioural Approaches in Human Geography*, 2nd edition. New York: Longman Scientific and Technical.

Ward, C. and Fyson, A. (1973), *Streetwork: The Exploding School*. London: Routledge & Kegan Paul.

Ward, H. (ed.) (1999), *Acting Locally: Concepts and Models for Service Learning in Environmental Studies*. Washington, DC: AAHE.

Wiegand, P. (1992), *Places in the Primary School: Knowledge and Understanding of Places at Key Stages 1 and 2*. London: Falmer.

Wilmsen, C., Elmendorf, W., Fisher, L., Ross, J., Sarathy, B. and Wells, G. (eds) (2008), *Partnerships for Empowerment: Participatory Research for Community-Based Natural Resource Management*. London: Earthscan.

Wood, P. (2009), 'Locating place in school geography – experiences from the pilot GCSE', *International Research in Geographical and Environmental Education*, 18, 5–18.

Wright, J. K. (1966), *Human Nature in Geography: Fourteen Papers, 1925–1965*. Cambridge, MA: Harvard University Press.

After the Crisis . . . Place, Space and Identity 6

John Morgan

Writing now, at the end of the first decade of a new millennium, it is difficult for those of us who lived through it not to think back to another decade when much of what is now crashing to the ground was first established in its dominance. The 1980s, that epochal decade of Thatcherism and Ronald Reagan, of the establishment of a new dispensation in which individualism and competition, finance and financialisation, privatisation and commercialisation were hammered home as the only possible ways of being in a 'modern' economy and society.

Massey, 2009, p. 136

Introduction

Geography teachers have long taught about places and spaces. However, the turn towards 'theory' in the social science and human geography since the 1970s means that we can longer take these terms at face value (for accessible introductions see Cresswell (2004), Holloway and Hubbard (2002)). To adopt the language of the times, 'place' and 'space' must be regarded as social constructions. In practical terms, this means that geography teachers are increasingly urged to think carefully about the way they use these concepts in teaching (Lambert and Morgan, 2010, ch. 6). This chapter is about the *politics of place*. It explores the question of how geography educators can think about place in the light of contemporary economic, social and cultural change. It does so through the use of various theoretical and empirical examples in order to weave one particular argument about places.[1] The central idea here is that of the socio-spatial dialectic. This refers to the idea that society and space are mutually constituted. Social life does not take place on the head of a pin. Space is not the mere backdrop to social action. Instead, geographically varied space provides contexts that shape the nature of social life. Where we are affects our actions and our actions in turn shape space. The narrative of the first part of this chapter is the unfolding of this socio-spatial dialectic in the United Kingdom, with particular reference to that moment to which Massey refers: to the 'establishment of a new dispensation in which individualism and competition, privatisation and commercialisation were hammered home as the only possible ways of being in a "modern" economy and society'. The second part of the chapter focuses on the question of what comes next, after much of this is, in Massey's words, 'now crashing to the ground'.

Spatial fixes

As Massey suggests, the 1980s was a period in which a new economic and social 'settlement' was forged, and one in which an older geography of places was swept away to make space for a new geography – a new 'spatial fix' (Harvey, 1982). During the post-war period, a distinctive modern geography of Britain came to be represented in schools. It was effectively a regional geography, which described the basis of economic activity across the UK space. It focused on the distribution of primary and secondary activity – agriculture, mining and fishing, steel-making, brewing, chemicals, as well as the development of transport networks and modes of communication. There was little need for politics in the telling of this geography. Indeed, some feared that there was little need for geography, and the subject underwent a 'scientific turn' which allowed for the spatial modelling of the economic processes that shaped these landscapes. With hindsight we can recognize this as the 'geography of the Keynesian Welfare State' to signal the mode of regulation which involved a settlement between capital, labour and the state, and was designed to provide the conditions of full employment. It had three features. First, it assumed that the national state is the essential unit of economic and political organization. Second, the state acted to secure a high degree of spatial centralization of the domestic economy. Third, the state sought to be spatially redistributive in order to stabilize regional inequalities (Martin and Sunley, 1997). As an aside, because it will become important later in this chapter, it is interesting to reflect on the fact that social geography – an area concerned with the relationships between people, social groups and space – was largely absent from these geographical representations of places, as well as the environment.

The post-war consensus that had shaped Britain's economic and political landscape crumbled in the 1970s. A series of economic events served to undermine the Keynesian Welfare settlement. The OPEC Oil Crisis of 1973–1974 led to price inflation and demands for higher wages, and the protracted struggle between the miners and the Conservative government led by Edward Heath resulted in the rationing of energy supplies and the 'three-day week', with people needing to consult their newspapers to learn when they would have power. The worsening fiscal crisis led to the Labour government calling in loans from the International Monetary Fund in 1976. The resumption of war in Northern Ireland, and growing calls for nationalist settlements in Scotland and Wales, added to the sense of disorder, and 1978–1979 was dubbed by the popular press as the 'Winter of Discontent' as the Callaghan government's attempts to limit wage demands sparked successive waves of industrial and public service strikes, forcing the government to back down and appear to be weak. In the second half of the decade the opposition tapped into a public mood that appeared to favour strong government and offer a new direction, and the end of the decade saw the election of a Conservative government committed to radical change. This involved a rejection of the idea that the main role of government is to regulate capitalism, rejecting the idea of a social contract with organized labour, and seeking to withdraw the state from economic and social intervention. In the 1980s nationalized industries were privatized, failing industries (so-called lame ducks) were allowed to fail, trade union power curtailed and effectively broken in the decisive industrial dispute of the decade, the Miners' Strike of 1984–1985. In line with a belief that the market offers better solutions to how to live, council housing was made available for private purchase (the 'Right to Buy'), and private heath care was encouraged. Public spending on health, education and welfare was squeezed, although the overall size of public expenditure was the same, but redistributed to areas such as defence, law and order, and providing unemployment benefits for the 3 million or more unemployed. The medicine was tough, but the Conservative government could point to the fact that, following the deep economic recession of 1979–1982, Britain experienced an economic boom, based on the growth of financial services and foreign investment. However, this was a period of deep social division, marked by mass unemployment, riots in many large urban centres, rising crime, homelessness and increased poverty. In effect, the notion that governments should seek to redistribute wealth was rejected, and replaced with the promise that increased wealth would eventually 'trickle down' to the poorer sections of society.

The physical changes to the landscape, the feel of places and the social and cultural climate that occurred in the 1980s were striking, and amounted to nothing less than a revolution in what it meant to live in Britain. Ball et al. (1989) saw that what was distinctive about political debates in the 'Thatcher era' was the emergence of a new set of social beliefs. Notions of collectivism were on the wane, being replaced by beliefs about the efficacy of markets. Individual actions in markets were claimed to promote personal satisfaction and the greatest common good. The idea of collective provision by the state came to be seen as inefficient and 'old-fashioned', while market-related individualism was 'new and exciting'. These values were aided considerably by the resurgence in economic growth after the recessions of the early 1980s and the rise in real incomes that left many people better off. In the geographies written of the 1980s there is much attention to the changes that were wrought by 'Thatcherism'. The focus was increasingly on social geographies or what Mohan called 'cartographies of distress' (Mohan, 2001). Examples of such works by geographers include: Cloke (1992); Hudson and Williams (1985); Martin and Rowthorn (1986); Short (1984); Champion and Townsend (1989). The idea that geography (as part of the social sciences) could offer a neutral or a-political view of the world was increasingly challenged, and the subject emerged from this period with a strong focus on political and social issues.

While geographers contributed to the analysis of the politics of 'Thatcherism' in the 1980s, by the 1990s it was becoming common to argue that the developments of that decade should be understood as part of a more general global shift. For many on the political left it was important to understand Thatcherism as in some way capturing the 'hearts and minds' of ordinary people in a way that the parties of the left had signally failed. It was argued that Britain was undergoing a fundamental transformation or epochal shift. This was described in various ways, for instance, the shift from Fordism to post-Fordism, or from 'Organized' to 'disorganized capitalism' (Lash and Urry, 1987). Whatever the label, it was clear that we were living in 'new times', an argument closely associated with the work of the magazine *Marxism Today* (Hall and Jacques, 1989):

The New Times argument is that the world has changed not just incrementally but qualitatively, that Britain and other advanced capitalist societies are increasingly characterised by diversity, differentiation and fragmentation, rather than homogenisation, standardisation and the economies and organisations of scale which characterised modern mass society.

For these writers the new times were welcomed in as far as they appeared to offer the prospect for a new politics beyond that of the older forms of class conflict. In particular they drew attention to the new identities that were being shaped as the older settlements broke down. These seemed to chime with a more 'modern' Britain that was emerging in the spaces of leisure and consumption as economic growth returned and the expansion of credit allowed for more and more people to join in the 'brave new world' of late capitalism (see, for example, Mort, 1996). Although there is no simple connection between economic realities and academic ideas, it is possible to argue that the study of places became increasingly informed by the optimistic mood of cultural transformation in the 1990s. It is surely no coincidence that geography took a distinctive 'cultural turn' during this period? As Shurmer-Smith (2002) noted:

Not only in the universities, but also in the media and in private encounters, virtually everyone, everywhere, became increasingly conscious of the problem of creating meaning in situations in which so many of the parameters of economic, political and social life had shifted.

This was reflected in what geographers chose to examine. Thus, urban geographers became interested in the new sites of consumption and heritage that were rising – phoenix like – in the derelict spaces of inner cities; rural geographers became interested in how the lifestyles of the professional middle classes were reflected in the post-productivist countryside; economic geographers became interested in the cultures of organizations and the performance of work; most importantly, this period saw the increased centrality of consumption as the focus of geographical study. These developments reflected the rise of identity as a political project. No longer was it possible to argue that identities were fixed and stable. Instead identities are seen as a construction. All was fluid and liquid – there was no single geography but instead multiple geographies. In all of this geographers were in step with the *zeitgeist*, a growing consensus that Britain has become a different place in the light of these economic transformations, and this is reflected in the lifestyles, values and attitudes of the population. This is reflected in the 'flagship' new sites of consumption that are transforming cities, and the new suburban estates in which people spend larger proportions of their leisure time; it is reflected in patterns of leisure and travel – the rise of budget airlines enabling most of us to escape to the sun for at least part of the year; new forms of work. The changes have been cultural too – some talk of a dramatic shift in gender relations and sexuality (Weeks, 2007); the decline of Christian Britain (Brown, 2001); apparently, we are less deferent, more open to new experiences (see, for example, Marr, 2007; Weight, 1998). Cultural geographers have mapped these patterns and new developments. They have not done so uncritically, since they have been concerned to understand how the categories of social life are constructed and to draw attention to the processes of inclusion and exclusion, but much of this work is concerned to describe what it means to live in a post-manufacturing, consumer society.

The economic context in which this focus on the geographies of culture has occurred is important, with economic geographers arguing that there has been a fundamental shift in the nature of economic organization which means that the *what*, the *how* and the *where* of production shifted. The crisis of accumulation of the 1970s required a new mode of regulation. Harvey (2005) usefully discusses the idea of embedded liberalism to describe the relative stability of the Fordist period. Markets were surrounded by a web of social and political constraints and a regulatory environment that set the parameters for economic development. The goal of 'neoliberalism' (as it has become commonly known) has been to disembed markets from these regimes in order to enable capital to circulate more quickly and over increasing distances. The upshot is that the fast world of the global economy is characterized by an intense connectedness that ties together a billion or so people through global networks of communication and knowledge, production and consumption. The competitive drive of capitalism leads to an endless drive to seek out new markets and reduce the turnover time of capital. As countless advertisements remind us, time costs money, and the inevitable result is the acceleration of everyday life. The commodification thesis holds that more and more of the things that people do are bought and sold, so that it becomes necessary to have employment to earn money to provide the goods and services advertised. In order to secure access to the 'good life', there is a lengthening of the working day, and households depend on more than one income, with resulting stresses on domestic life and the emergence of the 'work-life balance' as personal and policy problem.

The effects on people's 'maps of meaning' are profound. People's notions of self-worth are increasingly organized around consumption. The work-spend cycle has become fundamental to the economic and social dynamics of contemporary society. Speed has become a hallmark of many aspects of consumption – as reflected and prompted by advertising. Speed and busy-ness of schedules are transformed from negatives into symptoms of laudable, well-adjusted and fulfilling lifestyles. Capitalism literally delivers: speed of delivery, speed of service, speed of cook-time, speed of bill-paying, speed of opening-cans, speed of gratification (Knox and Mayer, 2009).

Places are hooked into the spatial logic of this economic system. Economically, there is a tendency to shift production overseas and to intensify consumption within the wealthier home markets. The supply chains of goods and services are spread out over the globe but the trends towards the concentration of capital and ownership lead towards the dominance of a number of high profile brands and stores.

The socio-spatial dialectic shapes identities and behaviour, and these 'act back' to create and re-create spaces and places. The past 20 years have given strong messages that there are no alternatives to capitalist forms of place-making. However, in the aftermath of the financial crisis of 2008 which heralded a global economic recession, the question of what types of places, spaces and identities we can develop for the future is posed with increased urgency.

After the crisis . . .

On 10 February 2010 BBC Breakfast carried a news item which showed how, in the wake of the credit crunch and economic recession, many planned developments in large cities were being delayed (http://news.bbc.co.uk/1/hi/england/8507598.stm). It showed footage of boarded up sites, and members of the public were interviewed and expressed their concern that these sites were an eyesore and were not great adverts for the towns and cities. In the light of this, the report went on to show how these sites are being reclaimed for other uses – including urban gardens (allotments), football pitches and walkways, with seats and public art. While these were heralded as being a positive development by many, the report ended by stating, 'These alternatives to rubble-strewn holes are all just temporary. The sport, greenery and gardening will all go when the economy picks up.' The first time the report was shown, one of the presenters commented that it was a pity that these things would be lost. However, she was quickly corrected by her co-presenter that of course, it was more important to get the economy back to normal. When the report was repeated an hour later, the presenters made no comment. This is an interesting moment, since it represents a moment when, to appropriate the words of

Roland Barthes the gleaming capitalist garment gaped. People could see that the drive to get the economy back to normal would invariably lead to the replacement of something people wanted and needed (green space, conviviality, engagement with nature) by something they already feel they have enough (of retail outlets, expensive city-centre flats). Jim Stanford (2008) begins his book *Economics for Everyone: A Short Guide to the Economics of Capitalism* with the following words:

> Most people think economics is a technical, confusing, and even mysterious subject. It's a field best left to the experts: namely, the economists.
>
> But in reality, economics should be quite straightforward. After all, economics is simply about how we work. What we produce. And how we distribute and ultimately use what we've produced. Economics is about who does what, who gets what, and what they do with it.

There is a very important question to be asked about where the socio-spatial dialectic will take us next; how places will be made or remade in the coming years. As Doreen Massey intimated in her essay, one of the great tricks of the past decade was to persuade people that there was no alternative to the present way of organizing economic and social life and, in fact, life was *so* good that there was no need to imagine alternatives. This is perhaps reflected in the popularity of the idea of social exclusion and inclusion, which served to suggest that any continuing problems of exclusion were experienced only by a minority. In the past two years, it has been revealed that we have been living on what Larry Elliott and Dan Atkinson (2008) call 'Fantasy Island', and the extent to which the neoliberal policies pursued have led to the emergence of a global 'super-rich' class who effectively live in a different world. Massey reminds us that this world, to which there was apparently no alternative, was relatively short-lived, and was not set in place without a struggle. The question of what comes next is being posed daily, in the media, politics and the spaces of 'everyday life'. Grahame Thompson (2009) has usefully summarized some of the narratives that are currently on offer to frame the causes of the financial crisis and what comes after the crash:

1. Business as usual – the main task is to resecure the stability of the financial system, stimulate the consumer boom once again, recapitalize the banks so they can get credit flowing into the economy and hopefully, restimulate the housing market. This argument does not see any major problem with sustaining the making of capitalist places.

2. The globalization frame – which is to blame the collapse on the forces of globalization. This is difficult, because it was globalization that was seen as having solved the problems associated with cycles of boom and bust. However, there is some possibility of the emergence of a new 'international financial architecture' which would presumably limit the flows of finance capital around the globe and hold the banking sector more accountable to the rest of society (e.g. the so-called Robin Hood Tax).

3. The happy Scandinavian frame – involves a strong critique of the emphasis on greed and profits and growth at any cost. Instead we should pay attention to well-being and happiness and sustainability. This is found in a variety of places, and the idea is gaining ground that we cannot go on in the same way. It is reflected in books such as Madeline Bunting's *Willing Slaves*, Richard Wilkinson and Kate Pickett's *The Spirit Level: Why More Equal Societies Almost Always Do Better*, and the psychologist Oliver James' *Britain on the Couch* and *Affluenza*.

4. The conservative frame – this involves a refusal to provide more bail-outs for bankers, a willingness to lead the market do its clean-out of unprofitable enterprises, and to enact cuts in the budget deficit.

All of these assume that the places and spaces that emerge in the aftermath of the financial crash will by and large resemble what came before, not least because they assumed the continued dominance of the market economy. There are other possibilities though: one of these is that the types of 'already-existing' alternative economic spaces that have continued to operate at odds with and despite the power of neoliberal capitalism will gain sustenance from the financial crisis and become to be more important. In the late 1980s ands early 1990s John Huckle developed a curriculum project called *What We Consume*. It consisted of a series of 10 units that explored the social use of nature and environment and sought to link pupils' everyday consumption choices to people and environments in a global economy. It was uncompromising in its insistence that the 'treadmill of consumption' that had accelerated in the post-war period was ultimately destructive of cultures and ways of life and provided superficial pleasures rather than sustainable futures. An important element of Huckle's approach was to draw attention to alternative forms of economy and social production. This type of education for sustainability remained marginal in the decade that followed. Though students are encouraged to adopt altruistic and citizenly ethics, they are prepared for a work-world where competitive self-interest and an uncritical commitment to profit win the highest esteem and reward. Geography teachers, tied to regimes of performance management which ensures that they 'teach to the test' and meet students' needs by ensuring that they get their '5 A*–C' grades, contribute to this.

It is perhaps time to revisit these approaches, and to finish, I want to discuss some perspectives that may allow for the development of a more open-ended sense of place in geography education. A starting-point is the work of J-K. Gibson-Graham, whose 1996 book *The End of Capitalism (As We Knew It)* argues that much economic geography, concerned with mapping the power of capitalism, obscures the fact that much of what goes on in the world is not driven by the imperatives of profit maximization or gain. When we talk of capitalist schooling or the capitalist family, we neglect to recognize all of the other motives and activities that are done for love, for friendship, and so on, with non-monetary reward. This is driven by the idea that ideas such as the 'market' should be seen as abstractions – they do not exist in real life. This holds the possibility that economies can be made otherwise. Gibson-Graham suggests that there are 'already-existing' non-capitalistic spaces that can offer models of alternative forms of economic and social life. This is something that geographers have started to explore in recent years. In *A Commodified World? Mapping the Limits of Capitalism* (2005) Colin Williams sets out to examine the argument that the 'market' dominates all aspects of life in what he calls 'advanced economies':

> The notion that we live in a 'capitalist' society organized around the systematic pursuit of profit in the marketplace is something commonly assumed by business leaders, journalists and academic commentators of all political hues. (p. 14)

He notes how this process of commodification is usually seen as a natural or organic process. For example, markets are often described as buoyant, calm, depressed, expectant, hesitant, nervous. The pound is said to have 'had a bad day'. This is not simply a way of making economics more comprehensible to the public by financial journalist. It is a way of imbuing them with the force of nature, even a reflection of divine will.

The prime achievement of Williams' book is to carefully examine empirical evidence about the extent to which market relations dominate our lives. He examines subsistence work, non-monetized exchange and not-for-profit mon-etized exchange, showing that these are growing in importance. In addition, he examines the uneven contours of commodification, showing how these are shaped by socio-economic status, geography and gender. His evidence is that:

> for all the talk of a hegemonic, enveloping, dynamic, pervasive and totalizing commodified realm, there exists in the heartlands of commodification – the

advanced 'market' economies – a non-commodified sphere that is not only as large as the commodified sphere but also growing relative to it. (p. 268)

Williams is careful not simply to argue for a headlong rush to develop the non-commodified sphere, since he suggests that this is not simply a case of the populations of the advanced economies expressing their discontent with a commodified world by voting with their hands and minds to engage in alternative ways of living. Indeed, the growth of the these activities is also in part a product of capitalism seeking to off-load the social reproduction of those no longer of any use to it.

The arguments discussed in the last part of this chapter cannot easily be dismissed as those of 'extreme' neo-Marxist geographers, but can be seen as contributing to attempts to rethink the practical politics of place and space. Geography, as part of an education for the future, has an important part to play in helping students think and understand the processes through which places, spaces and identities are made and remade.

Note

[1] In fact this chapter is really concerned with the *cultural politics of place* since I would argue that this is the work that geography teachers are engaged in when they offer representations in classrooms. This is my interest in this chapter, and it is based on an argument that geography education is concerned with providing students with 'imaginative spaces in which to dwell'. This may sound obvious in these post-modern times when we are apparently all comfortable with the fact that there are different readings or meanings of texts, but we should remember that this is a relatively recent shift. Until the advent of the 'cultural turn' in human geography, it was quite possible to teach about places in the belief that what was offered was a mimetic representation of the 'real world'. This is no longer viable. At the other extreme we should think of the dangers of the post-modern conversation which suggests that there are unlimited versions of places and that it is impossible to decide or adjudicate between them. This brief note on the politics of place should alert readers to the fact that the argument here is not final. Indeed, the title of the article by Doreen Massey from which the quote at the top of this chapter comes is called 'Invention and Hard Work', and this is precisely what I argue is needed if geography education is to be able to fulfil its promise of providing something worthwhile in these times.

References

Ball, M., Gray, F. and McDowell, L. (1989), *The Transformation of Britain; Contemporary Social and Economic Change*. London: Fontana.

Brown, C. (2001), *The Death of Christian Britain: Understanding Secularisation 1800–2000*. London: Routledge.

Bunting, M. (2004), *Willing Slaves: How the Overwork Culture is Ruling Our Lives*. London: Harper.

Champion, A. and Townsend, A. (1990), *Contemporary Britain: A Geographical Perspective*. London: Edward Arnold.

Cloke, P. (ed.) (1992), *Policy and Change in Thatcher's Britain*. Oxford: Pergamon Press.

Cresswell, T. (2004), *Place: A Short Introduction*. Chichester: Wiley-Blackwell.

Elliott, L. and Atkinson, D. (2008), *Fantasy Island: Waking Up to the Incredible Economic, Political and Social Illusions of Blair*. London: Constable and Robinson.

Gibson-Graham, J-K. (1996), *The End of Capitalism (As We Knew It)*. Oxford: Blackwell.

Hall, S. and Jacques, M. (eds) (1989), *New Times: The Changing Face of Politics in the 1990s*. London: Lawrence and Wishart.

Harvey, D. (1982), *The Limits to Capital*. London: Verso.

—. (2005), *A Brief History of Neoliberalism*. Edinburgh: Edinburgh University Press.

Holloway, L. and Hubbard, P. (2001), *People and Place: The Extraordinary Geographies of Everyday Life*. London: Prentice Hall.

Hudson, R. and Williams, A. (1985), *Divided Britain*. Chichester: Wiley.

James, O. (2007), *Affluenza*. London: Vermilion.

—. (2010), *Britain on the Couch*, 2nd edition. London: Vermilion.

Knox, P. and Mayer, H. (2009), *Small Town Sustainability: Economic, Social and Environmental Innovation*. Basel: Birkhauser.

Lambert, D. and Morgan, J. (2010), *Teaching Geography 11–18: A Conceptual Approach*. Maidenhead: Open University Press.

Lash, S. and Urry, J. (1987), *The End of Organized Capitalism*. Cambridge: Polity Press.

Marr, A. (2007), *A History of Modern Britain*. London: Macmillan.

Martin, R. and Rowthorn, B. (eds) (1986), *The Geography of De-Industrialisation*. Basingstoke: Macmillan.

Martin, R. and Sunley, P. (1997), 'The post-Keynesian state and the space economy', in R. Lee and J. Wills (eds), *Geographies of Economies*. London: Arnold, pp. 278–289.

Massey, D. (2009), 'Invention and hard work', in J. Pugh (ed.), *What Is Radical Politics Today?* Basingstoke: Palgrave Macmillan, pp. 136–142.

Mohan, J. (2001), *A United Kingdom? Economic, Social and Political Geographies*. London: Arnold.

Mort, F. (1996), *Cultures of Consumption*. London: Routledge.

Short, J. R. (1984), *The Urban Arena*. Basingstoke: Macmillan.

Shurmer-Smith, P. (2002), *Doing Cultural Geography*. London: Sage.

Stanford, J. (2008), *Economics for Everyone: A Short Guide to the Economics of Capitalism*. London: Pluto Press.

Thompson, G. (2009), 'What's in the frame? How the financial crisis is being packaged for public consumption', *Economy and Society*, 38, (3), 520–524.

Weeks, J. (2007), *The World We Have Won; the Remaking of Erotic and Intimate Life*. London: Routledge.

Weight, R. (2002), *Patriots: National Identity in Britain 1940–2000*. Basingstoke: Pan Macmillan.

Wilkinson, R. and Pickett, K. (2009), *The Spirit Level: Why More Equal Societies Almost Always Do Better*. London: Penguin.

Williams, C. (2005), *A Commodified World? Mapping the Limits of Capitalism*. London: Zed Books.

Discussion to Part 2
Charles Rawding

The three chapters contained within this part of the book clearly demonstrate the wide-ranging characteristics of place and the importance of the concept to the study of geography in the school classroom. As such, it is important here to stress how nuanced considerations of place – physical, environmental, social, cultural, political and economic – are essential if a dynamic, relevant and topical understanding of contemporary geography is to be achieved. Above all else, place is a human production, one in which we are all involved irrespective of age, wealth or economic and social power. As a result of our unavoidable involvement with place, it provides a direct and extremely important link between the experience of the pupil and the academic subject of geography. The study of place provides a very effective way into the subject and an opportunity for educators which must be maximized.

As Eleanor Rawling rightly points out in Chapter 4, place needs to be considered emotionally as well as analytically in order to give pupils a meaningful experience of it. Place is an outcome of historical processes (Pred, 1986) and is constantly being remodelled by contemporary societies, both in terms of its physical fabric and our changing perceptions of it. John Morgan (Chapter 6) clearly positions his analysis in the context of the changing socio-political framework of the second half of the twentieth century and the early years of this century, something which is not always made clear in classrooms where children do not have the sense of historical perspective which is acquired both through age and learning. The discussion by Alun Morgan (Chapter 5) of potential synthesis between the approaches of the geographer to place and 'place-based education' highlight a potentially fruitful realm for a more effective and powerful consideration of place, while at the same time exposing the vulnerability of the subject to alternative constructions of the curriculum. The tricky issues that arise from a combination of a 'cultural turn' in geography and a 'spatial turn' in the social sciences are ones that particularly perplex geographers defending their position within a politically structured curriculum. (Geographers within the Academy seem much less concerned with clear-cut definitions of their subject, although see Bonnett, 2008.) Overall, such an approach may well achieve a version of Geertz's[1] 'thick description' enabling us to discover and reconstruct deep layers of meaning in human interaction (Geertz, 1973).

The work of the Commission for Architecture and the Built Environment (CABE) and the 'Places Matter' initiative (www.placesmatter.co.uk) demonstrate an integrated approach which can prove fruitful in classroom situations. One further example might be cited here in the form of the joint Geographical Association/CABE project 'Where will I live?' which provided teachers and pupils in Lancashire and Cambridgeshire with opportunities for an effective evaluation of their own places and the futures of those places (www.geography.org/projects).

In many ways, such initiatives hark back to the earlier geographies of Vidal de la Blache (1845–1918) and his concept of 'pays' which result in the development of distinctive lifestyles (genres de vie) (Rawding, 2007). While it would be unwise to carry this analogy too far; John Morgan's point about the changing nature of society applies even more strongly when using theories derived from analyses of nineteenth-century France; nevertheless it is clear that there is a very real need among pupils to develop an understanding of the meaning of their places and the places of others. An understanding such as this will enable pupils to develop an appropriate and informed sense of place and to advance their geographical imagination.

At one level, such an approach might be seen as overly phenomenological, leading to criticisms for an absence of social theory. However, if we incorporate such approaches within an overtly socio-economic, environmental and political framework it becomes possible to avoid the pitfalls of both phenomenological approaches and the excesses of process-based studies which have a tendency to leave people (and particularly pupils) out of the equation. At the same time, such an approach enables us to move beyond the local towards constructions of Massey's (1993) 'progressive sense of place'.

Note

1 Clifford Geertz (1926–2006) was himself an anthropologist.

References

Bonnett, A. (2008), *What is Geography ?* London: Sage.

Geertz, C. (1973), *The Interpretation of Culture.* New York: Basic Books.

Massey, D. (1993), 'Power-geometry and a progressive sense of place', in J. Bird, B. Curtis, T. Putnam, G. Robertson and L. Tickner (eds), *Mapping the Futures: Local Cultures, Global Change*. London: Routledge.

Pred, A. (1986), *Place, Practice and Structure*. Cambridge: Polity Press.

Rawding, C. (2007), *Theory into Practice: Understanding Place as a Process*. Sheffield: Geographical Association.

Part 3
Mediating Forms of Geographical Knowledge
Roger Firth

This part is about the importance of knowledge in education. It considers knowledge in societal, disciplinary and educational contexts. In modern education systems knowledge is central to education, but we are seeing a major shift in ideas about what knowledge is and how and why it is important in terms of what is now widely known as the 'knowledge society'. This has obvious implications for education. Each chapter considers the importance of subject knowledge in different ways. Lambert makes the case for geography in the school curriculum, describing geography as a vehicle for education, emphasizing its potential for developing young people's intellectual capabilities. Brooks is concerned with teachers' knowledge and argues why it is important to understand subject knowledge (both academic and school geography) as dynamic knowledge. Finally, Firth draws attention to recent debates within education about the question of knowledge, the importance of social theories of knowledge and discusses some implications for the geography education community. The part speaks to significant and current issues and problems and offers an assessment of ideas that have long been, and continue to be, influential in education.

Reframing School Geography: A Capability Approach

7

David Lambert

Introduction

> *. . . children are no longer seen as able to cope with* education *. . .*
> *Ecclestone and Hayes, 2009, p. 383; original emphasis*

It is impossible to imagine an educated person who does not possess some geographical knowledge and understanding (and, some would say, values). It is for this reason that some observers of contemporary education debates express surprise at the sense of vulnerability of geographers and geography in schools. And yet the subject in school is threatened.

The threat can be from overt, conscious attacks from those who for many years have concluded that 'traditional subjects' are part of the problem in education and who favour 'integrated' knowledge in child-centred settings. More serious, however, is the more covert and subtle threat arising in the current *zeitgeist* described by Furedi and others as a 'therapy culture' (Furedi, 2003) in which it is argued that concern for feelings and emotional well-being of young people have eroded education. The effect has been to undermine how the system sees children and young people as potential agents in the world *and* its view on what they are to be taught (and are expected to learn). Ecclestone and Hayes (2009) are forthright about this: 'Curriculum shifts towards "learning", rather than the acquisition of what is now routinely dismissed as "soon to be outdated knowledge", are the commonest expression of the attack on knowing' (p. 383).

The emphasis on skills, which is now deep seated in schools and expressed through innovations such as 'Learning to Learn', 'Personal Learning and Thinking Skills', 'Building Learning Power' and others besides, appears to adopt a deficit view of the learner – as basically a fragile being in need of support to build resilience and other desirable dispositions, attitudes or behaviours. This is an attack on young people as 'knowers'. It is also an attack on subjects such as geography. Even when subjects are not dismissed entirely, or replaced by a thematic or skills led programme, the subjects are distorted by the softer therapeutic aims of the 'emotionally literate school' (Weare, 2004). In geography, therefore, we might stress the language of care for the environment, empathy with the 'other' and personal responsibility through actions such as fair trade or recycling.

This chapter is a constructive and progressive response to this scenario. It makes the case for geography in schools, but avoids the self-serving trap of merely asserting geography as a justifiable and timeless end in itself (cf. Standish, 2009). In describing geography as a vehicle for education rather than emotional literacy, I shall emphasize its potential for developing young people's intellectual capacities based on knowledge making and understanding, in the context of developing young people's capabilities. This chapter draws from, and then builds on, Lambert and Morgan's earlier discussion of a capabilities perspective (Lambert and Morgan, 2010, ch. 4).

Framing the subject in a hostile climate

The Geographical Association's 2009 'manifesto' *A Different View* (GA, 2009) is a challenging and complex statement about geography, education and the future. In it we are asked to accept geography as a 'curriculum resource' to be used by primary and secondary school teachers in their role as 'curriculum makers'. Along the way we are introduced to the notion of 'thinking geographically' and the rebranding of school geography as *living* geography (which incorporates a futures dimension). We are reminded of the role of fieldwork, exploration and enquiry, not only as key elements of geography's heritage but also as expressions of its contemporary educational power. Finally, and possibly most contentiously, we are introduced to 'young people's geography' which emphasizes the importance of tapping into the lived experience of children and young people, while allowing their questions and interests to help shape the curriculum.

Though not necessarily made explicit, what underpins this manifesto is a broadly liberal humanist educational philosophy – broad enough, that is, to encompass the radical idea of education as a potentially 'subversive activity' (Postman and Weingartner, 1971). Young people are equipped intellectually to think critically and autonomously to detect falsehoods or inadequacies in what they read or hear – what Postman and Weingartner in 1971 famously referred to as 'crap detection'. Geography, according to the manifesto, is a subject *discipline* for making sense of the world (albeit arguably quite an unruly one!). Teachers use geography lessons to introduce children to disciplined thought and argument, putting reported fact and information about the world into a conceptual frame. It is the latter that enables us to make sense of the world geographically: in other words, geography in school seeks to help students *understand* aspects of society and environment, and people and places. The manifesto places emphasis on this by distinguishing the 'vocabulary' of geography (such as its terminology, features and place-names) from its 'grammar' in the form of its principles, processes and key concepts (such as place, space and scale).

The manifesto claims that geography is for *all* children and young people, not just for the few. This is both ambitious and progressive. It can be aligned with Michael Young's (2008) call to 'bring knowledge back in', for there was a time when school subjects like geography was thought to be overly 'academic' and (therefore) elitist and only relevant to a minority. Indeed, Ivor Goodson (1993) showed how a subject such as geography strengthened its position in the curriculum specifically through articulating its academic credentials. Working-class children, especially those in deprived wards of the big cities, were often thought to be better off doing something more applied and accessible, such as integrated humanities or social studies. And to this day the geographical pattern of GCSE geography entries is revealing in this regard

(Weeden and Lambert, 2010) with the lowest candidatures generally found in urban comprehensives and academies. The anti-intellectual (anti-subject) sentiment, which as Young argues actually denies sections of the community access to disciplined knowledge and the critical capacities alluded to above, is therefore still apparent. For example (and I think astonishingly), in *Subject to Change*, the Association of Teachers and Lecturers (ATL) (a teachers' union) informs us that: 'Education is assumed to be primarily about the development of the mind', *but* this is a 'misunderstanding' (Johnson et al., 2007, pp. 69–70). The authors continue,

> Most people are not intellectual. Most people do not lead their lives predominantly in the abstract. It is not clear that it is preferable to do otherwise: the world cannot survive only through thought. (ibid., p. 72)

This second assertion maybe a statement of the obvious, but it is used mistakenly to undermine the idea of education. In effect it expresses a loss of hope and is deeply pessimistic. It is an invitation to teachers to stop thinking carefully about the purposes and goals of what they do, and instead submit to something more therapeutic and altogether less challenging than 'education', as we discussed in the introduction. In such a scenario, it is likely that geography can only ever hope to make a contribution of a list of 'vocabulary' and a limited range of 'skills' to children. And yet, growing up in the world and thinking about ourselves *in* the world, now and in the future, surely requires young people to engage in a search for understanding. Without the disciplinary 'grammar' and the ambition that comes from a deeper idea of education-for-understanding, surface knowledge and skills remain relatively inert and useless.

The ATL position is just one case in point reflecting contemporary trends that have exerted a powerful influence on schools. The influence, arguably embodied by the official 'big picture' of the Qualifications and Curriculum Development Agency (QCDA, 2008) which strongly promotes cross-curricular 'dimensions' and the notion of successful learners and confident individuals, has shaped how many school leadership teams understand the curriculum. Under relentless pressure to innovate for the twenty-first century, and against a backdrop of a persistent narrative of school failure, headteachers have often been persuaded by the seductive claims of innovation which focus on learning. Education has to some degree become usurped by 'learning'. Learning is a word that is now heard almost ubiquitously, being preferred to 'teaching' certainly, but also to 'education'. Writings that support such trends include those such as Charles Leadbeater (2008) and academics such as Guy Claxton (2002, 2005). In the field of geography education, the influence is perhaps epitomized by David Leat's enormously successful *Thinking through Geography* (Leat, 2001) and *More Thinking through Geography* (Nichols et al., 2001) in which the geography is in very soft focus compared to the cherished 'thinking skills' for everyday life.

The problem with 'learning' is that it is morally a fairly empty term, unlike education which cannot be understood as an idea without a moral context. Learning can be measured quite readily. Education has to be debated. They are certainly not synonymous terms. We know that learning can take place of a kind that under no circumstances could be described as educational.

These distinctions are important. For without them we risk being left with a lot of learning without too many questions being asked about the quality of that learning, or what it is all for. Indeed, Ecclestone and Hayes (2009) concluded:

> There seems to be a growing view that liberal humanist goals of learning a body of worthwhile, inspiring knowledge as a route into a world outside oneself, both in order to understand the human subject and to recognize its potential for agency in the world, and perhaps aspiring to excel in those goals, are irrelevant and oppressive. (p. 384)

In attempting to frame geography in the contemporary school curriculum, therefore, the GA's manifesto aims to retrieve a strong sense of moral purpose, and these are unashamedly within a broad liberal humanist tradition of education. What should we teach and why? The subject discipline is a resource which helps us answer such questions.

Restating the idea of education

So far, this chapter has argued that an expansive, challenging idea of education, taking up and developing some of the ideas mapped out by education thinkers of the mid-twentieth century, has been seriously undermined in England in recent years. For example, following Richard Peters' idea of education as initiation (Peters, 1965; see also Lambert, 2009) and the profound conclusion that all worthwhile education in the final analysis has to be 'self-education', we can take it as axiomatic that education cannot be spoon-fed, dumbed-down or taught-to-the-test. And yet in an age of intense scrutiny on 'what works', as instanced by measurements of 'learning gain' resulting from specific interventions, schools have adopted strategies and techniques designed precisely to raise test scores. At the same time they have also tried to respond to the fluidity and therapeutic needs of the times, introducing creative and flexible curriculum innovations. Often these competing pressures cause tension and stress – and are, in the terms outlined here, on the whole anti-educational.

The idea of education therefore needs rediscovering and renewing for the current age. We need to remind ourselves about what geography in schools is for, by articulating educational outcomes. For example, we should remind ourselves how education is different from propaganda (and the role subject disciplines play in this regard – see Marsden, 1997), how we can distinguish it from training, and why these distinctions matter. We should remind ourselves of the agency of the learner and the role education plays in enhancing this agency through intellectual engagement and development.

One way to think about the key argument in this chapter is to focus not so much on pedagogy as on the role the subject plays in curriculum formation. Unless we take the view that children can learn best without their teachers (and this may be a growing viewpoint in the context of affordances offered by information technology, although not one shared by many pupils: see the Harris Federation Student Commission on Learning[1]), teachers need to teach *something*. Guiding their selection within the broad framework of the national curriculum, ought to be a sense of what the teaching is *for* in educational terms, opening up for scrutiny a whole network of relationships – between teachers, children, parents and wider society and the subject knowledge deemed significant and worthwhile enough to teach. What we need is a mechanism or device to help us keep this sophisticated educational mix of competing priorities in some form of meaningful balance. The rest of this chapter offers a critical exploration of 'capability' as a means to provide a conceptual basis for geography contributing to what Vic Kelly (2009) calls an 'educational curriculum'.

Capability and the contribution of geography

The idea of 'capability' derives from the conceptual framework developed by the economist Amartya Sen (1985) and the US philosopher Martha Nussbaum (Nussbaum and Sen, 1993) in the field of human welfare and development economics. There is clearly not the space here to expand on this in great detail.

It is a fairly complex field which has more recently been taken up as a 'new space to evaluate what is of value in education' (Hart, 2009, p. 391; see also Hinchliffe, 2007a, 2007b).

Perhaps the key idea is the extent of what is termed *well-being freedom* afforded by a person's capability set. This is the extent of the freedom a person has as an autonomous agent in pursuing his or her well-being. This is not to be confused with a therapeutic or emotional sense of well-being in the form of, say, happiness. It is more to do with the real opportunities the individual has to lead a valued life, or the freedoms he or she has to achieve the particular 'beings and doings' they have reason to value. According to Hinchliffe (2009), a key aspect of exercising such freedom is the mental act of deliberation, defined as the 'critical assessment of ends and means in respect of well-being' (p. 404).

Sen's very broad idea has been shaped, with Martha Nussbaum (Nussbaum and Sen, 1993), to include the identification of ten capabilities which, apart from fairly obvious matters to do with the right to life and health, include items such as:

- *Senses, Imagination, and Thought*: Being able to use the senses, to imagine, think, and reason – and to do these things in a 'truly human' way, a way informed and cultivated by an adequate education, including, but by no means limited to, literacy and basic mathematical and scientific training.
- *Practical Reason*: Being able to form a conception of what is good and to engage in critical reflection about the planning of one's life.
- *Affiliation*: For example, being able to live with and towards others, to recognize and show concern for other human beings, to engage in various forms of social interaction; to be able to imagine the situation of another.
- *Control over one's Environment* (in the broadest sense): For example, the political – being able to participate effectively in political choices that govern one's life; having the personal right of political participation, protections of free speech and association.

Thus, capability in its broadest sense is not a simple measure of material possession and access to services. The capability framework emphasizes human *functioning* or what are called 'substantial freedoms' such as the ability to live to old age, engage in economic transactions, or participate in political activities. Thus, poverty is understood not in terms of low income but as capability deprivation, meaning lack of choice and ignorance as much as lack of financial resources. This approach to human welfare, with its stress on freedom and choice, diversity and human possibility or potential, clearly has a profound educational dimension. It is also possible to see how educationists at a system level, working in both richer and poorer countries, can apply a capability perspective to the education process itself, in terms of capability building of both individuals and societies. Some educationists have begun to explore this (for an introduction, see Hinchliffe, 2007a, 2007b). In this chapter I am interested not so much in the system but the potential of a capabilities perspective in helping articulate the curriculum, and in particular the contribution of school geography.

If capability in its original sense is not merely 'a measure of material possessions and access to services' as stated in the previous paragraph, then in educational terms capability is not a simple measure of examination success or 'value added' using performance indicators. It is an idea that embraces a much broader conception of outputs than specific skills or competences, important though these are. What is proposed here is a focus on human 'functionings' that values the individual and their intellectual development. In Hinchliffe's (2009) discussion, he makes two points that are helpful in establishing the significance of this. First, he points to Sen's distinction between desiring something and valuing it, and the importance of giving priority to the latter. Thus examining one's values becomes a key component of education: 'it implies that the agent is someone who thinks about her life in terms of ends' (Hinchliffe, 2009, p. 405). 'Living geography' (as expressed in the GA's manifesto: GA, 2009) encapsulates a worthwhile educational goal in this regard as it explicitly encourages individuals to examine their values in relation to change, sustainable development and alternative futures. In other words, it asks young people to think about their life in relation to themselves in the world, and what may become – an impossible undertaking without the deep description of the world offered by geography. Geography does not tell us how to live; but thinking geographically and developing our innate geographical imaginations can provide the intellectual means for visioning ourselves on planet earth.

Such grand thinking takes us to Hinchliffe's second point. He writes,

> Capability development relates both to the creation of opportunities and to the ability to make the best of those opportunities. The former aspect is dependent on social and political processes usually not under the direct control of individuals, but the other aspect – what might be called the agency aspect of capability – is very much of direct concern to the individual. (Hinchliffe, 2009, p. 406)

The form of agency proposed in this passage cannot be reduced to specific competencies or particular skills – again, important though these are. Capability refers to larger 'generic' – or what Hinchliffe calls 'type' – functionings, which provide the context or setting for more specific 'beings and doings', or 'token' functionings. In geography, an example of a subject-specific perspective at the level of 'generic' functioning maybe thought of as the intellectual values and dispositions that flow from the concept of a 'global sense of place' (Massey, 2008). This asks us to imagine place with porous and perhaps flexible boundaries, as meeting points of ideas, goods and people, taking in ideas such as power geometries and the operation of scale (see Lambert and Morgan, 2010, chs 5, 6 and 7). In other words, this is a big idea and helps us theorize – that is, it provides a framework for understanding – ourselves in the world. It is an idea that grows and develops cumulatively through a careful and suitably resourced geography education. Significantly, it provides the basis in terms of wider understanding, values and intellectual dispositions for undertaking more specific deliberations – such as on the shopping patterns in a local high street, where to site a nuclear power station, etc. It provides meaning and purpose to these more specific topics and enquiries. It enables particular instances to be understood more fully in terms of implications and wider interdependencies. Is this to say one cannot undertake the specific deliberation without first putting in place the big picture? Of course not. But it is to say that an individual's capability set is restricted somewhat without providing the means to develop the broader intellectual contexts and the possibility of *a different view* (GA, 2009). This is less likely to be achieved if one sticks solely to specific instances – or, far worse, learning and thinking skills development as if these were in themselves a worthwhile 'end'.

I am proposing the idea that geography education can contribute to developing the capability of young people. This is to argue that the value of geography in schools is its contribution to the enhancement of human capability in particular ways. The main point of making such an argument is to provide a conceptual basis for expressing the idea of geography in education that is ambitious, sophisticated and multidimensional, and which has its roots in the notion of human potential – to become self-fulfilled and competent individuals, informed and aware citizens and critical and creative 'knowledge workers'.

Although capability refers to what people are able to do, it is worth repeating that it does *not* equate exactly with the narrower notion of skills (or what are sometimes called competences in skills led curricula such as the RSA's Opening Minds). Capability certainly includes skills, but a lot more besides, enhancing people's individual freedoms, particularly with regard to making choices about how to live. Rather than discrete skills, capability rests on acquiring and developing a range of broader 'functionings' which contribute to human autonomy in thought and action and which are based on conceptual development and understanding. Part of the appeal of this approach is the realization that people with similar capabilities may derive these from different sets of functionings. Furthermore, whereas skills are often said to be value free, capabilities are value-laden, emphasizing what lies at the moral heart of teaching – a strong sense of aims and purpose. Teachers can infer from this that capability draws not only from 'knowledge' of particular instances, but from some engagement with the chosen epistemological roots of the subject discipline also. In other words, what is learnt, and how it is learnt, matters. Teachers as the curriculum makers are in a position to make choices about what to teach, and why. Softer learning outcomes, of the kind that appear to be highly valued in a 'therapy society' such as collaborative group work, are not ignored and indeed are valued. But they are not given pride of place. This is reserved for the tough work that aims to develop intellectual capability.

To what extent is capability a beguiling concept?

The 'space of capabilities' is essentially a liberal concept as I have already openly acknowledged. But it for this reason that it is possible to regard it as lacking in some ways, or as Dean suggests, as a beguiling distraction (Dean, 2009). This critique comes from the social policy arena rather than education, but nevertheless may cause some pause for thought. While acknowledging the widespread influence of the concept of capabilities, Dean points out the possible delusion of an idea that is essentially based on the 'human capital' approach which encourages us to imagine 'a consensus by which the ability of the poor to 'succeed' is construed too readily as a property or characteristic of individuals' (ibid., p. 265). Thus, he argues, the idea of capabilities is in itself constrained and abstracted from key drivers of inequality and poverty, which in turn reduces the 'critical purchase of the concept' (ibid., p. 267). This critique translates readily to the classroom. We need a more sophisticated sociological analysis than that which supposes the individuals we encounter in classrooms are free of all economic and other interdependencies or that all have equal possibility of exercising the individualistic capabilities we have been describing.

Indeed, we should also be wary of the very notion that educational development is necessarily a wholly individualistic process. Human beings may well desire personal autonomy, and there is a sense in which all worthwhile education is in the end self-education. But they also value recognition and solidarity (ibid., p. 269), not least we could add when they are learning about what it means to be human living on planet earth. Dean shows that while capability certainly encompasses the notion of public deliberation and participation, the problem may be that it does so in an essentially beguiling sense, in a world where individuals are members of a single undifferentiated public and the operations of capitalist relations are ignored or assumed to be benign. As Dean concludes:

> The capabilities approach is well suited to a consensual approach, but the politics of need should be about struggle, not consensus: the struggle for the recognition of unspoken needs; the struggle for more direct forms of political participation; the struggle against exploitation and the systemic injustices of capitalism. (ibid., pp. 274–275)

The validity of this position is perhaps less readily translated to classrooms. This is not to say that classrooms need to be consensual places – indeed I have argued many times about the need for geography in schools to be a resource for nurturing a 'culture of argument' (rather than merely promoting an answer culture). But classrooms are not necessarily the places to site a struggle for more direct political participation. My view is that educational settings are justifiable places for exploring with young people their knowledge and understanding of environment, society and economy. Their capabilities regarding future voting decisions, or decisions to join certain struggles (or not), depend heavily on their knowledge base and conceptual means to make sense of economic, social and environmental disputes. We should care very much about what we teach our children and young people and the ideas they are exposed to: to be able to think geographically (see Jackson, 2006) is a valuable part of this as we anticipate living in the world for the rest of the twenty-first century.

In an earlier chapter on capabilities Lambert and Morgan (2010) proposed, albeit tentatively, the notion of geo-capability, as a means of cementing the capabilities perspective in geography education. This was posited in the context of an impoverished education in which young people are denied the opportunities afforded by geography to support the development of their capability to understand and think critically and creatively about themselves in the world; this was even characterized as a form of capability deprivation.

Geo-capability was described in terms of how geography lessons might contribute to the development of young people's intellectual functioning. This took the form of a threefold framework:

- Capabilities concerned with enhancing individual freedoms (understanding autonomy and rights)

- Capabilities concerned with choices about how to live (understanding citizenship and responsibilities)
- Capabilities concerned with being creative and productive in the 'knowledge economy' (understanding economy and culture).

Each of these contains a full range of learning elements – that is of knowledge, understanding, skills and values. Of course, it cannot be claimed that geography is the only subject that can support the development of capabilities through an orientation of this kind. However, Lambert and Morgan (2010) also provided some examples of how such capabilities may be developed in geography lessons. Overall, it can be argued, a capability perspective on geography in education evokes a subject that can contribute to young people's:

- deep descriptive 'world knowledge'
- theoretically informed relational understanding of people and places in the world
- propensity and disposition to think about alternative social, economic and environmental futures.

It would be expected that such learning will be achieved through teaching strategies that emphasize the application of geographical understanding, often in realistic decision-making contexts. This requires us to give young people opportunities to acquire, develop and apply a range of key ideas and principles, and ultimately to make judgements about particular issues or themes through thinking geographically. Capability development is therefore to do with providing opportunities to practice the mental process of *deliberation* (Hinchliffe, 2009), underpinned by geographical knowledge and understanding. It is worth noting that the process of deliberation has long been identified as a component of a 'moral education' – for example, by John Wilson (1990) who described the twin processes leading to the main outcomes of an education oriented to moral development: namely, the ability to form judgements enabling 'worthwhile distinctions' to be made and the formation of 'healthy allegiances'. The idea of a moral education allows us to link geography education and the acquisition of the ability to think geographically to a capabilities approach.

Conclusion

School subjects such as geography are often understood in a more restricted way than I have attempted to describe in the previous section. When this is so it is hard to imagine their contribution to young people's developing capability in anything more than in a fairly modest way. In the case of geography, this is sometimes reduced to a partial description of the world and some rudimentary knowledge of a selection of human and physical processes. This may be one reason why currently it is so easy for some influential voices to dismiss subjects altogether – as being nineteenth-century constructs which have now outlived their usefulness in a post-disciplinary world. Such a restricted view overemphasizes the 'vocabularies' of the subject and rather underplays the 'grammar', or in the terms used in this chapter a curriculum for understanding. Capability in geography requires both. When an appropriate balance is struck, geography in schools can help young people not only to see the world anew but also with a means to engage with basic questions about the world, their place in it and conversations about possible futures (Hicks, 2007).

In a sense the capabilities approach serves to provide a link between geography and education, two big, important ideas that have been under threat in recent times. The implications are significant. As with a first, quick reading of the GA's 'manifesto' the full implications may not be self-evident. However, what the approach implies is little short of a radical reframing of how we see the role of geography as a subject discipline contributing to the school curriculum and the educated capability of young people.

Note

1 See www.harrisvoice.org.uk or www.harrifederation.org.uk Although students were critical of many teaching methods, they strongly endorsed the view that teachers were very important, particularly ones who knew their subject and how to communicate their enthusiasm.

References

Claxton, G. (2002), *Building Learning Power*. Bristol: TLO.

—. (2005), 'It ain't what you do, it's the way that you do it: a debate about learning to learn'. Battle of Ideas, Conference paper, London: RSA (29 October 2005).

Dean, H. (2009), 'Critiquing capabilities: the distractions of a beguiling concept', *Critical Social Policy*, 29, (2), 261–273.

Ecclestone, K. and Hayes, D. (2009), 'Changing the subject: the educational implications of developing emotional wellbeing', *Oxford Review of Education*, 35, (3), 371–389.

Furedi, F. (2003), *Therapy Culture: Cultivating Vulnerability in an Uncertain Age*. London: Routledge.

GA (2009), *A Different View*. Sheffield: Geographical Association (also available at via www.geography.org.uk/adifferentview).

Goodson, I. (1993), *School Subjects and Curriculum Change*, 3rd edition. London: RoutledgeFalmer.

Hart, C. S. (2009), 'Quo vadis? The capability space and new directions for the philosophy of education research', *Studies in Philosophy and Education*, 28, 391–402.

Hicks, D. (2007), 'Lessons for the future: a geographical contribution', *Geography*, 92, (3), 179–188.

Hinchliffe, G. (2007a), 'Beyond key skills: the capability approach to personal development', *Prospero*, 13, (3), 5–12.

—. (2007b), 'Special issue on the concept of capability and its application to questions of equity, access and the aims of education', *Prospero*, 13, (3).

—. (2009), 'Capability and deliberation', *Studies in Philosophy and Education*, 28, 403–413.

Jackson, P. (2006), 'Thinking geographically', *Geography*, 91, (3), 199–204. Also available at www.geography.org.uk/resources/adifferentview/downloads/ (accessed 15 December 2009).

Johnson, M., Ellis, N., Gotch, A., Ryan, A., Foster, C., Gillespie, J. and Lowe, M. (2007), *Subject to Change: New Thinking on the Curriculum*. London: Association of Teachers and Lecturers (ATL).

Kelly, V. (2009), *The Curriculum: Theory and Practice*, 6th edition. London: Sage.

Lambert, D. (2009), 'Geography in education: lost in the post?' A Professorial Inaugural Lecture, London: Institute of Education, University of London.

Lambert, D. and Morgan, J. (2010), *Teaching Geography 11–18: A Conceptual Approach*. Maidenhead: Open University Press.

Leadbeater, C. (2008), *What's Next? 21 Ideas for 21st Century Learning*. London: The Innovation Unit. Available at www.innovation-unit.co.uk

Leat, D. (2001), *Thinking Through Geography*, 2nd edition. Cambridge: Chris Kington Publishing.

Marsden, B. (1997), 'On taking the geography out of geography education: some historical pointers', *Geography*, 82, (3), 241–252.

Massey, D. (2008), 'A global sense of place', in T. Oakes and P. Price (eds), *The Cultural Geography Reader*. Oxford: Routledge.

Nichols, A., Kinninment, D. and Leat, D. (eds) (2001), *More Thinking through Geography*. Cambridge: Chris Kington Publishing.

Nussbaum, M. C. and Sen, A. (eds) (1993), *The Quality of Life*. Oxford: Clarendon Press.

Peters, R. (1965), 'Education as initiation'. An Inaugural Professorial Lecture. London: Institute of Education.

Postman, N. and Weingartner, C. (1971), *Teaching as a Subversive Activity*. Harmondsworth: Penguin.

QCDA (2008), *The National Curriculum 'Big Picture'*, published online at http://curriculum.qcda.gov.uk/uploads/BigPicture_sec_05_tcm8–15743.pdf (accessed 23 July 2010).

Sen, A. (1985), *Commodities and Capabilities*. Oxford: Oxford University Press.

Standish, A. (2009), *Global Perspectives in the Geography Curriculum: Reviewing the Moral Case for Geography*. London: Routledge.

Weare, K. (2004), *Developing the Emotionally Literate School*. London: Paul Chapman.

Weeden, P. and Lambert, D. (2010), 'Unequal access: why some young people don't do geography', *Teaching Geography*, 35, (2), 74–75.

Wilson, J. (1990), *New Introduction to Moral Education*. London: Cassell Educational.

Young, M. (2007), *Bringing Knowledge Back In: From Social Constructivism to Social Realism in the Sociology of Education*. London: Routledge.

Debates about Knowledge and the Curriculum: Some Implications for Geography Education

8

Roger Firth

Introduction

Over the last decade in education there has developed an agenda to reinstate, reclaim or recover knowledge (Barnett, 2009). That such an agenda has currency anywhere in educational settings should surely be an occasion to query; yet it poses important questions for policy makers, curriculum theorists, school subject communities and all involved or interested in education in the United Kingdom and elsewhere. Its emergence within the sociology of education has been as much a critical response to social constructivism and post-modernism in education and the increasingly instrumental focus of educational/curriculum policy as the endeavour to advance a 'social realist' tradition.

Michael Young[1] and others[2] have developed a formidable critique of social constructivist and post-modernist views of knowledge and truth and the various forms of relativism they associate with them (Balarin, 2008, p. 507) that have for a long time now been influential in education, as well as more broadly across the social sciences. These theoretical developments have been paralleled by educational policy developments that have their roots in neoliberal politics and its celebration of markets; of which they are also highly critical. Their arguments have focused on the way knowledge has been undermined by recent trends in educational theory and curriculum policy-making, such that the role of schools in its transmission[3] and acquisition has been neglected.

One might, of course, question the idea that knowledge has been absent from education. The disciplines of knowledge and the selection of 'subjects' for the school curriculum are one of those enduring matters of debate in education and in recent decades they have been the source of much disputation. The hegemony of the traditional disciplines, for example, legitimized by traditional and established forms of authority has frequently been challenged by sociologists of education for 30 years or more, as have the outcomes of education and the concerns to produce equal opportunity and social cohesion. The influence of Young's earlier work and the development during the 1970s of the so-called new sociology of education[4] in England is noteworthy here.

Recent educational policy has been strongly influenced by the notion of the 'digital economy' and the premise that the United Kingdom (along with other advanced capitalist societies) is becoming a knowledge society. In this sense the question of knowledge has been thrown into sharp relief again. It seems a major shift in ideas about knowledge is taking place, in the way in which it is defined and operationalized in society. This alternative way of thinking about knowledge is summarized by Gilbert (2005) where she emphasizes that knowledge is increasingly seen as a process rather than a product; it is performative in the sense that it is used to make things happen. It is dynamic and changing and collectively produced rather than the possession of individual experts and resists being codified into subjects and disciplines, which are seen as imposing unnecessary limits on our thinking. These recent changes in understanding are seen as an opportunity to think differently about the nature of the curriculum and teaching and learning.

According to this analysis schools operate with an outmoded view of knowledge and need to change. Leadbeater (2008) captures these arguments in stating that 'schools are out of kilter with the world children are growing up in' (p. 147). Currently there are a number of examples of projects, such as the RSA *Opening Minds*, which involve schools in organizing learning in ways that emphasize competences and skills that students will need to thrive in the knowledge society and downplay the importance of subjects such as geography and science. It is worth pointing out that Ball (2008) thinks that the 'empirical evidence for the knowledge economy is still weak at best' (p. 23).[5] Here, Young draws attention to an apparent contradiction. On the one hand, 'knowledge' has undoubtedly become the major organizing category in educational policies in the United Kingdom and of many other governments and international organizations. On the other hand the category 'knowledge' appears to be used in an almost entirely rhetorical way. As Fuller (2007) argues, one of the most insidious features of knowledge society discourse is the devaluation of knowledge, where the category has been emptied out.[6] One of the ironies, not to say deep concerns for Young about the so-called knowledge society is not just the way in which the meaning of knowledge might be changing or the marginalization of knowledge in debates about education; but rather that education itself is ill-equipped to contribute to debates about knowledge and the future of the school curriculum. What it critically lacks, he emphasizes, is a robust theory of knowledge.

All of these ideas about knowledge raise important questions about how schools and the school curriculum are organized, the most important of which for Young (2008a) and Moore (2004) is: what should we teach? The purpose of this chapter is to draw attention to this agenda and to the basic tenets of the social realist project before connecting it to recent discussion in the geography education literature and a brief discussion of some of its implications for the geography education community and how geography teachers in school might respond.

Bringing knowledge back in

In *Bringing Knowledge Back In: From Social Constructivism to Social Realism in the Sociology of Education* Young argues that the question of knowledge has been neglected both by policy makers and those working in education (Young, 2008a, p. xv). Along with others Young emphasizes how, in recent years, the secondary school curriculum has given increasing emphasis to the idea that education should be about preparing young people for employment and to be good citizens.[7] It has involved narrowing the aims of education to economic and social purposes and led to a focus on competencies and skills, and the shift in learning towards personalization and learning outcomes. In all of this, abstract, formal or disciplinary knowledge is being increasingly marginalized in the curriculum in all sectors of education and in many countries.

Within the default settings of contemporary curriculum policy and debates, it is argued, it is 'virtually impossible to defend a *knowledge*-based model of education . . . without that attempt being dismissed as inherently conservative and reactionary – as a defence of entrenched privilege and power relations' (Moore, 2004, p. 174; original emphasis). The importance of promoting young people's intellectual development, where 'the acquisition of knowledge is the key purpose that distinguishes education . . . from all other activities' (Young, 2008a, p. 81), is stressed. Learning this disciplinary or specialist knowledge is fundamentally more powerful than that gained from everyday life.[8] Access to such knowledge is both an epistemological and a social justice issue. Basically, the key goal is to reduce inequality by providing all students with equal access to, what is seen as, the best and most powerful knowledge[9] (Young, 2008c, 2009b) within society. It takes students beyond the local and the experiential (their own everyday or context-dependent knowledge), to knowledge which they would be unlikely to have access at home, at work or in the community (Young, 2009b). Running through this argument is an emphasis on the *differentiatedness* of knowledge.

Young people should have 'epistemic access' (Young, 2009a) to such knowledge; it initiates them into the intellectual traditions and gives them a language and provides them with reliable explanations and ways of thinking which they need to make their way in society. Young (2009b) does acknowledge that while schools can make a difference to young people's life chances, schools are not always successful, and in some cases, they actively reproduce social inequalities. He argues, however, that it does disadvantaged students no service to construct an alternative curriculum around their experience on the grounds that this will work best for them, and as a result leave them there. 'School may be the only opportunity that they have to acquire powerful knowledge and be able to move, intellectually at least, beyond their local and particular circumstances' (Young, 2009b, p. 15).

It should be emphasized that Young and others do not see this as an argument for a return to a conservative view of education and the purposes of schools. As Young points out, the traditional elite curriculum was grounded in absolutist views of disciplinary knowledge and the idea of the intrinsic value of certain bodies of knowledge (Hirst and Peters, 1970) that denied the historicity and sociality of knowledge, by which we are left with a false objectivity based on the givenness of knowledge. For Young (2009a) there is 'a clear distinction between a content based curriculum which treats knowledge as given and one which recognises that knowledge changes and treats contents as carriers of concepts not ends in themselves'. And while Young acknowledges that 'the idea of education as the transmission of knowledge has, with some justification, been heavily criticized (2009a, p. 13), the transmission metaphor does not have to mean the 'mechanical one-way and passive model of learning' (ibid.); rather, it can 'explicitly presuppose the active involvement of the learner in the process of acquiring knowledge' (ibid.).

Their interest is not in the school curriculum *per se* and Young (2008a) avoids a defence of 'any particular expression of a subject-based or disciplinary curriculum' (p. 85). Instead, it is the deeper issues raised by the recognition of the social basis of knowledge and with curriculum theory at the policy and institutional level: with the very principles that shall inform it and which express a conception of what schooling should be for with respect to society. The key issues concern the epistemological basis for an appropriate curriculum for the twenty-first century and the nature of that curriculum.

Such arguments capture something important about education, what Moore (2004) describes as 'knowledge as the basis of the intelligibility and integrity of education' (p. 1). Traditionally schools have been understood as having a unique role in reproducing human societies and in providing the conditions which enable them to innovate and change through the transmission and acquisition of knowledge. The quintessence of this relationship between knowledge and education is referred to by Oakeshott (1972) as a civilized inheritance of enduring traditions of thinking, and Kelly (2009) 'a truly educational curriculum', where 'schools, in addition to meeting the vocational needs of pupils and the economic needs of society, should be seeking to provide all pupils with an education in the full sense of the term' (p. xv).

While disciplinary knowledge and the capacity for abstract thought is seen by many as a means by which people escape the limitations of the context into which they are born, there are question marks over how far academic knowledge alone can prepare young people for life in the twenty-first century.

What is apparent today is the very strong questioning of the suitability of school subjects and 'traditional' underpinnings for curriculum in school. As Pring (2005) points out, there seems to be an ever widening gap 'between those who see the curriculum to be essentially constituted of subjects and those who want very different principles of organisation' (p. 1). What now of schools, the curriculum and the meaning of knowledge at the beginning of the twenty-first century?

From the new sociology of education to social realism

In arguing against constructivism and post-modernism and the recent trends in curriculum policy, Young and others seek to 'bring knowledge back in' to the curriculum and into the sociology of education through a social realist approach that recognizes the social basis of knowledge as intrinsic to its epistemic status. The aim is to provide a theoretical basis for the possibility of objective social knowledge and a knowledge-based curriculum that can be supported for socially progressive purposes, by drawing on the work of sociologists Emile Durkheim and Basil Bernstein, psychologist Vygotsky and others.[10]

The starting-point for Young is to acknowledge the social origins of knowledge, a position that Young took in *Knowledge and Control* (1971), a seminal collection of essays written with Basil Bernstein and Pierre Bourdieu among others. The book quickly became canonical in teacher education and contributed to what became known as the 'new sociology of education'. Previously, sociologists were concerned with the uneven distribution of educational outcomes. Young et al. brought to the fore the process of cultural transmission that lay at the heart of the specific role of formal education and schooling in modern societies, and the interplay of knowledge, the curriculum and power.

Only, Young has rethought his position. He now views the 'new sociology of education' and its social constructivist assumptions as an important, albeit, a seriously flawed attempt to establish a sociological basis to debates about the curriculum, though it undoubtedly represented an advance on the uncritical acceptance in England of the idea of liberal education (Hirst and Peters, 1970) based on the forms of knowledge thesis (Young, 2008a, p. 200). It was an 'over socialized' approach which neglected the question of truth. The idea of the social was no more than the standpoints or perspectives of particular social groups which reduces questions of epistemology to 'who knows'. Such a reductionist and relativistic approach, Young emphasizes, could offer no constructive rationale or direction to schools. It 'led to an over-politicised and instrumental view of the curriculum as something that could always be changed if political purposes changed. In concentrating on the link between the social construction of the knowledge structures of the curriculum and the politics of changing them . . . sociologists of education were led away from identifying the social basis of the knowledge structures themselves' (Young, 2008c, p. 3). At best, it is argued, these critiques offer only pragmatic and not epistemological grounds for distinguishing knowledge from experience. If all knowledge is reducible to perspectives and standpoints we are denied the possibility of demarcation criteria for the selection of knowledge that should be taught in schools (Young, 2008a, pp. 22–23; Moore, 2004, p. 155).

In the last decade a distinctive social realist research tradition has begun to emerge in the United Kingdom and elsewhere. The underlying claim of social realism is that 'education presupposes the possibility of both knowledge and truth' (Young, 2008a, p. 83). The arguments, as Hartley states (2007), 're-direct us back towards a modernist view that re-engages the Enlightenment project without falling for a naive realism' (p. 821); in other words the need for a form of epistemological realism that recognizes the social basis of knowledge.

Social realism places emphasis on the conditions and collective practices of knowledge generation that enable communities of experts/scientists within the social institutions in which they are located to construct knowledge that transcends its origins. It relies on a regulatory rather than an absolute notion of truth, which recognizes the indeterminacy (underdetermined by the evidence) of theories and the fallibility of even the most reliable knowledge. This does not, however, rule out the possibility of demarcating between 'good' and 'not so good' theories that does not take us back to relativism. This is not, they argue, a trivial return to some kind of foundationalism. It should rather be seen as a version of 'structural objectivity' (Daston and Galison, 2007) where the structures of expert/scientific practice owe something to the schemes of intelligibility that people use to identify them as such. In this sense, knowledge, truth and objectivity have to be recognized as fundamentally social categories, where knowledge about the world is based on the best evidence and the most powerful theories as rationally arrived at within communities of experts/ scientists who can legitimately contribute to the rational consensus. Here communities of experts/scientists are a logical proposition, not an empirical one (Young and Muller's response to Balarin, 2008, p. 520).

The logic of the argument begins with the structural *differentiation* of knowledge. If the differentiation thesis is accepted, Young argues, it follows that the curriculum must recognize this differentiation, even as the particular social and political circumstances of the time as well as global changes will inevitably shape how this differentiation is expressed. The emergent, non-reducible and socially differentiated character of knowledge has significant implications. These include:

- the distinction between curricula and pedagogy
- the inescapably hierarchical nature of pedagogy

- the crucial importance of subject-specific content
- the non-arbitrariness between knowledge domains and between school and non-school knowledge
- the 'objective' basis of the authority and professionalism of teachers
- the conditions for, and definitions of, creativity and innovation
- the epistemological constraints on the scope of policies for widening participation and promoting social inclusion
- the limits of 'generic skills' as a model for 'general education'.

(Muller and Young, 2008, p. 5)

The thesis provides for social realists a principled basis for a curriculum, where the key curriculum questions will be concerned with:

- the differences between different forms of specialist knowledge and the relations between them,
- how this specialist knowledge differs from the knowledge people acquire in everyday life,
- how specialist knowledge and everyday knowledge relate to each other, and
- how specialist knowledge is pedagogized.

(Young, 2009b, p. 14)

In emphasizing the social differentiation of knowledge, 'social realist approaches challenge the widely shared assumption that boundaries are always barriers to be overcome rather than also conditions for innovation and the production and acquisition of new knowledge' (Muller and Young, 2008, p. 6). Social theories of knowledge are important because they put people back into knowledge. By focusing on the social production of knowledge and the idea of a naturalized rather than a normalized epistemology this can help us rethink how we might approach knowledge in schools. In this way new questions can be raised about knowledge and education.

The school curriculum and geography

Whereas Young and other sociologists of education have placed emphasis on the very principles and theory that should inform curriculum policy, structure and organization, the geography education community has, perhaps inevitably, been more concerned with the place of geography in the school curriculum and with curriculum making at the classroom level. In *Is the Future Secure for Geography Education?*, however, Butt (2008) does raise similar questions about recent trends in education and curriculum policy. He ponders whether government policy makers have now lost interest in the 'fine tuning' of the academic content of subjects taught in schools and suggests that 'despite the statutory responsibility to teach a national curriculum which is constructed of subjects, the importance to the curriculum of many of these subjects, including geography, is being questioned' (p. 159). In conclusion, worryingly, he argues, 'we are approaching a time when the 'toe hold' that geography and geographers have held on to for the education of young people in schools might be lost forever' (p. 164).

Lambert (2008) has engaged with the contemporary debate on school subjects, arguing for the importance of subjects and the need to have a deeper understanding of subject disciplines in the school curriculum. He is rightly concerned about the intellectual vacuum that can lie at the heart of practical curriculum making when subjects no longer take a leading part. The type of geography curriculum appropriate to young people growing up in Britain in the twenty-first century is discussed by Morgan (2008) with the intention to stimulate wider discussion in the geography education community.

In *Corrupting of the Curriculum? The Case of Geography* Lambert and Morgan (2009) engage with a particular critique of the curriculum in English secondary schools made by the think tank Civitas (see Whelan, 2007). The Civitas argument is that since the early 1990s the school subjects of the curriculum in UK schools have been appropriated for extrinsic purposes, often by government, and thus 'corrupted' from their true educational purpose. Standish (2007, 2009) has applied these arguments with reference to geography. He argues that the school geography curriculum in UK and US schools is being 'politicized' by educational policy makers, professional associations and subject leaders with a serious effect on the intellectual development of students. Geography is becoming an ethics-based subject concerned with the promotion of environmentalism, cultural diversity and social justice. These developments are fundamentally undermining the intrinsic educational value of the subject and the freedom of young people to shape the world in which they live.

Standish seems to be making a case for 'education for its own sake'; to promote young people's intellectual development. Reflecting scientific, humanistic and intellectual traditions, he seeks to 'train young people in the virtues of disciplines, such that they gain wisdom and insight into both the outside world and humanity itself' (p. 5). Standish argues for a more rigorous school geography and deeper learning. But in all of this, Standish's theoretical position in relation to knowledge is not entirely clear, nor fully articulated. He also fails to engage with epistemological developments in geographical thought.

While appearing to acknowledge the social basis of knowledge, he seems to favour an absolutist view of knowledge which supports his view of geography as being an end in itself. He seems not to appreciate the relevance and importance of enabling young people to come to understand the social basis of knowledge, and for teachers to develop pedagogic approaches that can take on and work with the social basis of knowledge in the classroom.

The subject discipline connects us to a range of more or less distinct intellectual traditions on how best to think geographically. Young people need grounding in these traditions. The pedagogic implications of the need for school geography to take into account epistemological developments within the academic discipline have been discussed by Firth (2007). The social realist agenda has largely ignored the relation between knowledge and pedagogy in its concern with broader epistemological concerns in relation to the curriculum, though Young does acknowledge that 'the sociology of education must also develop a theory of pedagogy' (Young, 2008a, p. 80). It remains to be seen whether such theory will be concerned not only with 'the activities of teachers and students that provide the necessary conditions for students to acquire powerful concepts' (ibid.), but also a more 'politicized' appreciation of the social basis of knowledge as emphasized here (see Firth, 2007).

Supporting practising and prospective teachers to refocus on the subject discipline, Morgan and Lambert (2005) and Firth (2007) suggest, is probably one of the most important developments that needs to take place within the geography education community, especially at a time when England has a national curriculum framework which asserts an asocial view of knowledge, and where through government strategies generic concepts of pedagogy dominate. This will not be easy and the work required to bring to school geography the necessary theoretical clarity has arguably not been done during the years since the establishment of the national curriculum (Lambert and Morgan, 2009, p. 155). I would suggest that geography educators need to extend this theoretical clarity beyond the subject to the strategic policy level – and to theorize geography in the school curriculum and how knowledge itself relates to the curriculum. There is a relative separation of school geography from broader discussions of educational developments that we need to address.

Discussion

There is a great deal to commend in Young's work. It makes a strong case for the power of formal or disciplinary knowledge (and the role of sociology in understanding the conditions that enable its development). Young persuasively demonstrates that schooling plays a unique role in initiating students into the intellectual traditions that enable them to think for themselves. If we accept this starting-point for curriculum policy and school curriculum design, it raises a number of important questions for the geography education community. These would include: in what ways is geographical knowledge powerful knowledge? What aspects of such knowledge do we want young people to acquire? How should such knowledge be organized within the school curriculum? Such questions immediately come to mind, but as yet, we have hardly begun to consider these questions within a framework that recognizes the historical and social basis of geography as an academic discipline.

In answering such questions it is necessary to make the conceptual distinction between the academic discipline and the subject-matter of the school subject and recognize a range of possibilities regarding the relationship between the two (Stengel, 1997). Different views of the academic discipline and school subject relation will impact on how geography educators might answer these questions. What needs emphasis here is that over the last two decades there has been little connection between the academic discipline and the school subject (Butt, 2008). Due to curriculum centralization school teachers have not been encouraged to take forward curriculum thinking by working at depth with the academic discipline. That this needs to be done is as Lambert and Morgan (2009) argue, 'increasingly apparent, for the curriculum is increasingly at risk of being diminished – at worst, to a pedagogic adventure with a high value placed on skills and competence, at the expense of knowledge and understanding (p. 155). Extending this argument, I also emphasize below that school geography would be in danger of becoming socially and epistemologically irrelevant.

The chapter now focuses on the following three important and interrelated questions that emphasize how we might work with the academic discipline:

1. How subject-specific pedagogies might develop in an era where generic concepts of pedagogy dominate education?
2. How specialist and everyday knowledge might relate to each other at a curriculum level?
3. How university-based subject specialists and their school-based colleagues might relate to each other?

(One and three are questions that Young asks (2009a), the second is not a question that Young is likely to acknowledge as being significant).

How subject-specific pedagogies might develop in an era where generic concepts of pedagogy dominate education?

In some respects secondary school teachers do need to know and understand similar things, but in terms of subject specialist teaching pedagogical development needs to reflect the disciplinary context. Traditionally, classroom teaching has been understood in terms of transformation (Shulman, 1986, 1987) or transposition (Banks et al., 1999). Here, geography teachers work with and transform/transpose their subject knowledge of the academic discipline into the subject-matter of a school subject embodied in various pedagogical representations, teaching strategies and learning activities that are pedagogically powerful. Pedagogical content knowledge or pedagogic knowledge is seen as central to the transformation. It is a kind of knowledge that allows the teacher to transform the disciplinary knowledge she or he possesses into appropriate pedagogical forms and yet which are adaptive to the variations in 'ability' and background of the students. The transformation process is also informed and shaped by the teacher's knowledge and beliefs about the purposes of schooling, about the school curriculum, about national strategies and about the school context. In other words, transforming the subject-matter of an academic discipline into the subject-matter of a school subject is construed as an essential pedagogical task undertaken individually or collectively by classroom teachers. Teaching young people how to reason geographically requires a specific understanding of the nature of the geography discipline and the ability to frame learning experiences in ways that help form geographical understanding.

However, there is more to it than this. In placing emphasis on the importance of the epistemic question of what it means to know the subject-matter of the academic discipline, geography educators are only beginning to engage with more recent epistemological developments in the academic discipline: developments that recognize the social basis of knowledge (though see Firth, 2007; Morgan and Lambert, 2005). Geography, like the other disciplines, in recent decades, has devoted considerable attention to the production of knowledge and knowledge controversies and has seen a productive rethinking of the epistemological basis of research and knowledge as a product of its sustained engagement with the philosophy and sociology of science. This is nothing new of course; geographers have long entertained their own discussions about the nature of knowledge, science and the disciplinary status of geography as part of the process of refinement and redefinition (Livingstone, 1992).

In many respects school geography ignores the social basis of its own discipline and its knowledge. Given central control of the curriculum and all the constraints and demands on school teachers' time, it is unlikely that teachers are familiar with epistemic developments in the discipline. In epistemological terms, school geography clearly presupposes a realist epistemology, which is not made explicit. And more to the point, it is a naive realism; one which has none of the philosophical rigour of earlier analytic forms of realism, and more importantly here, none of the sociological sophistication of the more recent forms of realism. The significance of this, from an educational point of view, is that it prevents school students from appreciating the developmental nature of geographical knowledge, and of thinking critically about the production and justification of knowledge claims. This raises a question about the underlying messages given to students about knowing the world?

In recognizing the social basis of knowledge I am saying that knowledge is always already pedagogically pre-inscribed (Segall, 2004). Emphasizing this is not simply to suggest that the subject-matter of geography lessons is important or that content and pedagogy need to come together to provide for creative and effective teaching, such an argument has already been forcefully made by those writing about pedagogical content knowledge in the last three decades (based on the original work of Shulman, 1986, 1987). Rather, it is to argue that content and pedagogy are already interrelated and that creative and effective teaching is an outcome of recognizing that interrelationship (Segall, 2004). Knowledge does not only tell students something about the world, but also positions them to know of and to be in the world in particular ways. This idea does not negate the primary role that teachers have in creating pedagogical opportunities for learning. Neither am I implying that teachers necessarily hold or endorse foundation list and absolutist views of subject knowledge, though their teaching and assessment methods usually seem to presuppose it. It does, however, suggest the need for teachers to reconceptualize pedagogy.

The nature of subject teaching in schools today and the emphasis on generic teaching strategies suggest that attempts to shift teachers' thinking towards a more sophisticated sociological conception of pedagogy that recognizes the pedagogic nature of subject-matter will not be easy and that teachers will need professional support. As a geography education community, we therefore have to find the right ways to support school teachers to take ownership of reform and develop their pedagogic knowledge. In this respect, teachers need to spend more time on subject knowledge and epistemological developments in their concern with student learning; and in order to do this they need an appreciation of contemporary social views of knowledge. The problem is that as a community we know very little about how these characteristics of knowledge might contribute to actual teaching practices or students' geographical learning. Research in geography education needs to give a strong emphasis to such issues.

Geography in the school curriculum would be educationally the poorer without this vital dialectic linkage; without such engagement school geography is 'in danger of becoming epistemologically and socially irrelevant' (Fien, 1999, p. 141). Geography teachers need to engage with questions about the production and nature of knowledge if they are to enable their students to make sense of how geography helps them to make sense of the world. An aim of geography education should be to develop school students' understanding of the nature of geographic knowledge so that they can become intelligent consumers and users of that knowledge. This has never really been an explicit aim of geography education.

If the discipline, therefore, is to be more than a framing reference for pedagogy – rather it actually nurtures and feeds the forms of pedagogy that evolve to serve the purposes of education – then an ongoing debate is needed across the geography education community that supports the development of a theory of subject-specific pedagogy. And how might the professional standards across the careers of school teachers be reformulated in ways which recognize and encourage the growth and development of such pedagogy?

In the discussion so far transformation is construed as primarily a pedagogical task in terms of transforming the subject-matter of an academic discipline into pedagogic forms. As we know, however, there is another dimension. Transformation is also a complex curricular task (Deng, 2007). This curricular transformation necessarily precedes the pedagogical task. This has usually involved subject specialists, curriculum experts, educational theorists and classroom teachers (ibid., p. 289) in the establishment of subject curricula. Since 1988 and the establishment of the national curriculum and the extension of controls over GCSE and A-level specifications in England the government has maintained strong centralized control of the school curriculum and its development. In this case, what geography teachers have primarily worked with for the last two decades is not the subject-matter of the academic discipline, but the subject-matter of the school subject embodied in nationally prescribed programmes of study and examination specifications, government exemplification and the initiatives and the work of advisory and regulative authorities, all of which control or frame the complex curricular endeavour (see Rawling (2001, 2003) for a useful account and overview of the impact of curriculum centralization of national educational policies on the school subject of geography between 1980–2000).

The subject-matter of the school subject 'that results from the selection, framing and translation of cultural knowledge for educational purposes' (Deng, 2007, p. 290) challenges the conflation of school subject and the academic discipline embedded in much of the discussion about the nature of school geography within the education literature. With regard to curriculum developments over the last two decades the broader curriculum question of what constitutes the subject-matter of the school subject is of greater significance. Such an emphasis makes clear that viewing subject-matter in this way is also an essential issue of curriculum inquiry. Consequently, there is a broader discussion to be had within the geography education community with particular attention to the formation of school subjects and subject-specific pedagogy.

There are two points here. The first is the imposition of central curriculum control has changed the processes of curriculum change at the national level, the nature of the school subject and has also changed the nature of the subject teacher's task in terms of curriculum planning. In short, since 1988 the curriculum work of geography teachers has become increasingly tied to subject-matter of the school subject and the needs of the economy and other social purposes of the government. This goes some way to explaining the continued gap between geography as taught in schools and geography as taught at universities. The second is that the school subject needs to creatively re-engage with the academic discipline and with epistemology.

How specialist and everyday knowledge might relate to each other at a curriculum level?

The concept of knowledge differentiation, for Young and others, is a principled way of distinguishing between school and non-school knowledge, which they argue is important at the policy/institutional level in the design of the curriculum. It also has a specific importance in making clear the distinction between the curriculum (at the intermediate/programmatic level) and pedagogy (classroom level): between the conditions for acquiring new knowledge and the process of acquisition. For Young (2009b), while pedagogy necessarily takes seriously the non-school knowledge that students bring to school, such knowledge can never be a basis for the curriculum. Equally, this does not mean that the teacher's pedagogic authority does not need to be challenged, but it does mean that some form of authority relation is intrinsic to pedagogy and to schools (pp. 14, 16).

Contemporary curriculum policies, discourses and flagship projects such as the RSA's Opening Minds are tending to weaken the boundaries between school and non-school knowledge through emphasis on sets of competences or life skills that students will acquire through a range of experiences. Such frameworks are seen as offering a more flexible, accessible and a more economically relevant and socially purposeful curriculum so that young people are prepared for the real world of the twenty-first century. Such initiatives focus attention back on the learner and challenge a National Curriculum widely criticized for being weighed down with content. The message is clear: schools that concentrate on teaching a body of knowledge need to change their focus. At this point, a note of caution needs to be introduced. This is not to say that we should forget all about the possibility of radical change in education systems and curricula, but rather warn against the danger of thinking that schools must simply respond to large-scale forces such as globalization and economic change. We still need to think about what we mean by the 'real world' of the twenty-first century and how we understand knowledge and how it will relate to this world.

Within geography education the question has been approached in a different way from the initiatives referred to above. As part of a vision for renewing school geography and how young people benefit from geographical learning, the emphasis has been on the idea of 'living geography'. 'Living geography captures ways in which geography in the secondary school curriculum presents young people with a basis to understand living in the world' (Lambert, 2009, p. 1). The Young People's Geographies Project (Firth and Biddulph, 2008, 2009a, 2009b) is an example of this approach, concerned as it is with the geographical lives of young people and how their lives offer the possibility that classrooms could be reconfigured to allow young people and their teachers to be co-creators of the geography curriculum and of geographical knowledge.

The aim of the Young People's Geographies Project is to recognize the rich repositories of accumulated knowledge embedded in young people's everyday lives and explore how and whether teachers and students working together could start from young people's own cultural experiences and funds of knowledge (Gonzales et al., 2005; Moll et al., 2001) and connect these to the concepts and ideas from the academic discipline to build up a more critical understanding of the forces that shape students' own lives within an understanding of the wider world. Important here is the notion of ongoing conversations between teachers and students as a basis for developing the geography curriculum and a subject-specific pedagogy. By adopting an historical-cultural lens in viewing students' own lives, teachers are able to view geography up close and personal. In this way teachers and students can transform the learning that counts as school/intellectual success.

The project builds on the research of academic geographers over the last two decades, which has begun to redress the absence of young people from the academic discipline (Valentine et al., 1998). Today, the geographies of children, youth and families constitute a distinct research agenda within the academic discipline in the United Kingdom. It reflects an increasing interest in the diverse socio-spatial contexts and issues of young people's lives through which young people's identities and knowledge are made and remade, as well as all forms of socio-spatial inequality and hitherto 'hidden' and 'neglected' geographies (Matthews and Limb, 1999; Philo, 1992, 2000).

A particularly important area of development around young people's geographies in the academic discipline has been the increasing interest in the methodologies used in research with children and young people. One of the key aims is to develop mechanisms promoting children-centred research, creating an opportunity for children and young people, through their own voices, to discuss experiences within their lives. Geographers have contributed to the growing body of research that highlights that children/young people are not simply passive objects dependent on adults, but are competent social actors that make sense of and actively contribute to their environment. These geographies can be located within a wider dominion within the academic discipline, namely public geographies. These geographies are concerned with producing popular knowledge relevant to 'academics' and 'non-academics' through the co-construction of knowledge. Such geographies offer meaningful engagement to a wider public. The growing trend in the academic discipline and more widely to conceptualize young people as social actors in their own right, as well as the notion of public geographies, has implications not only for research with young people, but for ideas about disciplinary knowledge and knowledge production, for classroom practice and curriculum policy and theorization.

The curriculum boundaries between formal and informal knowledge that are being eroded here are likely to be defended by Young, arguing that such an approach, in appearing to be democratic and even populist both in its deference to experience and in its critique of expertise, falsely holds out equality between knowledges that are not equal (Young, 2008a, p. 16). In Young's terms, there is incoherence in the structuring of the curriculum; one that fails to distinguish the conditions by which students may acquire powerful knowledge. However, we do not have to accept this dichotomous approach. It is here, I begin to appreciate more fully some limitations of Young's conception of the sociology of knowledge. Stripped to its essentials due to lack of space, I raise three questions. The first is about the 'normative' and 'functionalist' orientations of social realism based on its structural model of knowledge progression. A second is whether Young would appreciate the substance of recent research work in the academic discipline of geography and elsewhere and if this appreciation of actual scientific practice is not a necessary part of any approach to the sociology of knowledge. Finally, if comparisons between different sciences suggest that there exists a variety of scientific practices, of 'sociologies' in the cultural order of each of these sciences, whether social realism as a metatherory best serves education and the curriculum?

How university-based subject specialists and their school-based colleagues might relate to each other?

The discussion so far entails the need for a stronger relationship between university- and school-based geographies. Since the establishment of the national curriculum in England, however, the notion of a 'divide' between university and school geography has become commonplace (for a useful overview see Hill and Jones, 2010). Any thoughts about a creative re-engagement (there have been much stronger links in the past) with the academic discipline, let alone issues of epistemology (not that these should be seen as separate), may have seemed antithetical to both university- and school-based geography teachers. There are a number of reasons for this, but space prevents me from going into detail here (for a discussion of the reasons see Hill and Jones (2010) and Firth (2007)). More recently, however, there has been some activity to reconnect university- and school-based geographies, including the GA and RGS-IBG (professional associations) beginning to combine forces to support and lead the future development of the discipline.

The social basis of knowledge will need to be a central part of this exchange and building of communities. Debates in the academic discipline have often centred upon what constitutes admissible ways of knowing the world, whether through theory, observation or experience. Over recent decades, there has been a growing engagement between university geographers and those in cognate disciplines interested in the sociology of scientific knowledge, the nature of knowledge controversies and the diversity of knowledge practices. Attention to the production of knowledge and knowledge controversies has given a new vitality and momentum to the subject.

As a result of geographers' sustained engagement with these philosophical issues geographical knowledge has become more fragmented over time, especially since the great divide in the social sciences between post-positivist and post-structuralist epistemologies, underpinned by realist, idealist and materialist ontologies respectively. There are now a plurality of geographies within the academic discipline and it is 'impossible to understand geography as a body of knowledge unless one understands recent shifts in scholarly conceptions of the relation between representations and reality, on the one hand, and the concrete, material conditions in which geographers produce geographical knowledge, on the other' (Hannah, 2005, p. 152). The nature of change in geographical knowledge will be important in helping to understand the nature of curriculum development in school geography.

Realistically, what is possible? Forging cross-sectoral partnerships will require considerable staff time and commitment, financial resources, as well as appropriate professional development and recognition. Ultimately, the real challenge as Hill and Jones (2010) emphasize is in 'creating an equitable exchange of ideas between university academics and school geography teachers, leading to mutually constructed learning communities that re-connect school and university geographies' (p. 30). Are we up for this?

Final thoughts

My purpose has been to raise some questions about the relationship between academic discipline and school subject and their conceptual, historical and social basis as well as broader educational issues concerning the curriculum role of subjects and whether subjects have relevance and educational value in a curriculum for the twenty-first century. My view is the knowledge agenda does speak to significant current issues and dangers in education and raises important questions about how social theories of knowledge impact on curriculum policy, the school curriculum and pedagogy. While it does not exhaust the ways we can think about knowledge in its relation to educational goals, it does emphasize that our underlying view of knowledge must be part of our considerations of the school curriculum. It also underlines the need for a theory of pedagogy that directs our attention to the production of knowledge.

As for social realism, it is acknowledged that it is an ongoing project (Young, 2009a; Young and Muller, 2007). It is recognized too that a social theory of knowledge that offers grounds for the very possibility of objective knowledge 'has its dangers' (Young, 2009a). 'It can easily slip from providing grounds for the authority of knowledge to being a licence for authoritarianism and losing its claim to be critical' (Young, 2008a, p. xviii). In his review of *Bringing Knowledge Back In* Keating (2008) 'is left with a slight feeling that the social realist theory of knowledge has not been fully revealed, or even remains a little elusive' (p. 436). It is an initial work that confronts and challenges education policy as well as significant theoretical and practice issues in the curriculum and pedagogy, respectively. While I agree with the overall tenet of the argument of Young and others – the importance of our ideas and theorization of knowledge for education – the approach taken can be debated. The theoretical arguments deserve close attention, but, I ask whether the desire to impose such an overall design (or, presumably paradigm) an opportunity or an impediment for clear thinking about the issue of knowledge and the curriculum at the beginning of the twenty-first century?

As a geography education community how might we respond to this knowledge agenda? Do we begin to take up the challenge Young and others have set us – to defend a knowledge based model of the curriculum and make a credible case for preserving our intellectual traditions in a changed social context and thus give weight to the idea that schools are not agents of social control but potentially a force for intellectual liberation. Do we go with the current 'curriculum flow'? Or do we think otherwise?

Notes

1 In this chapter the main focus is the work of Michael Young.

2 The work is quite extensive now. See Young (2000, 2003, 2008a, 2008b, 2008c, 2009b); Young and Muller (2007, 2010); Moore (2000, 2004); Moore and Maton (2001); Moore and Muller (1999, 2002); Moore and Young (2001); Maton and Moore (2010); Muller (2000, 2009); Wheelahan (2007, 2008). Whenever I refer to 'Young and others', it is a reference to these authors. They have two main agendas. The first and most important is the revival of the sociology of education, and in particular a realist sociology of education that places knowledge at its centre. The second is to use this realist sociology of knowledge as a basis for critiques of a range of educational innovations that have characterized recent times.

3 The cultural transmission of knowledge that is associated with education is understood as a much more complex process than a one-way 'passing on' of knowledge that the term transmission is usually used to describe. The research literature, Young and Muller (2007) suggest, mistakenly polarizes these two meanings of transmission. They give the example of Sfard's (1998) well-known essay on metaphors of learning that has been influential in education. Sfard distinguishes between the transmission/acquisition metaphor and the participation metaphor; but they emphasize, the analysis leaves the polarity unresolved because she treats learning as a generic process separable from what is learned (p. 5).

4 The motivation of the 'new sociology of education'(and 'critical curriculum studies' in the United States) in the 1970s was a concern for equality of provision and an awareness that the traditional form of the subject-based curriculum, founded on absolutist conceptions of human knowledge was inimical to these aims.

5 He argues that the 'main areas of recent economic growth and expansion of jobs' rests 'not on knowledge but on 'service' (p. 24).

6 For Fuller a second most insidious feature is the assimilation of democratic processes to market processes.

7 Contemporary education policies are underpinned by two main concerns: preparation for life in a knowledge society and social cohesion.

8 Basil Bernstein (2000) argued that fair access to theoretical knowledge was important for democracy because it is the means society uses to conduct its conversation about itself and about what it should be like. Society uses theoretical knowledge to imagine alternative futures through thinking the unthinkable and the not-yet-thought. This is why theoretical knowledge is socially powerful knowledge. Access to abstract theoretical knowledge is thus a question of distributional justice. School curriculums should be structured so that they provide students with this access.

9 Young distinguishes between 'knowledge of the powerful' and 'powerful knowledge'. 'Knowledge of the powerful' refers to what Young once termed 'high-status' knowledge and Bourdieu (1986) would describe as the 'cultural capital' of the dominant or ruling classes. Many sociological critiques of school knowledge have focused on the dominant relations between knowledge and power and the inequalities that have been embodied historically in the disciplinary and subject basis of school curricula. The concern has been with the legitimation of knowledge (who legitimizes what counts as knowledge) and who has access to it. However, the fact that some knowledge is 'knowledge of the powerful', Young argues, tells us nothing about the knowledge itself. The term 'powerful knowledge' refers to what the knowledge can do: move young people, intellectually at least, beyond their local and particular circumstances. Sociological critiques of school knowledge have neglected the extent to which the knowledge from which the disadvantaged are disproportionately excluded – disciplinary knowledge – is not just the knowledge of the powerful, which it has for too long been, but it is also, in an important sense, 'knowledge itself', that is 'powerful knowledge' (Young, 2008c, 2009b) that is valued in particular ways within society.

10 The work has drawn on a number of wider theoretical developments in sociological theory (Alexander, 1995; Collins, 1998, 2000; Shapin, 1994), the sociology of science (Collins and Evans, 2007; Ward, 1996, 1997), and philosophy (Cassirer, 1996, 2000).

References

Alexander, J. C. (1995), *Fin de Siecle Social Theory: Relativism, Reduction and the Problem of Reason*. London: Verso.

Balarin, M. (2008), 'Post-structuralism, realism and the question of knowledge in educational sociology: a Derridean critique of social realism in education', *Policy Futures in Education*, 6, (4), 507–519.

Ball, S. (2008), *The Education Debate*. Bristol: Policy Press.

Banks, F., Leach, J. and Moon, B. (1999), 'New understandings of teachers' pedagogic knowledge', in J. Leach and B. Moon (eds), *Learners and Pedagogy*. London: Paul Chapman, pp. 89–110.

Barnett, R. (2009), 'Knowing and becoming in the higher education curriculum', *Studies in Higher Education*, 34, (4), 429–440.

Bernstein, B. (2000), *Pedagogy, Symbolic Control and Identity: Theory, Research, Critique*, 2nd edition. Oxford: Oxford University Press.

Bourdieu, P. (1986), 'Forms of capital', in J. Richardson (ed.), *Handbook of Theory and Research for the Sociology of Education*. New York: Greenwood.

Butt, G. (2008), 'Is the future secure for geography education?' *Geography*, 93, (3), 158–165.

Cassirer, E. (1966), *The Philosophy of Symbolic Forms: Volume 4, The Metaphysics of Symbolic Forms*. Trans. J. M. Krois. New Haven: Yale University Press.

—. (2000), *The Logic of the Cultural Sciences: Five Studies*. Trans. S. G. Lofts. New Haven: Yale University Press.

Collins, R. (1998), *The Sociology of Philosophies: A Global Theory of Intellectual Change*. Cambridge, MA: The BellKnap Press of Harvard University Press.

—. (2000), *The Sociology of Philosophies*. Cambridge, MA: Harvard University Press.

Collins, H. and Evans, R. (2007), *Rethinking Expertise*. Chicago: University of Chicago Press.

Daston, L. and Galison, P. (2007), *Objectivity*. New York: Zone Books.

Deng, Z. (2007), 'Transforming the subject matter: examining the intellectual roots of pedagogical content knowledge', *Curriculum Inquiry*, 37, (3), 279–295.

Fien, J. (1999), 'Towards a map of commitment: a socially critical approach to geographical education', *International Research in Geographical and Environmental Education*, 8, (2), 140–158.

Firth, R. (2007), *Geography Teachers, Teaching and the Issue of Knowledge*. Nottingham: Nottingham Jubilee Press. Available at: http://www.nottingham.ac.uk/Education/Research/JubileePress/Publications/2007Firth.aspx

Firth, R. and Biddulph, M. (2008), *Young Peoples Geographies*. Sheffield: Geographical Association, GTIP Think Pieces. Available at: http://www.geography.org.uk/gtip/thinkpieces

—. (2009a), 'Whose life is it anyway? Young people's geographies', in D. Mitchell (ed.), *Living Geography: Exciting Futures for Teachers and Students*. London: Optimus Education.

—. (2009b), 'Young people's geographies and school geography', *Teaching Geography*, Spring, 32–34.

Fuller, S. (2007), *The Knowledge Book: Key Concepts in Philosophy, Science and Culture*. Stocksfield: Acumen.

Gilbert, J. (2005), *Catching the Knowledge Wave? The Knowledge Society and the Future of Education*. Wellington: NZCER Press.

Gonzales, N., Moll, L. and Amanti, C. (2005), *Funds of Knowledge: Theorising Practice in Households, Communities and Classrooms*. Mahwah NJ: Lawrence Erlbaum Associates.

Hannah, M. (2005), 'Representation/reality', in N. Castree, A. Rogers and D. Sherman (eds), *Questioning Geography*. Oxford: Blackwell.

Hartley, D. (2007), 'Extended review', *British Journal of Sociology of Education*, 28, (6), 817–822.

Hill, J. L. and Jones, M. (2010), '"Joined-up geography": connecting school-level and university-level geographies', *Geography*, 95, (1), 22–32.

Hirst, P. and Peters, R. (1970), *The Logic of Education*. London: Routledge & Kegan Paul.

Keating, J. (2008), 'Book review', *Journal of Education and Work*, 21, (5), 435–437.

Kelly, A. V. (2009), *The Curriculum: Theory and Practice*, 6th edition. London: Sage.

Lambert, D. (2008), 'Why are school subjects important?' *Forum*, 50, (2), 207–213.

—. (2009), 'Introduction – part 1: what is living geography?' in D. Mitchell (ed.), *Living Geography*. London: Chris Kington Publishing.

Lambert, D. and Morgan, J. (2009), 'Corrupting the curriculum: the case of geography', *London Review of Education*, 7, (2), 147–157.

Leadbeater, C. (2008), *We-Think: Mass Innovation Not Mass Production*. London: Profile.

Livingstone, D. (1992), *The Geographical Tradition*. Oxford: Blackwell.

Maton, K. and Moore, R. (eds) (2010), *Social Realism, Knowledge and the Sociology of Education: Coalitions of the Mind*. London: Continuum.

Matthews, H. and Limb, M. (1999), 'Defining and agenda for the geography of children: review and prospects', *Progress in Human Geography*, 23, (1), 61–90.

Moll, L., Amanti, C., Neff, D. and Gonzalez, N. (2001), 'Funds of knowledge for teaching: using a qualitative approach to connect homes and classrooms', *Theory Into Practice*, 31, (2), 132–141.

Moore, R. (2000), 'For knowledge: tradition, progressivism and progress in education – reconstructing the curriculum debate', *Cambridge Journal of Education*, 30, (1), 17–36.

—. (2004), *Education and Society*. Cambridge: Polity Press.

Moore, R. and Maton, K. (2001), 'Founding the sociology of knowledge: basil Bernstein, intellectual fields and the epistemic device', in A. Morais, L. Neves, B. Davies and H. Daniels (eds), *Towards a Sociology of Pedagogy: The Contribution of Basil Bernstein to Research*. New York: Peter Lang.

Moore, R. and Muller, J. (1999), 'The discourse of "voice" and the problem of knowledge and identity in the sociology of education', *British Journal of Sociology of Education*, 20, (2), 189–206.

—. (2002), 'The growth of knowledge and the discursive gap', *British Journal of Sociology of Education*, 22, (4), 445–461.

Moore, R. and Young, M. (2001), 'Knowledge and the curriculum in the sociology of education: towards a reconceptualisation', *British Journal of Sociology of Education*, 22, (4), 445–461.

Morgan, J. (2008), 'Curriculum developments in "new times"', *Geography*, 93, (1), 17–24.

Morgan, J. and Lambert, D. (2005), *Geography: Teaching School Subjects 11–19*. London: Routledge.

Muller, J. (2000), *Reclaiming Knowledge: Social Theory, Curriculum and Education Policy*. London: Routledge.

—. (2009), 'Forms of knowledge and curriculum coherence', *Journal of Education and Work*, 22, 205–227.

Muller, J. and Young, M. F. D. (2008), *Three Scenarios for the Future – Lessons from the Sociology of Knowledge*. DCSF and Futurelab: Beyond Current Horizons. Available at: http://www.beyondcurrenthorizons.org.uk/three-scenarios-for-the-future-lessons-from-the-sociology-of-knowledge

Oakeshott, M. (1972), 'Education: the engagement and its frustration', in R. Dearden, P. Hirst and R. Peters (eds), *Education and the Development of Reason*. London: Routledge & Kegan Paul.

Philo, C. (1992), 'Neglected rural geographies: a review', *Journal of Rural Studies*, 8, (2), 193–207.

—. (2000), 'The corner-stones of my world, editorial introduction to special issue on spaces of childhood', *Childhood*, 7, (3), 243–256.

Pring, R. (2005), 'The strengths and limitations of subjects', Nuffield 14–19 Review. Available at: http://www.nuffield14–19review.org.uk/cgi/documents/documents.cgi?a=118&t=template.htm

Rawling, E. (2001), *Changing the Subject: The Impact of National Policy on School Geography 1980–2000*. Sheffield: Geographical Association.

—. (2003), 'Connecting policy and practice: research in geography education', BERA Professional User Review of UK Research. Available at: http://www.bera.ac.uk/files/reviews/geogpu1.pdf

Segall, A. (2004), 'Revisiting pedagogical content knowledge: the pedagogy of content/the content of pedagogy', *Teaching and Teacher Education*, 20, 489–504.

Sfard, A. (1998), 'On two metaphors for learning and the dangers of choosing just one', *Educational Researcher*, 27, 4–13.

Shapin, S. (1994), *A Social History of Truth: Civility and Science in 17th Century England*. Chicago: Chicago University Press.

Shulman, L. S. (1986), 'Those who understand: knowledge growth in teaching', *Educational Researcher*, 15, (2), 4–14.

—. (1987), 'Knowledge and teaching: foundations of the new reform', *Harvard Educational Review*, 57, (1), 1–22.

Standish, A. (2007), 'Geography used to be about maps', in R. Whelan (ed.), *The Corruption of the Curriculum*. London: Civitas.

—. (2009), *Global Perspectives in the Geography Curriculum*. London: Routledge.

Stengel, B. (1997), '"Academic discipline" and "school subject": contestable curricular concepts', *Journal of Curriculum Studies*, 29, (5), 585–602.

Valentine, G., Skelton, T. and Chambers, D. (1998), 'Cool places: an introduction to youth and youth cultures', in G. Valentine, T. Skelton and D. Chambers (eds), *Cool Places: Geographies of Youth Cultures*. London: Routledge.

Ward, S. (1996), *Reconfiguring Truth*. Lanham, MD: Rowman & Littlefield.

—. (1997), 'Being objective about objectivity: the ironies of standpoint epistemological critiques of science', *Sociology*, 31, 773–791.

Wheelahan, L. (2007), 'How competency-based training locks the working class out of powerful knowledge: a modified Bernsteinian analysis', *British Journal of Sociology of Education*, 28, 637–651.

—. (2008), 'A social realist alternative for curriculum', *Critical studies in Education*, 49, (2), 205–210.

Whelan, R. (2007), *The Corruption of the Curriculum*. London: Civitas.

Young, M. (2000), 'Bringing knowledge back in: a curriculum for lifelong learning', in A. Hodgson (ed.), *Policies, Politics and the Future of Lifelong Learning*. London: Kogan Page.

—. (2003), 'Durkheim, Vygotsky and the curriculum of the future', *London Educational Review*, 1, (2), 100–120.

—. (2008a), *Bringing Knowledge Back In: From Social Constructivism to Social Realism in the Sociology of Education*. Abingdon: Routledge.

—. (2008b), 'Education, globalisation and the "voice" of knowledge'. Paper presented at the second seminar in the ESRC Series Education and the Knowledge Economy, University of Bath 26/27 June 2008.

—. (2008c), 'From constructivism to realism in the sociology of the curriculum', *Review of Research in Education*, 32, (1), 1–28. Available at: http://rre.sagepub.com/content/vol32/issue1

—. (2009a), 'Alternative educational futures for a knowledge society'. Available at: http://socialismand-education.wordpress.com/2009/12/06/alternative-educational-futures-for-a- knowledge-society

—. (2009b), 'What are schools for?' in H. Daniels, H. Lauder and J. Porter (eds), *Knowledge, Values and Educational Policy*. London: Routledge, pp. 10–18.

Young, M. and Muller, J. (2007), 'Truth and truthfulness in the sociology of educational knowledge', *Theory and Research in Education*, 5, (2), 173–201.

—. (2010), 'Three educational scenarios for the future: lessons from the sociology of knowledge', *European Journal of Education*, 45, (1), Part I: 11–27.

Geographical Knowledge and Professional Development 9
Clare Brooks

Chapter Outline

Introduction

Literature in education often refers to teachers' knowledge, or teachers' subject knowledge without further elaboration or explanation. In fact, teachers' knowledge is not an unproblematic term and can be used in education to mean a variety of things. A cursory glance at the literature will reveal a range of terms used sometimes interchangeably: subject expertise, subject knowledge, subject content, the subject, the subject discipline. When these terms are used without explanation they can belie assumptions about teachers' knowledge which sees it as reified, independent of the knower, timeless, objective and universal (see Kelly, 2009). Kincheloe and Steinberg summarize this as a positivist approach and argue:

> To the positivist educator there is only one *correct* way to teach and one *correct* body of subject matter. (Kincheloe and Steinberg, 1998, p. 4)

There are, of course, alternative approaches to understanding knowledge which believe it to be socially constructed, context dependant and imbued with notions of power and authority, as is reflected in much work in curriculum and teaching (see, for example, Kelly, 2009). But ideas around teachers' knowledge are still dominated by traditional notions of knowledge and this influences how we understand how teachers use their subject knowledge.

In this chapter I explore why viewing teachers' knowledge as bounded and objective limits our understanding of how teachers use their subject expertise. I argue that understanding both academic and school geography as dynamic knowledge constructs means that we have to re-evaluate how we understand teachers' subject knowledge and subject expertise. I explore alternative ways of viewing teachers' knowledge and argue that these reflect a conceptualization of knowledge that can be helpful for teachers preparing students for a postmodern world.

Describing teachers' subject knowledge

One of the most popular ways of understanding teachers' knowledge has been developed by Lee Shulman who argued that teachers have seven discrete knowledge bases, one of which he called pedagogical content knowledge (PCK), the particular domain of teachers. This concept became a popular way of understanding and conceptualizing the role and influence of subject knowledge in teachers' practice. In this section, I explore this idea's popularity and how it conceptualizes teachers' knowledge.

Shulman's aim was to draw attention to what he called 'the missing paradigm' in the study of teachers' knowledge: that of understanding teachers' subject knowledge. He identified seven knowledge bases for teaching: content knowledge, general pedagogical knowledge, pedagogical content knowledge, curricular knowledge, knowledge of learners, knowledge of educational contexts, knowledge of the philosophical and historical aims of education. PCK was given special attention as a key knowledge base for teachers.

Shulman defined pedagogical content knowledge as: 'subject matter *for teaching*' (1986, p. 9; original emphasis). The term was used as separate from content knowledge in that it describes 'the most useful forms of [content] representation . . . , the most powerful analogies, illustrations, examples, explanations, and demonstrations – in a word, the ways of representing and formulating the subject that makes it comprehensible for others' (Shulman, 1986, p. 9) making it the specific domain of the subject specialist teacher. In Shulman's later paper (Shulman, 1987) his elaboration of the knowledge bases for teaching elevated PCK to an equal status with the other knowledge bases (Gess-Newsome, 1999). He also described it as:

> that special amalgam of content and pedagogy that is uniquely the providence of teachers, their own special form of professional understanding . . . Pedagogical content knowledge . . . identifies the distinctive bodies of knowledge for teaching. It represents the blending of content and pedagogy into an understanding of how particular topics, problems, or issues are organised, represented, and adapted to diverse interests and abilities of learners, and presented for instruction. Pedagogical content knowledge is the category most likely to distinguish the understanding of the content specialist from that of the pedagogues. (Shulman, 1987, p. 8)

PCK has been very popular, both with teacher education courses and educational researchers. Nelson (1992) described it as promoting a cottage industry of research into PCK, much of which was subject-specific research which sought to identify what teachers needed to teach their subject effectively (Wineburg and Wilson, 1988; McDiarmid et al., 1989; Grossman et al., 1989; Ormrod and Cole, 1996). It was adopted largely uncritically by many teacher education programmes (McEwan and Bull, 1991).

Part of PCK's appeal was that it 'felt right' to many researchers. For example, Rosie Turner-Bisset describes how she first encountered PCK, which then went on to feature as an important part of her research:

> [Shulman's] conceptualisation of it [PCK] as an amalgam between content and pedagogy resonated with me immediately. I recalled the PE lesson and realised what I had been missing in terms of knowledge. (Turner-Bisset, 2001, p. 12)

PCK therefore seems to describe something which teachers are familiar with. Its popularity can be seen in how many initial teacher education courses are structured to combine pedagogy and content knowledge. For example, most Geography PGCE[1] courses do not teach geographical content or pedagogical processes separately: but unite them, emphasizing how content and pedagogy work together.

By identifying PCK as a separate and unique knowledge construct to describe teachers' subject knowledge, Shulman was not only responding to criticisms of the work of educationalists at the time, but was also demonstrating that there was something unique that teachers did with academic knowledge that was different to other subject specialists.

Gess-Newsome (1999) notes, however, that the recognition of this phenomena as a separate knowledge has brought conceptual difficulties. She reports how research has been unable to agree on how PCK is developed, or how it relates to its constituent parts of content knowledge and pedagogical knowledge (ibid.). Consequently, the lack of clarity over how PCK is developed makes the concept difficult to understand (Sockett, 1987; Meredith, 1995; Segall, 2004). Grossman's work highlights the difficulty of defining PCK as it is unclear how it can be differentiated from other types of knowledge. This difficulty is grounded in how it represents teachers' knowledge. By defining the phenomena of how teachers use their subject knowledge as a separate knowledge construct, Shulman was ascribing it with the attributes of knowledge rather than as a process. Carlsen (1999) argues that PCK is grounded in a structuralist view of knowledge. As such, there is an implicit assumption in PCK that content is static (Banks et al., 1999). Others have noted that it does not enable a constructivist conception of learning (Meredith, 1995; Geddis, 1993), or accommodate how teachers' responses may vary due to differing contexts (Carlsen, 1991).

These observations limit the usefulness of PCK to understand teachers' subject knowledge. For example, teachers change their understanding of knowledge through teaching. Grossman's (1990) and Hillock's (1999) work shows how English teachers' values about the subject affect what they perceive as English 'content' or knowledge. Their definition of 'English' affects how they construct sequences of lessons and individual lessons. Turvey (2005) also shows how the act of teaching can change teachers' subject knowledge as they encounter different perspectives on text through working on it with children. Carlsen's (1991) work with science teachers shows that their perception of the subject also varies depending on context and the people involved. Teachers actively construct and develop their subject knowledge through the process of teaching, suggesting that their subject knowledge is dynamically developed and under constant review.

The conceptual problems with PCK are partly due to the inadequacies of the word 'knowledge' to describe this aspect of teachers' work. Fenstermacher (1994) describes 'knowledge' as a word that gives power and authority. He questions if the type of 'knowledge' to which PCK refers is clearly defined as a form of knowledge (Fenstermacher, 1994). In fact, Fenstermacher notes the epistemic difficulties with defining knowledges, particularly the knowledge held by others, and differentiating them from beliefs. Indeed, Pajares (1992) notes the complexity of researching teachers' beliefs and knowledge, and being able to make firm statements about the influence of either. As such, defining

PCK as a knowledge becomes problematic. Carlsen (1999) argues that we need a more general term that reflects the dynamic nature of subject knowledge, teachers' personal relationship with it and with pedagogy.

The conceptual difficulties associated with PCK can therefore be attributed in part to the problems associated with defining it as a knowledge. Regarding what teachers know in this way prevents teachers and teacher educators from recognizing the dynamic way that knowledge is developed both in disciplinary communities and in individuals. In the next section, I look specifically at geographical knowledge suggesting that it is more useful to consider geography teachers' subject knowledge as subject expertise.

Academic geography and school geography

Academic geography, as a discipline, is a human creation, defined and maintained by people (Johnston, 1991). Goodson notes that this social construction is a dynamic process:

> Subjects are not monolithic entities but shifting amalgamations of subgroups and traditions that through contestation and compromise influence the direction of change. (1987, p. 64)

Johnston (1991) argues that such rivalry of ideas and influences can come from both inside and outside the discipline. Therefore, how 'geography' has been understood changes over time and reflects what society considers valuable knowledge (Johnston, 1991; Unwin, 1992; Livingstone, 1993). These changes have affected *how* geography was studied and *what* content was considered valuable. This reflects different geographical knowledges (or epistemologies) as well as different methodologies.

This is not to suggest that there is always agreement about what constitutes geographical knowledge at any given time or place. Academics will hold different views about what geography is at any given time, and what its contribution is to our social, political, cultural and academic understanding. Consequently, while definitions of geography are subject to change, there is some agreement about key concepts which are geographical. For example, Jackson (2006) has argued that there is some consensus that the concepts of space, place and scale are agreed to be geographical. His elaboration of what it means to 'think geographically' is especially useful as it places emphasis on relational thinking and key geographical concepts. However, acknowledging the contested nature of academic geography, makes defining school geography – or 'what' geography should be taught to young people – even more complex.

How does this changing definition of academic geography affect the school subject? Lambert (2009a) has argued that the perceived gap between academic and school geography is in fact widening. This is perhaps unsurprising as academic geographers play less of a role in constructing school geography, while government policy and public examination boards play an increasing role in defining the school curriculum. Walford (2001), analysing school geography from 1850–2000, observes that the school subject has been influenced by broad changes and developments in pedagogy such as progressive notions of teaching and learning. Graves (2001), focusing on school geography textbooks from the same period, makes similar observations stating: '[Geography school] textbooks tend to follow society, rather than lead it' (p. 157). Rawling (2001) also highlights how ideological perspectives of key players have had a significant impact on education policy and how it defines school subjects (particularly geography). Such trends and foci affect how school geography can be defined independently of developments in the academic discipline.

The relationship between the discipline and the school subject

The relationship between the academic and school subject is then characterized as a relationship between two shifting, dynamic entities. It is not surprising therefore, that geography graduates consider school geography to be different from their undergraduate studies (Lambert, 2002). Undergraduate geography courses rarely cover all areas of geographical content covered in the school curriculum, so geography teachers do not necessarily have a detailed knowledge of all the topics required to teach geography at 'A' level (Bale and McPartland, 1986). Opportunities to reflect on subject knowledge development post qualification are limited (Prentice, 1997).

Research in geography education has tried to identify the link between undergraduate specialism and practice. For example, Barratt-Hacking's (1996) research looked at 16 teachers in their PGCE year and concluded that geography teachers' geographical 'persuasions' are often suspended when they teach geography. Jewitt's (1998) work contradicts these findings. Her work on one geography department suggests that the individual's practice is underpinned by values, mainly developed through their academic geography experience, which affects how they perceive school and academic geography. One of the reasons for this lack of clarity may be due to the narrow way that geography is defined in these studies (i.e. through undergraduate specialization). A broader conceptualization of subject expertise that goes beyond undergraduate knowledge or experience could illuminate the relationship between how teachers understand geography and how they teach it.

Teachers' subject knowledge is not fixed upon graduation. Brooks and Morgan (2006) argue that the experience of living in the world makes geographers out of all of us. Such a notion suggests that geographical knowledge is created and recreated on a daily basis through learners (inside or outside a formal learning context) thinking geographically. This learning can be influenced by a variety of media, including portrayals of geographical or global phenomena of distance places, and through independent travel. This is especially the case for geography teachers who have received an academic training in the discipline. Rynne and Lambert (1997) argue that geography graduates have the intellectual capacity to develop new understandings through their ability to think geographically. These ideas are developed further in Martin's (2006) work which demonstrates the complexity of defining teachers' understandings of geography. Her concept of ethnogeographies emphasizes how teachers' engagement with geographical phenomena beyond formal education is an important component of their geographical understanding and pedagogical toolkit:

> Ethnogeography reflects the view that all learners are geographers because they all live in the world. They all negotiate and interact with a variety of landscapes (human and natural) on a daily basis. What they don't perhaps recognise is that this knowledge is useful geographical knowledge and a point from which deeper conceptual understanding is developed. (Martin, 2006, p. 183)

Therefore, experienced teachers may have highly developed geographical imaginations, which can influence their understanding of the subject, and consequently their teaching. Therefore to talk about teachers' geographical knowledge or subject knowledge may be inaccurate and it may be more useful to consider teachers as having a range of geographical knowledges. The knowledge base (or bases) that teachers can draw upon when deciding what to teach and what is valuable geographical knowledge will be broad. Teachers are informed by their own geographical understanding, their geographical imaginations and their formal knowledge of the academic subject. This combination goes beyond an understanding of teachers' geographical knowledge to that of teachers' subject expertise.

Subject expertise and its influence on practice

Understanding teachers' knowledge as subject expertise enables a more constructivist approach to knowledge creation and development. PCK is not able to reflect changes in subject knowledge development, but a more flexible approach to teacher's subject knowledge – such as viewing it as subject expertise – acknowledges that knowledge can be created in classrooms, and credits teachers with geographical knowledge that is developed beyond formal academic contexts.

Exploring what this looks like in a classroom setting, Lambert (2009b) has advocated an approach that he describes as 'living geography' which enables a constructivist and critical approach to geographical knowledge and geography education. He argues that this encompasses three different geographical knowledges: academic geography, school geography and popular geography (ibid.).

> Living geography is created when teachers use the subject discipline . . . and their knowledge of children and young people . . . to make sense of the world. Living geography
>
> - embraces 'young people's geographies' – that is young people's experiences and encounters with the world and takes seriously what they make of these things
> - certainly recognizes the past, including the deep past (how else would we understand mountains for example), but is also current and futures oriented, encouraging young people to envision and project into the future
> - often 'local' but always set in wider (global) contexts, requiring practice and steadily deepening awareness of interlocking scales
> - investigates processes that bring change to environments – these can be grouped as environmental (or 'physical'), social, economic and political
> - encourages a critical, conceptual understanding of a range of key ideas such as 'sustainable development'. This foregrounds the nature of geography as a synthesis across the physical and human worlds. (ibid.)

Lambert's explanation of living geography describes an approach that seeks to combine geographical concepts alongside local knowledges while advocating constructivist pedagogies such as geographical enquiry (see Roberts, 2003). Lambert's definition also incorporates learners' geographical experiences which can be developed as part of their geographical education. Such a vision of geography and teaching geography is underpinned by a view of knowledge that acknowledges that it is plural, constructed, can be critical and can be developed through a teaching/learning interaction.

Innovative and plural approaches to geography education that take into account pupils' views and locally derived knowledge have not received universal approval. Concerns have been raised about the quality of the geographical content in some similar initiatives. For instance, Marsden (1997) has argued that some approaches to teaching geography (e.g. the issues-based approach) place too much emphasis on the social or educational considerations at the expense of due consideration of the content. He warns of the geography being taken out of geography education. Lambert criticizes the thinking skills movement in geography for its light consideration of geographical content (see Chapter 7 in this volume). Standish (2009) takes this argument even further. He suggests that recent developments in school geography have been hijacked by a liberal agenda that has effectively removed the essence of what geography is. Both of these arguments are useful warnings to geography educators about the geographical integrity of what is being taught (Lambert, 2008).

Such concerns are echoed by Young (2008) who notes how trends in education, such as the emphasis on targets, access and participation, have resulted in a lack of attention to knowledge. These trends have diverted our attention away from questions about what is worthwhile knowledge and what knowledge should be taught. Young recognizes the importance of knowledge in society. He argues that:

> a 'curriculum of the future' needs to treat knowledge as a distinct and non-reducible element in the changing resources that people need access to in order to make sense of the world. (ibid., p. 90)

This emphasis on the importance of knowledge is echoed by Gardner (2007) in his consideration of 'minds of the future', where he argues that 'disciplinary thinking' will be important as it distinguishes between those that have factual knowledge without disciplinary sophistication. For Gardiner, the disciplines are ways of understanding the world, and understanding and interpreting 'facts' about the world. In this sense the disciplines help us to differentiate between knowledge and information. (Gardner also notes the importance of 'being disciplined' as part of disciplinary thinking.) Therefore, it is important not to underestimate the significance of disciplinary knowledge and its inclusion in the school curriculum. The challenge remains to understand how such views of academic disciplines are reflected and how they influence the school subject.

Goodson (1987) has noted that the case of geography is unique as the subject started being taught in classrooms before graduating to university status. In the school subject of science, it has been suggested that the academic and school subjects are not the same subject discipline (Kind and Taber, 2005). In fact, as Stengel's (1997) work demonstrates, the relationship between the school subject and its academic parent is not always straightforward. Stengel suggests that academic and school subjects are linked in one of the following ways:

1. that academic disciplines and school subjects are essentially continuous
2. that academic disciplines and school subjects are essentially discontinuous
3. that academic disciplines and school subjects are different but related in one of three ways:
   a. academic discipline precedes school subject
   b. school subject precedes academic discipline, or
   c. the relationship between the two is dialectic.

Her analysis shows that the relationship between academic and school subject is not necessarily linear. Recognizing this complexity indicates that subject specialist teachers need to have a critical understanding of both the academic discipline and the school subject. In practical terms, this means understanding the disciplinary origins of the content of school curricular and school texts. Such an understanding can help teachers to make the decisions necessary to ensure that what they are teaching is both geographically accurate, up-to-date and suitable for their students. It is this dynamic that PCK sought to describe. However, as McEwan and Bull (1991) highlight this is more of a dynamic process conducting 'in-action', than a knowledge. This distinction is significant as it requires a shift in how we think about knowledge in classrooms. The shift is away from a technical delivery model of instruction, to a more dynamic process where the teacher guides her students to a greater and deeper understanding through her own expert knowledge of the subject. This is a different model of subject expertise which recognizes the various ways in which teachers use their subject expertise. Its roots were explored by John Dewey, and returning to his analysis is useful here.

Psychologizing subject-matter

Dewey had a nuanced understanding of the nature of teachers' subject expertise. He distinguished between academic subjects and how we learn them because he suggested they were developed differently. Dewey argued that subjects or disciplines were the result of academics debating and clarifying arguments over time. Consequently academic subjects are organized and presented 'logically'. They are the finished product of all the work that has gone on before, presented in the most logical way. In contrast, Dewey argued that children learn from experience, which he described as 'psychologically'. Dewey represents this with a specific example from geography:

> We must discover what there is lying within the child's present sphere of experience [or within the scope of experiences which he can easily get] which deserves to be called geographical. It is not the question of how to teach the child geography, but first of all the question *what* geography is for the child. (Dewey, 1972 [1897], p. 169)

Dewey deliberately placed the child's experience first, and the subject discipline as a way of helping that child to make sense of that experience. Dewey suggested that teachers could do that by 'psychologizing subject-matter' to enable children to make sense of their experience (Dewey, 1972 [1897]). However, understanding what this psychologizing means has proved to be challenging. For example, Shulman (1986) has argued that it is this process of psychologizing that pedagogical content knowledge seeks to describe. McEwan and Bull (1991) have been critical of his interpretation of Dewey highlighting how Dewey's description of 'psychologizing' is of a process that a teacher does with their subject knowledge, alongside their knowledge of students, rather than as a separate knowledge base.

Research into teachers' psychologizing subject-matter often uses metaphors to illustrate the pivotal role of subject knowledge. For example, Smith and Girod (2003) use an analogy of a map to illustrate the process. In their description, the teacher's subject knowledge is the base of the map. Upon that base map, teachers can orientate both the intended final destination (i.e. what is to be learnt), and the locations of where their students currently reside (i.e. the students' prior and current knowledge and experience). Connecting the final destination and the students' current location is the process through which teachers can help to connect their students with the lesson content.

Other descriptions of excellent teachers' practice have described this process as a bridge, such as Wineburg and Wilson (1988), in their examination of the use of subject knowledge in history teachers:

> Though diverse, all of these representations shared one feature: Each attempted to build a bridge between the sophisticated understanding of the teacher and the developing understanding of the student. (p. 332)

Both metaphors are useful to visualize how teachers can use their subject expertise, but only go some way in illuminating the relationship between teachers' subject knowledge and how they teach. They successfully illuminate that psychologizing requires teachers to begin with their knowledge of students. Smith and Girod (2003) emphasize this in their work, noting how the blind acceptance of 'bought' or 'legislated' curriculum is not acceptable as the curriculum authors are not able to design curricula for individual children and their needs. Smith and Girod argue that it is teachers' responsibility to adapt and design curricula for their individual students. Only in this incidence can they psychologize the subject-matter.

Deng (2007) has explored what teachers need to know about their subject in order to psychologize it in this way. He argues that teachers need a broad conception of a subject discipline which should encompass five dimensions: the content, the psychological aspects, the pedagogical aspects, the epistemological aspects and the socio-cultural dimensions. To psychologize the curriculum, teachers have to move beyond the 'content' of the curriculum or examination specification, and also consider its epistemological assumptions, what the children's experience of the subject would be, any misconceptions they may have of it and also public perceptions that may be relevant. These five dimensions make up a broad definition of subject expertise that can enable teachers to move beyond 'delivering' the curriculum.

In my own research (Brooks, 2007, 2010) into geography teachers' subject expertise I observed six 'expert' geography teachers who used three strategies in their lessons to connect learners with the lesson content:

- tuning into the students' personal geographies
- making connections with students' previous geographical knowledge or experiences
- using the teachers own geographical experiences as an example or story.

In the lessons I observed, these strategies were used flexibly and appropriately depending on the student, the lesson topic and the particular difficulties students were experiencing. The use of these strategies showed teachers making nuanced decisions about their teaching that reflect the kind of subject expertise described by Deng: one that takes into account where the knowledge comes from and how students understand it. Each of these strategies requires the teacher to apply their subject expertise in a unique and context-dependant way. This decision-making process has been described by Rice as synoptic capacity (although in a higher education context):

the ability to draw strands of a field together in a way that provides both coherence and meaning, to place what is known in context and opens the way for connections to be made between the knower and the known. (1992, p. 125)

This way of understanding teachers' subject expertise is useful for many subjects, but particularly for geography as a discipline that can draw upon the teacher's and students' own lived experiences. A geography teacher using their synoptic capacity will be able to draw upon the learners' geography experience and will use the disciplinary tools (or concepts) to help students develop a deeper understanding of the world around them and the connections they have with the world that may not be immediately visible to them. This is not an aspiration notion, but a description of a teacher using and engaging with her subject expertise.

Final words

In this chapter I have argued for a broad conception of geography teachers' subject expertise, that encompasses their formal and informal geographical knowledge. Such a broad definition enables us to understand that for a teacher, knowing the subject is not enough. Teachers need to understand the concepts that underpin knowledge in their field, alongside engaging with what their students know about the subject, their experience of it and how they can make sense of their experience. This is especially true for geography as students live and experience the world, and the school subject can help them to understand that experience. But teaching geography is more than helping young people to understand the commonplace. 'Living geography', as described by David Lambert (2009a), reminds us that to do this, teachers have to draw upon geographical concepts and theories about the world. These concepts and theories are developed and refined in the academic discipline. Teachers are the gatekeepers to that discipline, and as such can use the academic discipline as a geographical resource to help students understand more than their local experience. Modelling how teachers use their subject expertise is not easy, and as this chapter has shown many educationalists have attempted to do so. But as Rynne and Lambert (1997) argue, teachers as graduates of geography have the intellectual capacity to support students to think geographically. The theories outlined in this chapter, and particularly that of psychologizing subject-matter, can support geography teachers in developing this kind of subject expertise in their practice.

Note

1 PGCE – Post-Graduate Certificate of Education: the post-graduate teacher training certificate for England and Wales.

References

Bale, J. and McPartland, M. (1986), 'Johnstonian anarchy, inspectorial interest and the undergraduate education of PGCE geography students', *Journal of Geography in Higher Education*, 10, (1), 61–70.

Banks, F., Leach, J. and Moon, B. (1999), 'New understandings of teachers' pedagogic knowledge', in J. Leach and B. Moon (eds), *Learners and Pedagogy*. London: Paul Chapman, pp. 89–110.

Barrett-Hacking, E. (1996), 'Novice teachers and their geographical persuasions', *International Research in Geographical and Environmental Education*, 5, (1), 77–86.

Brooks, C. (2007), 'Towards understanding the influence of subject knowledge in the practice of "expert" geography teachers'. Unpublished Ph.D. thesis, Institute of Education, University of London.

—. (2010), 'Developing and reflecting on subject expertise', in C. Brooks (ed.), *Studying PCGE Geography at M Level*. London: Routledge.

Brooks, C. and Morgan, A. (2006), *Theory into Practice: Cases and Places*. Sheffield: Geographical Association.

Carlsen, W. S. (1991), 'Subject-matter knowledge and science teaching: a pragmatic perspective', in J. Broby (ed.), *Advances in Research on Teaching*. Greenwich, CT: JAI Press Inc, vol. 2, pp. 115–143.

—. (1999), 'Domains of teacher knowledge', in J. Gess-Newsome and N. G. Lederman (eds), *Examining Pedagogical Content Knowledge*. Boston: Kluwer, pp. 133–146.

Deng, Z. (2007), 'Knowing the subject matter of a secondary-school science subject', *Journal of Curriculum Studies*, 39, (5), 503–535.

Dewey, J. (1972 [1897]), 'The psychological aspect of the school curriculum', in J. A. Boydston (ed.), *The Middle Works of John Dewey, 1882–1898*. Carbondale, IL: Southern Illinois University Press, vol. 5 (1895–1898), pp. 164–177.

Fenstermacher, G. D. (1994), 'The knower and the known: the nature of knowledge in research on teaching', *Review of Research in Education*, 20, 3–56.

Gardner, H. (2007), *Five Minds for the Future*. Boston, MA: Harvard Business School Press.

Geddis, A. (1993), 'Transforming subject-matter knowledge: the role of pedagogical content knowledge in learning to reflect on teaching', *International Journal of Science Education*, 15, (6), 673–683.

Gess-Newsome, J. (1999), 'Pedagogical content knowledge: an introduction and orientation', in J. Gess-Newsome and N. G. Lederman (eds), *Examining Pedagogical Content Knowledge*. Boston: Kluwer.

Goodson, I. (1987), *School Subjects and Curriculum Change: Studies in Curriculum History*, 2nd edition. London: Falmer Press.

Graves, N. (2001), *School Textbook Research: The Case of Geography 1800–2000*. London: Institute of Education.

Grossman, P. L. (1990), *The Making of a Teacher: Teacher Knowledge and Teacher Education*. Columbia University: Teachers College Press.

Grossman, P. L., Wilson, S. M. and Shulman, L. (1989), 'Teachers of substance: subject matter knowledge for teaching', in M. C. Reynolds (ed.), *Knowledge Base for the Beginning Teacher*. Oxford: Pergamon Press, pp. 23–36.

Hillocks, G. J. (1999), *Ways of Thinking, Ways of Teaching*. New York: Teachers College.

Jackson, P. (2006), 'Thinking geographically', *Geography*, 91, (3), 199–204.

Jewitt, L. (1998), 'Personal experiences, values and the teaching of geography'. Unpublished MA dissertation, Institute of Education, London.

Johnston, R. J. (1991), *Geography and Geographers: Anglo-American Human Geography since 1945*, 4th edition. London: Edward Arnold.

Kelly, A. V. (2009), *The Curriculum*, 6th edition. London: Sage.

Kincheloe, J. L. and Steinberg, S. R. (eds) (1998), *Unauthorised Methods: Strategies for Critical Thinking*. London: Routledge.

Kind, V. and Taber, K. S. (2005), *Teaching School Subjects 11–19: Science*. London: Taylor & Francis.

Lambert, D. M. (2002), 'Teaching through a lens: the role of subject expertise in teaching geography', in Y. C. Cheng, K. T. Tsui, K. W. Chow and M. M. C. Mok (eds), *Subject Teaching and Teacher Education in the New Century: Research and Innovation*. Hong Kong: The Hong Kong Institute of Education, Kluwer Academic Publishers.

Lambert, D. M. L. (2008), 'Review article: the corruption of the curriculum', *Geography*, 93, (3), 183–185.

—. (2009a), 'Geography in education: Lost in the post?' Inaugural Professorial Lecture delivered at the Institute of Education, University of London, June 2009.

—. (2009b), 'What is living geography?' in D. Mitchell (ed.), *Living Geography*. Cambridge: Chris Kington Publishing.

Livingstone, D. (1993), *The Geographical Tradition*. Oxford: Blackwell.

McDiarmid, G., Ball, D. L. and Anderson, C. W. (1989), 'Why staying one chapter ahead doesn't really work: subject specific pedagogy', in M. C. Reynolds (ed.), *Knowledge Base for the Beginning Teacher*. Oxford: Pergamon Press.

McEwan, H. and Bull, B. (1991), 'The pedagogic nature of subject matter knowledge', *American Educational Research Journal*, 28, (2), 316–334.

Marsden, W. E. (1997), 'On taking the geography out of geographical education', *Geography*, 82, (3), 241–252.

Martin, F. (2006), 'Knowledge bases for effective teaching: beginning teachers' development as teachers of primary geography', in D. Schmeink (ed.), *Research on Learning and Teaching in Primary Geography*. Karlsruhe: Padagogische Hochschule Karlsruhe, pp. 149–184.

Meredith, A. (1995), 'Terry's learning: some limitations of Shulman's pedagogical content knowledge', *Cambridge Journal of Education*, 25, (2), 175–187.

Nelson, B. (1992), 'Teachers' special knowledge', *Educational Researcher*, 21, (9), 32–33.

Ormrod, J. E. and Cole, D. B. (1996), 'Teaching content knowledge and pedagogical content knowledge: a model from geographic education', *Journal of Teacher Education*, 47, (1), 37–42.

Pajares, M. F. (1992), 'Teachers' beliefs and educational research: cleaning up a messy construct', *Review of Educational Research*, 62, (3), 307–332.

Geography, Education and the Future header

180 Geography, Education and the Future

Prentice, R. (1997), 'Creating more contented teachers', in A. Hudson and D. M. Lambert (eds), *Exploring Futures in Initial Teacher Education*. London: Institute of Education.

Rawling, E. (2001), *Changing the Subject: the Impact of National Policy on School Geography 1980–2000*. Sheffield: Geographical Association.

Rice, R. E. (1992), 'Towards a broader conception of scholarship: the American context', in T. Whiston and R. Geiger (eds), *Research and Higher Education: The United Kingdom and the United States*. Buckingham: SRHE/Open University.

Roberts, M. (2003), *Learning through Enquiry: Making Sense of Geography in the Key Stage 3 Classroom*. Sheffield: Geographical Association.

Rynne, E. and Lambert, D. (1997), 'The continuing mismatch between student's undergraduate experiences and the teaching demands of the geography classroom: experience of pre-service secondary geography teachers', *Journal of Geography in Higher Education*, 21, (1), 187–198.

Segall, A. (2004), 'Revisiting pedagogical content knowledge: the pedagogy of content/the content of pedagogy', *Teaching and Teacher Education*, 20, 489–504.

Shulman, L. (1986), 'Those who understand: knowledge growth in teaching', *Educational Researcher*, 15, (2), 4–14.

—. (1987), 'Knowledge and teaching: foundation of the new reform', *Harvard Educational Review*, 57, (1), 1–22.

Smith, J. P. and Girod, M. (2003), 'John Dewey & psychologizing the subject-matter: big ideas, ambitious teaching, and teacher education', *Teaching and Teacher Education*, 19, 295–307.

Sockett, H. (1987), 'Has Shulman got the strategy right?' *Harvard Educational Review*, 57, (2), 208–219.

Standish, A. (2009), *Global Perspectives in the Geography Curriculum*. London: Routledge.

Stengel, B. (1997), '"Academic discipline" and "school subject": contestable curricular concepts', *Journal of Curriculum Studies*, 29, (5), 585–602.

Turner-Bisset, R. (2001), *Expert Teaching: Knowledge and Pedagogy to Lead the Profession*. London: Fulton.

Turvey, A. (2005), 'Who'd be an English teacher?' *Changing English*, 12, (1), 3–18.

Unwin, T. (1992), *The Place of Geography*. Harlow: Longman Scientific and Technical.

Walford, R. (2001), *Geography in British Schools 1850–2000*. London: Woburn Press.

Wineburg, S. and Wilson, S. (1991), 'Subject matter knowledge in the teaching of American history', in J. Brophy (ed.), *Advances in Research on Teaching: Vol 2 Subject Matter Knowledge and Teaching*. Greenwich: JAI Press.

Young, M. F. D. (2008), *Bringing Knowledge Back In*. London: Routledge.

Discussion to Part 3
Michael Young

Fewer school students now take geography at GCSE and A level than used to. This disturbing trend, also true for history and foreign languages is somewhat evasively encouraged by the new National Curriculum proposals emphasize relevance, drawing on student experience and the importance of generic skills rather than on subject knowledge. Is this just a problem for geography teachers who may be made redundant? I don't think so. Is it a picture of the 'curriculum of the future' with the role of subjects like geography increasingly sidelined? If so, what kind of education are we offering the next generation and what are the likely consequences?

My own view is that we need to begin any debate about the future of a subject like geography by asking two basic questions. The first is 'what are schools for?' My answer to this question is that the primary (not the only) purpose of schooling is to give all students access to the 'powerful knowledge' that most of them will not have the opportunity to acquire at home. For me powerful knowledge means, knowledge that is reliable, fallible and potentially testable – knowledge that takes anyone *beyond their experience*. The second question is does geography (or any other subject) offer some of the powerful knowledge that we want all young people to acquire? Despite having myself given up geography at school at the age of 12, I have absolutely no doubt that it represents an important part of the knowledge that every pupil should have access to. It includes concepts that no twenty-first century citizen in our global world should be denied. Furthermore, there is absolutely no sign that our elite schools (private and state funded) are forgetting this. It follows that unless we take this argument seriously and reverse many current policies, we shall only find ourselves with new inequalities. What I find somewhat surprising is that although the authors of this book are as aware of and as concerned about the trends I have pointed to as I am, nowhere in these chapters do I find the powerful concepts that geography offers referred to. Is this a lack of confidence or are they taken for granted by geography educators? If the answer is the latter, then the authors have yet to work through the reinterpretation of the idea of the conceptual, historical and social basis of subjects that Firth outlines in his chapter. After outlining the broader sociological issues concerning the crucial curriculum role of subjects; he concludes his chapter with *three* crucial and largely neglected questions:

- How is a specialist approach to pedagogy in geography developed?
- What is the relationship between geography as a school subject and the everyday geographical knowledge that students pick up outside school?
- How are geography specialists in schools and universities brought closer together?

For me these are questions that all subject teachers and those involved in their initial and post-initial education should be concerned with.

Clare Brooks addresses Firth's questions by pointing out the popularity as well as the weaknesses Shulman's well-known concept of pedagogic *content knowledge*. As she indicates, it does little more than reassure teachers that what they know already is somehow 'unique'. Unfortunately by linking the inadequacy of Shulman's approach to his use of the word 'knowledge' in describing teachers what teachers do, Brooks avoids the questions that Shulman himself runs away from. This means she is unable or unwilling to address the basic questions facing geography teachers – 'what is geographical knowledge?' and 'why is it important that students should have access to it?'

Lambert's chapter begins by drawing on Furedi and Ecclestone's perceptive critique of therapeutic trends in current educational policy and argues for geography as a vehicle for education rather than for emotional literacy. He goes on to make a powerful case against the current anti-intellectualist trend associated with the QCDA and some teacher unions. Where he does not convince me is when he draws on Amartya Sen's concept of capability as a way of conceptualizing the role the subject (geography) plays in curriculum formation. Undoubtedly the concept has played an important role in broadening debates about paths to development, especially for poor countries. However, as a curriculum principle it is too general to underpin the crucial role of schools in transmitting the 'powerful knowledge' on which a student's future 'capability' will depend.

Paralleling my earlier comments on Clare Brooks's chapter, it seems inescapable that geographers must stipulate the distinctive conceptual content of geography. They must also argue that if learners are going to progress and develop their sense of identity as neophyte geographers, geography must be taught 'as a subject' and not as a collection of module choices. It is the importance of its concepts in the lives of young learners that gives geography its crucial role in the curriculum. If geographers cannot make these arguments, then it is difficult for us non-geographers to make the case for geography and to argue that in making it voluntary from the age of 14 we are in danger of undermining the next generation's future.

Part 4
Global Ethics, Environment and Citizenship
Fran Martin

This part highlights the relationship in geography education between ethics, environment and citizenship. Issues of sustainability and environmental protection have come to the fore in geography education in the past 20 years, both of which have a distinct geographical expression. The connections between these themes and the growing agenda for citizenship education in English schools have also become clearer, with geography educationalists now playing a key part in the development of this relationship in many schools. Together each of these themes has significant links to morality and ethics, both of which can be explored through the lens of geography education. Alun Morgan begins by exploring the relationship between morality and geography education and presents a powerful argument for 'ethical knowledge' to be added to the range of professional knowledges that are a part of teacher development. Fran Martin and Jessica Pykett then discuss in turn the global ethical issues that are raised through the relationships between sustainability and educational partnerships, geography and citizenship education. Thus the chapter authors explore not only the theoretical basis for relating ethics, environment and citizenship to geography education, but also issues arising for the professional development of teachers to promote the understanding and teaching of these themes.

Morality and Geography Education

Alun Morgan

Introduction

At a fundamental level education and teaching are deeply moral concerns which demand an ethical response (Peters, 1970; Hamm, 1989; Campbell, 2003). This is most obvious in terms of the interpersonal, and typically asymmetrical, power relationship between 'teacher and student' which give rise to moral and ethical[1] issues concerning the exercise of authority and discipline in and beyond the classroom. Less obvious, but perhaps more profound, are the necessary choices about appropriate 'educational aims, curricular content and implementation, teaching and classroom strategies' (Hamm, 1989, p. 2). Education is an inherently valuational concern in that it is deemed to be worthwhile, good, desirable and therefore morally right to pursue.

However, ethical decisions have to be made in terms of what *precisely* is educationally worthwhile? This quickly raises ethical issues about how to adjudicate a plurality of perspectives since one person's 'education' is another's 'mis-education'. To be an educator or teacher (geography or otherwise) is to occupy an extremely powerful position carrying great moral responsibility or '"moral agency" . . . in terms of both how teachers treat students generally and what they teach them of a moral and ethical nature' (Campbell, 2003, p. 2).

While each teacher or educator has an *implicit* philosophy of education which will have a bearing on their day-to-day practice, this is likely to remain unexamined since seldom are they given the opportunity, or direction, to undertake a deeper, reflective consideration of such practice. Consequently, 'teachers and school administrators, for the most part fundamentally good people, remain noticeably unaware and even unconscious of the ethical ramifications of their own actions and overall practice' (Campbell, 2003, p. 1). This is understandable in the high pressured context of the contemporary educational profession, yet highly regrettable. Without such ethical reflection pragmatic judgements about content and pedagogy, with real moral consequences, will be based on ill-considered moral intuition or 'received wisdom' and thereby prey to the vagaries and vicissitudes of the prevailing cultural, intellectual and/or political climate.

It goes without saying that the foregoing general discussion holds true for all teachers *including* geographers. Geography educators need, alongside all teachers, to have an understanding of the moral implications of their work and the ways in which their practice can be morally or ethically informed. They need, in short, to have as a crucial dimension of their professional knowledge alongside their generic pedagogical knowledge, specific subject knowledge and pedagogical content knowledge (Shulman, 1987) and 'ethical knowledge' (Hargreaves and Goodson, 2003; Campbell, 2003). However, the 'ethical knowledge' that this requires of a geography teacher goes far beyond generic considerations about classroom practice because of both the specific nature of the discipline itself and the wider education or societal role(s) to which it might be expected (legitimately or otherwise) to contribute.

This chapter is specifically concerned with these additional ethical dimensions of 'teaching geography'. The crucial questions posed by this chapter are: 'what, if any, is (are) the *moral* purpose(s) of geography education?'; and 'how should this (these) be accomplished?' Rather than seeking to provide any definitive answers the main purpose of this chapter is to challenge geography educators to arrive at a personally authentic response to these questions. The expectation is that in doing so they will be better equipped to teach geography in a 'morally careful' manner (Lambert, 1999; Morgan and Lambert, 2005). To support them in this task this chapter raises some salient issues and themes emerging from the two most pertinent fields – academic geography and moral education – with the aim that teachers can develop a more fully informed response to the intersections or synergies between them.

The pressing need for 'ethical knowledge' among geography educators

It is arguably more pressing and challenging for geography teachers to negotiate the exceedingly complex moral terrain of their specific subject teaching than for some other discipline specialists.[2] The specifically *geographical* moral imperative and challenge is that potentially all real-world ethical issues that students will encounter through their education will have a crucial geographical dimension since they occur 'someplace' and often exhibit complex relationships across space to other places and scales (either in terms of causes or effects, or more probably both). This is certainly the case in terms of so-called geo-ethics in which 'concepts central to geographical enquiry: landscape, location and place, locality, proximity and distance, space and territory, development and nature' (Smith, 2000, p. viii) are highly pertinent.

This may not apply to *all* ethical issues, but it certainly does those constellating around human-environment interaction; sustainability and development; conflict; globalization; global climate change; and spatially exclusionary practices based on gender, ethnicity, age, and so on. The challenge of such issues is increased significantly because they are inherently 'controversial' or 'wicked' (Rittel and Webber, 1973; Morgan, 2006b) – they are complex, not easily defined or resolved, and elicit a range of moral and ethical responses in pluralist societies as a consequence of different perspectives, divergent world-views and ideologies. The controversial nature of 'geo-ethics' or 'Wicked Geography' (Morgan, 2006a) demands of geography teachers sophisticated 'ethical subject knowledge'.

Furthermore, 'wicked' issues or problems cannot be solved through the simple application by individuals of reductionist and formulaic moral reasoning. Rather, they demand sophisticated, negotiated and contextual responses arrived at through collaboration within pluralist 'communities of enquiry' (Keen et al., 2005; Morgan, 2006a). This leads on to the crucial *educational* moral imperative and challenge in terms of the purpose of a subject such as geography in relation to broader societal goals and values. Is geography education morally worthwhile as an end in itself, or must it gain additional moral legitimacy by addressing the needs of society, chief among which are geo-ethical needs? Should school geography be directed towards passing on traditional geographical content, tools and techniques in a value-free way so that eventually an elite few graduates become expert decision makers on behalf of us all, as apparently argued by Standish (2009)? Or should the emphasis be placed on exploring pressing world issues and developing skills in problem solving and knowledge co-creation through enquiry and collaboration, so that all students will be empowered to take an active, participatory role as informed citizens? These are real and live issues for the geography education community and also ones which exercise the minds of policy makers.

Geography education around the globe is increasingly discussed as a potential vehicle for Education for Sustainable Development (ESD) and 'Civics' or Citizenship (especially in terms of Global Citizenship). The subject has also been identified as contributing to wider educational aims in terms of what is being referred to in the UK context as Personal Learning and Thinking Skills (PLTS) and in the United States as 'Partnership for 21st Century Skills' (P21)[3] which can be seen to be driven by vocational agendas. More contentiously still is the potential contribution of geography to overtly moral projects such as 'moral development', 'values education', and what the English National Curriculum refers to as spiritual, moral, social, and intellectual growth and development, and personal, social and health education (PSHE) (QCA, 2008) Many within the geography education community welcome this opportunity to demonstrate the worth of the subject at a time of falling rolls and allegedly uninspiring and irrelevant teaching (OfSTED, 2008). Others caution against jumping onto this 'relevance' bandwagon for the sake of subject integrity. It is imperative that geography teachers develop adequate generic and subject-specific 'ethical knowledge' to respond in a morally careful manner to these broader expectations and challenges.

The shifting moral ground of geography

An overt focus on the ethical dimension of the academic discipline of geography has increasingly been in evidence since the 1990s as part of a wider normative turn in the social sciences generally (Smith, 2000, 2004). Such a moral purpose has not always characterized the discipline. In the late nineteenth and early twentieth centuries, it attempted to model itself as a 'value-free' positivistic science concerned with objectively describing and explaining the world, although it was generally accepted that practical applications of knowledge so gained could be used to support the prevailing Modern/Western model of progress. As a consequence, geography has had an unfortunate historical association with the various and undeniable degradations to society and environment which have followed Western Imperial expansion, colonialism and industrialization and underlying beliefs such as 'environmental determinism' and 'social Darwinism' which legitimized racist practices and Western superiority. Such projects and perspectives were, by the standards of the time, deemed wholly appropriate and 'morally neutral', but are viewed today as morally reprehensible and at the root of many moral issues prevailing in the contemporary world.

There were dissenting voices, notably the anarchists Kropotkin, Reclus and others, who saw geography's and geographers' roles as the promotion of an alternative radical vision of human-human and human-environment relations (Blunt and Wills, 2000). In the 1970s such voices of dissent became more vocal as dissatisfaction with the prevailing paradigm gave rise to alternative humanistic and welfare approaches. Humanistic geography was concerned with the missing affective and values dimensions of human 'being' (e.g. Tuan, 1977; Buttimer, 1993; Relph, 1974) while welfare approaches were overtly concerned with uncovering situations of social *in*justice and *mal*development (e.g. Harvey, 1973). More recently the discipline has been influenced by post-modern and post-structuralist approaches which have had added greatly to the moral complexity of contemporary academic geography (Murdoch, 2006).

Today the list of moral issues, or 'geo-ethics', which might exercise ethically minded geographers is theoretically endless, including real-world moral issues such as conflict and terrorism; discrimination, exclusion and ethnic cleansing; poverty, development; human rights; environmental degradation and habitat destruction. An engagement with such issues is problematic because, as Smith notes, they raise a number of creative tensions or dialectics including 'those between general (thin) and specific (thick) moralities, between universalism and particularism, between global and local, space and place, between essentialism and individualism or difference, between the natural and the socially constructed, between ethical thought and moral practice, and between is and ought' (Smith, 1999, p. 275). Moral thinking in geography has benefitted from cross-fertilization with specialized philosophical fields such as 'ethics', and, more specifically still, 'environmental ethics' and 'development ethics' where such challenges and tensions are well rehearsed.

A key challenge is making sense of the plethora of ethical standpoints. One common philosophical approach is to consider the range of relevant ideological positions, often expressed as typologies, and explore their divergent moral and ethical implications. For example, Naess (1989), O'Riordan (1989), Fien (1995) and Dobson (1990) have all produced influential typo-logies of environmental thinking which either dichotomize perspectives into anthropocentric or ecocentric; or use broad political orientations (typically right-wing/conservative; liberal; and radical/left wing). Similarly, typologies of interpretations of the term 'development' have been proposed, the simplest contrasting 'economy first' (focusing on economic growth within neoliberal global markets) with 'people first' (focusing on human development and quality of life) (see, for example, Deneulin and Shahani, 2009). Alternatively, people have considered the ethical response of different cultures and belief systems to environmental and/or development issues around the world (see, for example, Solomon and Higgins, 2003; Sullivan and Kymlicka, 2007).

The contemporary ethical turn in geography is often associated with a 'relational' turn which emerged from post-modern and post-structuralist thinking (Murdoch, 2006). Such thinking resists reductive, rigid and mono-logical analyses in favour of fluid and dynamic conceptualizations. By way of illustration, 'relational' thinking has been applied to consider ways in which 'organic beings, technological devices and discursive codes, as well as people' (Whatmore, 1999, p. 26) are folded together as a 'hybrid collectif' (Callon and Law, 1995). While some might consider such intellectual efforts as frivolous 'navel gazing', they do carry profound moral implications for human-nature and human-technological relations. However, post-modern and post-structural approaches in geography have been criticized by Smith (2004) who argues that the tendency of the 'postmodern intellectual elite' (p. 203) to only privilege and celebrate difference and particularity undermines the basis for universal moral reasoning which he believes is crucial for moral judgement. He instead suggests that one can adopt a position of 'ethical naturalism or essentialism . . . [based on the] natural fact of human similarity' (p. 203). Smith therefore advocates that a 'context sensitive universalism' (p. 201) be applied to issues of moral geography.

(Education for) Place-based ethics?

Space precludes further detailed consideration of the many and emerging engagements of geography with morality, but a brief consideration of how one key geographical concept – 'place' – has provided a fruitful topic for ethical thinking is particularly worthwhile. Massey's 'progressive' or 'global sense of place' (Massey, 1991) represents a view of place which is relational but also crucially acknowledges structural forces (economic, political, social) operating across the globe. As such it represents a new intellectual conception of place which attempts to 'retain appreciation, and an understanding of the importance, of the uniqueness, of place while insisting always on that other side of the coin, the necessary interdependence of any place with others' (Massey, 1993, p. 146). This is a self-consciously normative conception of place which is 'extroverted, which includes a consciousness of its links with the wider world, which integrates in a positive way the global and the local' (Massey, 1991, p. 244). Such a conceptualization can trace its lineage to the 'welfare tradition' in geography and appears to sit well with calls for 'global perspectives' or 'Global Citizenship'.

The notions of 'place attachment' (Altman and Low, 1992) represents a different relational conception of place emerging from the more humanistic tradition and environmental psychology. *Geopiety* is the term used by Tuan (1976) to refer to a particularly virtuous type of place attachment in which a reverential and compassionate connection is developed between a person and their 'terrestrial home' (p. 12). It is characterized by an ethic of reciprocity in which ecology, territory and one's 'compatriots' are all important dimensions which are to be loved, nurtured, protected and served selflessly. Many environmental education and 'Place-Based Education' programmes are directed at developing this kind of ethical place attachment (Sobel, 2005; Van Matre, 1990; Cornell, 1987; see also Morgan, this volume).

However the notion of who or what constitutes a compatriot, or is worthy of 'moral consideration', is potentially problematic. In purely human terms, exclusivist, xenophobic identifications of the legitimate 'in group' in terms of ethnicity, religion, ideology, and so on would give rise to 'geographies of exclusion' (Massey, 1995) with the Third Reich providing the greatest caution against a 'land and blood' basis for place-based moral reasoning. Morally charged issues of 'inclusion' and 'community cohesion' which are key rationales behind 'citizenship' and PSD educational agendas become pertinent in terms of the development of a 'place attachment' based on a 'geography of acceptance' (Massey, 1995). However, inclusion might not be enough. The socially critical environmental orientations of 'environmental justice' and 'just sustainability' (Agyeman, 2005; Agyeman et al., 2003) reveal the various injustices experienced by particular communities in particular places to 'disproportionately affect people of color [*sic*] and low-income neighborhoods [*sic*]' (Agyeman, 2005, pp. 1–2). Consequently, more radical approaches to 'place-based education' which pay attention to issues of social and environmental justice are called for by some (Gruenewald, 2003; Gruenewald and Smith, 2008; Agyeman, 2005; Agyeman et al., 2003).

From a more ecocentric perspective 'inclusion' in terms of 'place-based' 'moral consideration' must extend beyond the purely human realm to include other species and even possibly ecosystems and landscapes. One attempt to provide an ecocentric 'Golden Rule' is Leopold's 'land ethic' which simply states '[a] thing is right when it tends to preserve the integrity, stability, and beauty of the biotic community. It is wrong when it tends otherwise' (1989, p. 225). The term 'biodiversity' describes more recent ethical concerns over protecting non-human, or what some prefer to call 'more-than-human' (Abrams, 1997), phenomena of places. Indeed, attention has more recently extended to focus on protecting abiotic features such as landscape under the rubric of 'geodiversity' (Gray, 2004) or 'spirit of place' (ICMS/CIMS, 2008).

Varieties of moral geography education

One purpose of this brief foray into 'place-based ethics' has been to reveal the complex moral and ethical systems which geography teachers might encounter either in terms of their teaching of 'place', or as ideologies underpinning some educational approaches and programmes which they are likely to encounter. This turns our attention to the second 'constituency' – the education community. For some it might be considered to be a thoroughly *bad* thing to address, or explore, ethical or moral issues in geography education. However, this represents a minority perspective both within and beyond the education community and 'moral development' has been an important albeit understated dimension or purpose of schooling since the inception of the English National Curriculum (UK-Parliament, 1998). Inman et al. (2003a) discuss the related concept of Personal and Social Development (PSD) as an overarching whole school responsibility to which all teachers, including geographers, should contribute. For them PSD is a challenging 'practice that expects young people and their teachers to confront issues in ways that enable them to question the taken for granted, to make connections between the personal and the social and political, to understand and explore their own emotions, and to locate themselves in changing worlds at personal, local, national and global levels' (Inman et al., 2003b, p. xix).

The contribution of geography education to such a wider vision has been advocated by geographers to a greater or lesser extent for a very long time, at least as far back as the 1885 in terms of Kropotkin's 'What Geography Ought to Be' (Kropotkin, 1996). The International Geographical Union's Charters on geographical education (IGU, 1992, 2000) and the Geographical Association's recent Position and Manifesto statements (GA, 1999, 2003, 2009) are replete with messages concerning the societal utility of geography education, some of which are specifically moral in nature, notably in terms of sustainable development and (global) citizenship. Statements such as these tend to advocate liberal and reformist agendas whereas others adopt a more radical 'socially transformative' vision of 'geography education for a better world' (e.g. Johnston, 1990; Huckle, 1997; Fien and Gerber, 1988).

Such moral visions, whether reformist or radical, are at odds with one which argues that it is *not* geography education's (nor any other subject, nor a school's) place to promote such societal/ethical agendas and which characterize those practitioners who advocate such a position as 'zealous campaigners' hell-bent on 'social engineering' at the expense of true education (see Furedi, 2007). Such a position is adopted most forcibly within the geography education community by Standish (2007, 2009) who argues that the subject's integrity is being fatally damaged by such externally driven and morally dubious instrumental agendas as developing a commitment to 'sustainable development', 'global perspectives' or exploring (or rather invading) students' inner consciences and values.

Thus there are a range of possible ethical positions for geography educators to adopt in relation to the subject's contribution to 'moral development/ education' ranging from outright rejection through to strong support. Individual teachers will have to develop and apply 'ethical knowledge' to position themselves as they see fit. However, an understanding of the variety of possible approaches to 'moral education' will provide a useful addition to their 'ethical knowledge' to support them in this task.

Approaches to moral (geography) education

This chapter cannot hope to do justice to the different forms of moral education which have developed but a cursory review is necessary in order to appreciate the possible ways in which geography education might be, or has been, implicated. Moral education is most often framed in terms of Values[4] Education. The key debate within Values Education has been between those that advocate the teaching or rather instilling of specific moral values or virtues[5] and those which advocate allowing pupils to explore and develop their own values (Halstead, 1996). The former 'virtues-oriented' approach, usually referred to as 'Character Education' which was popular in the United States in the 1920s and 1930s, has recently enjoyed a renewed popularity. It is specifically concerned with the instilling of particular 'virtues' which will lead to individual flourishing or the 'good citizen' (both being two sides of the same coin). While virtues accord with human nature, we are not born exhibiting them but rather come to develop them as good habits (and, equally, we can develop 'bad habits', or vices). Instruction and role models can be crucial in this respect. Hence the significance of 'education' (or what might be considered 'virtuous training') and a morally upstanding teaching profession answerable to 'codes of conduct' (GTC, 2009).

A significant challenge 'is that the composition of the list of virtues and the priorities given [*sic*] different virtues varies from one theory or practice to another' (Higgins, 1995, p. 55). In relatively homogenous cultures, or ones in which a particular tradition exhibits hegemony, this might not be so difficult since consensus is likely to reign.[6] However, it immediately becomes problematic where different cultural and/or ideological positions are represented, each arguing for a different set of virtues to be transmitted. Furthermore, there may be a clash between the virtues which are desirable for a particular societal end (such as 'a commitment to sustainability', 'social cohesion', etc.) and those for the intellectual flourishing of individuals (such as striving for autonomy and criticality). Finally, Character Education is predicated on training and inculcation of good habits. This might produce people who habitually do the right things, but it might not necessarily be for the right 'reasons' (Hamm, 1989). Thus many educators agree with Lambert who contends that 'simply promoting environmental values (recycling, picking up litter), whether overtly or covertly, is morally careless and does not contribute to pupils' moral development' (Lambert, 1999, p. 8). Rather, 'moral education' should be concerned with supporting people in moral 'reasoning' or 'judgement'.

The principle alternative to Character Education is Values Clarification. This starts from a very different premise and set of assumptions: 'that children will care more about values which they have thought through and made their own than about values simply passed down by adults; and that it is wrong, particularly in a pluralist society, to seek to impose values' (Halstead, 1996, p. 10). The goal of Values Clarification is to get young people to reflect upon their own previously unexamined values and alternative value systems and question them in terms of sources and inconsistencies. Such an approach is intended to equip learners with the confidence and critical faculties to interrogate various value positions thereby nurturing them as 'politically literate' or 'active citizens' (Slater, 2001), and is an approach that has been particularly influential in the United Kingdom.

Both approaches suffer from the challenge of relativism. For Character Education the challenge is justifying which values/virtues to promote. For Values Clarification the challenge might be in terms of how to adjudicate between contrasting and incompatible value systems; or how to challenge strongly held views which are deemed morally reprehensible since the individual's right to their values is sacrosanct. The issue of relativism presents itself within pluralistic, multicultural communities (including schools); within the discipline of geography; and in each 'wicked' or controversial issue. Hence the challenge is particularly acute in contemporary geography classrooms.

Approaches to moral development based on 'moral reasoning' have been developed in an attempt to overcome these challenges. Ultimately these might be seen as deriving from a Kantian[7] or Enlightenment emphasis on the application of sound reasoning underpinned by universally applicable 'constitutive moral principles' or concepts – such as justice, non-maleficence, beneficence, freedom and honesty (Hamm, 1989) – to arrive at an ethically defensible standpoint and basis for action. The goal of such an education is to nurture autonomous individuals with an authentic understanding of these principles. This approach is most associated with the developmentalist perspective of Kohlberg who identified three major sequential and universal stages of moral development from 'pre-conventional' (where morality is based on obeying an authority figure for rewards and to avoid punishment); through 'conventional' (where morality conforms to socio-cultural mores and norms); to the final 'post-conventional' level (where morality is based on autonomously accepted moral principles).

Kohlberg's theory of moral development has been applied in moral education through two approaches. The first involves presenting learners with 'dilemmas' intended to challenge or 'decentre' their existing moral frame to reveal its inadequacy and stimulate its reformulation. His 'just community' approach, by contrast, was focused on enhancing moral reasoning through participation in moral discussion and collaboratively building group norms and values. Kolhlberg has been extensively criticized from a number of standpoints. Some have questioned the invariance and universality of his stages across all cultures (Berry et al., 2002). Others have critiqued his emphasis on 'individual autonomy', 'justice' and 'rights-based' as implicitly biased towards 'Western' morality since those emphasizing 'social cohesion', 'duty' or 'filial piety' are more significant in non-Western contexts such as India and China (ibid.). A 'masculinist' bias is felt by many to underlay his emphasis on 'justice' in contrast to the supposedly more feminine ethical virtues of 'care' and 'responsibility' (Gilligan, 1982). Finally, following on from the above, there are those who argue that the prescription of a single universal 'right' way of thinking in all contexts and to all situations is fundamentally flawed. Such a perspective is more likely to subscribe to Habermas' 'communicative ethics' in which the 'right way of thinking' is negotiated in specific contexts by people in dialogue (Habermas, 1990).

Mindful of these criticisms, a number of educational approaches aimed at developing 'moral reasoning' have been applied to geography education. Many activities developed in the influential 'Thinking through Geography' movement, such as mysteries, lend themselves to this approach (Leat, 1998; Leat and Nichols, 1999). Alternatively, 'Philosophy for Children' (P4C) or 'community of philosophical enquiry' (Hannam and Echeverria, 2009) approach has been used to explore environmental issues in Morecambe Bay (Rowley and Lewis, 2003) and Global Citizenship in Cumbria (CDEC Project Team, 2005). Similarly, Lambert's call for a 'culture of argument' in contrast to a 'culture of answers' in geography classrooms (Lambert, 1999) has led to an increasing emphasis on 'argumentation' and 'dialogic argumentation' (Morgan, 2006a) and the application of approaches such as 'Open Spaces for Dialogue and Enquiry' (OSDE) (Andreotti, no date), particularly in relation to environmental and development issues.

One final approach to moral development worth mentioning is variously called 'service learning', 'community based learning' or 'active learning in the community' (Annette, 2000). Drawing on experiential learning theory, this is 'an educational method which provides a structured learning experience in civic participation which can lead to the development of the key skills necessary for being an active citizen. It also facilitates the acquisition of political knowledge and the ability to engage in reflective understanding which leads to personal development and civic virtue' (ibid., p. 82). Real potential exists for 'service learning' through geography and environmental education and engaged versions of 'place-based education' in terms of 'community based problem solving', 'participatory action research' and 'community based environmental management' (Stapp et al., 1996; Ward, 1999; Kindon et al., 2007).

Conclusion: setting the moral compass – applied ethics in geography education

A consideration of the ethical dimension of education generally and geography education specifically is particularly necessary at key moments when questions are raised concerning the nature of knowledge in relation to societal needs. We are presented by such a challenge internationally and across all educational phases in this early period of the twenty-first century when questions are crucially being asked about the purpose and aims of education partly in response to the various 'geo-ethics' noted above. In the United States significant concern has been raised over the past couple of decades about 'geographic illiteracy' in the population at large and particularly among K-12[8] students which has led to 'a rediscovery of the importance of geography in education in the United States' (Rediscovering Geography Committee of the National Research Council, 1997, p. 1). Such national debates raised significant challenges but also opportunities in terms of the moral relevance of geography.

A similar situation prevails in the schools sector in the United Kingdom. How 'geography' gained its place in the 'sun' as a foundation subject of the National Curriculum is telling in terms of the current discussion since, according to Walford (1997), the Thatcher government which was the original architect of the NC preferred geography's traditional subject identity as opposed to more overtly normative and 'critical' 'hybrid' candidate subjects such as 'peace studies' and 'world studies'. A more detailed description of the politically contested history of the Geography National Curriculum (GNC) has been provided elsewhere (Morgan, 2006c; Rawling, 2001) and it suffices to say that it has undergone a number of revisions since 1991, with a particularly significant change occurring from 1997 with the election of the Blairite 'New Labour' government. This gave rise to a so-called New Agenda for the revised curriculum launched in September 2000 (NC2000).

This New Agenda was framed in terms of an emphasis on Citizenship; Personal, Social and Health Education (PSHE); and Education for Sustainable Development. These presented a more overtly normative purpose to NC2000 and, for the first time, the whole curriculum had a rationale which included the phrase 'secure their [learners'] commitment to sustainable development at the personal, local, national and global level' (DfEE and QCA, 1999, p. 11). Furthermore, it contained many additional value-laden phrases such as: 'a more just society'; 'improving self-esteem'; 'challenging prejudice'; 'make a difference for the better'; 'understanding different beliefs and cultures'; 'international interdependence'; 'respect for the environment'; 'contributing to the common good' (ibid.). The most recent curriculum innovation within the schools' sector in the United Kingdom were the Secondary Curriculum Review (QCA, 2007) and the Primary Review. The former has increased the contribution of geography (along with other subjects) in terms of its contribution to broader aims of nurturing 'successful learners', 'confident individuals' and 'responsible citizens'; and achievement of the 'Every Child Matters' outcomes including 'to make a positive contribution'; and the 'cross-curricular dimensions' especially 'identity and cultural diversity', 'community participation' and 'global dimension and sustainable development'. These curriculum reforms also represent a potential opening up of greater teacher-autonomy.

However, greater teacher-autonomy makes greater demands on teachers which means they must believe their role is 'not merely to "deliver" the curriculum in the form of prefigured subject knowledge, but that they have an agentive role in making it' (Hardcastle and Lambert, 2005, p. x). This significantly increases their moral agency and it becomes incumbent on geography educators, whatever their moral or ethical persuasion, to engage with the crucial ethical debates and issues outlined in this chapter in order to establish an authentic and defendable stance based on 'ethical knowledge' appropriate to their subject and profession. Knowledge transmission and creation are ethical concerns. Geography education is demonstrably an ethical/political issue (Castree, 2005) and geography educators have a key responsibility in the shaping of learners' geographical world-views. This demands continuing personal and professional development in terms of the general and specific 'ethical knowledge' required to be a geography teacher in the twenty-first century.

Notes

1 For the purposes of this chapter the distinction made between morality vis-à-vis ethics is that the former represents any 'standards of conduct by which human action is right or wrong in an absolute sense, or better or worse in a relative sense . . . [whereas the latter implies] systematic intellectual reflection on morality in general, and specific moral concerns in particular' (Proctor, 1999, p. 3). Crucially, while morality – individual or collective – can be based on cultural mores and traditions in an unreflective and uncritical way, ethics implies rigorous intellectual reflection giving rise to personal autonomy and authenticity.

2 This is not to deny all teachers, whether subject specialists or otherwise, have profound 'moral agency' but to suggest that the nature and foci of geography and geography education add to its ethical significance.

3 Partnership for 21st Century Skills (P21) is an organisation in the United States which seeks to support the national education system by advocating the preparation of young people so that they can compete in the global economy.

4 Values are similar to beliefs in general but carry moral significance as 'principles, fundamental convictions, ideals, standards or life stances which act as general guides to behaviour or as points of reference in decision-making or the evaluation of beliefs or action and which are closely connected to personal integrity and personal identity' (Halstead, 1996, p. 5).

5 'Virtue' refers to 'a trait of character of a person that is good for that person to have' (Mizzoni, 2010, p. 23). Virtues are 'good habits' which contribute a person's 'flourishing'. Character traits that go against this flourishing are, as might be expected, the opposite of virtues, that is, 'vices'.

6 Such was historically the case in the United States and United Kingdom with a Christian, and predominantly Protestant mainstream advocating a particularly Protestant reading of Judaeo-Christian virtues along with Classical ones.

7 The philosophical system proposed by Immanuel Kant.

8 The period of free schooling from Kindergarten through to 12th Grade (generally the final year of Secondary or High School).

References

Abram, D. (1997), *The Spell of the Sensuous: Perception and Language in a More-Than-Human World.* New York: Vintage.

Agyeman, J. (2005), *Sustainable Communities and the Challenge of Environmental Justice.* New York: New York University Press.

Agyeman, J., Bullard, R. D. and Evans, B. (eds) (2003), *Just Sustainabilities: Development in an Unequal World.* London: Earthscan/MIT Press.

Altman, I. and Low, S. M. (eds) (1992), *Place Attachment.* New York: Plenum Press.

Andreotti, V. (no date), *Open Spaces for Dialogue and Enquiry: Methodology.* Nottingham: CSSGJ.

Annette, J. (2000), 'Education for citizenship, civic participation and experiential and service learning', in D. Lawton, J. Cairns and R. Gardner (eds), *Education for Citizenship.* London: Continuum, pp. 77–92.

Berry, J. W., Poortinga, Y. H., Marshall, H. S. and Dasen, P. R. (2002), *Cross-Cultural Psychology: Research and Applications,* 2nd edition. Cambridge: Cambridge University Press.

Blunt, A. and Wills, J. (2000), *Dissident Geographies: An Introduction to Radical Ideas and Practices.* Harlow: Prentice Hall.

Buttimer, A. (1993), *Geography and the Human Spirit.* Baltimore, MD: The John Hopkins University Press.

Callon, M. and Law, J. (1995), 'Agency and the hybrid collectif', *South Atlantic Quarterly,* 94, 481–507.

Campbell, E. (2003), *The Ethical Teacher.* Maidenhead, Berkshire: Open University Press.

Castree, N. (2005), 'Whose geography? Education as politics', in N. Castree, A. Rogers and D. Sherman (eds), *Questioning Geography: Fundamental Debates.* Oxford: Blackwell.

CDEC Project Team (2005), *Philosophy for Global Citizenship Project: Using P4GC to Support Learning in Global Citizenship.* Ambleside, Cumbria: CDEC.

Cornell, J. (1987), *Sharing Nature with Children.* Watford, Herts: Exely.

Deneulin, S. and Shahani, L. (eds) (2009), *An Introduction to the Human Development and Capability Approach: Freedom and Agency.* London: Earthscan.

DfEE and QCA (1999), *The National Curriculum.* London: DfEE/QCA.

Dobson, A. (1990), *Green Political Thought: An Introduction.* London: Unwin Hyman.

Fien, J. (1995), 'Ideology: orientation in environmentalism', in J. Fien (ed.), *Education for the Environment: Critical Curriculum Theorising and Environmental Education.* Geelong: Deakin University Press, pp. 23–29.

Fien, J. and Gerber, R. (eds) (1988), *Teaching Geography for a Better World.* Edinburgh: Oliver & Boyd.

Furedi, F. (2007), 'Introduction: politics, politics, politics', in R. Whelan (ed.), *The Corruption of the Curriculum.* London: Civitas.

GA (1999), *Geography in the Curriculum: A Position Statement from the Geographical Association.* Sheffield: Geographical Association.

—. (2003), *Geography: A Position Statement from the Geographical Association.* Sheffield: Geographical Association.

—. (2009), *A Different View: A Manifesto for the Geographical Association.* Sheffield: Geographical Association.

Gilligan, C. (1982), *In a Different Voice: Psychological Theory and Women's Development.* Cambridge, MA: Harvard University Press.

Gray, M. (2004), *Geodiversity: Valuing and Conserving Abiotic Nature.* Chichester: Wiley.

Gruenewald, D. A. (2003), 'The best of both worlds: a critical pedagogy of place', *Educational Researcher*, 32, (4), 3–12.

Gruenewald, D. A. and Smith, G. A. (eds) (2008), *Place-Based Education in the Global Age: Local Diversity.* Abingdon, Oxon: Lawrence Erlbaum Associates.

GTC (2009), 'Code of conduct and practice for registered teachers effective from 1 October 2009', in General Teaching Council, 22 (ed.), *P-CODE-1009.* London: General Teaching Council.

Habermas, J. (1990), *Moral Consciousness and Communicative Action.* Cambridge: Polity Press.

Halstead, J. M. (1996), 'Values and values education in schools', in J. M. Halstead and M. J. Taylor (eds), *Values in Education and Education in Values.* London: Falmer Press, pp. 3–14.

Hamm, C. M. (1989), *Philosophical Issues in Education: An Introduction.* New York: Falmer Press.

Hannam, P. and Echeverria, E. (2009), *Philosophy with Teenagers: Nurturing a Moral Imagination for the 21st Century.* London: Network Continuum.

Hardcastle, J. and Lambert, D. (2005), 'Series editor's preface', in J. Morgan and D. Lambert (eds), *Teaching School Subjects 11–19: Geography.* Abingdon, Oxon: Routledge.

Hargreaves, A. and Goodson, I. (2003), 'Foreword', in E. Campbell (ed.), *The Ethical Teacher.* Maidenhead: Open University Press, pp. ix–xiii.

Harvey, D. (1973), *Social Justice and the City.* Baltimore, MD: The Johns Hopkins Press.

Higgins, A. (1995), 'Educating for justice and community: Lawrence Kohlberg's vision of moral education', in W. M. Kurtines and J. L. Gewirtz (eds), *Moral Behavior and Development: An Introduction.* Boston: Allyn & Bacon, pp. 49–81.

Huckle, J. (1997), 'Towards a critical school geography', in D. Tilbury and M. Williams (eds), *Teaching and Learning in Geography.* London: Routledge.

ICMS/CIMS (2008), Québec Declaration on the Preservation of the Spirit of Place, at Québec.

IGU (1992), *International Charter on Geographical Education.* Washington, DC: IGU, USA.

—. (2000), *International Declaration on Geographical Education for Cultural Diversity.* Seoul, Korea: IGU-CGE.

Inman, S., Buck, M. and Tandy, M. (2003a), 'Personal, social and health education: challenging practices', in S. Inman, M. Buck and M. Tandy (eds), *Enhancing Personal, Social and Health Education: Challenging Practices, Changing Worlds*. London: RoutledgeFalmer, pp. 1–20.

—. (2003b), 'Preface', in S. Inman, M. Buck and M. Tandy (eds), *Enhancing Personal, Social and Health Education: Challenging Practices, Changing Worlds*. London: RoutledgeFalmer, pp. xix–xxii.

Johnston, R. J. (1990), 'The challenge for regional geography: some proposals for research frontiers', in R. J. Johnston, J. Haeur and G. A. Hoekveld (eds), *Regional Geography: Current Development and Future Prospects*. London: Routledge.

Keen, M., Brown, V. A. and Dyball, R. (2005), 'Social learning: a new approach to environmental management', in M. Keen, V. A. Brown and R. Dyball (eds), *Social Learning in Environmental Management: Towards a Sustainable Future*. London: Earthscan.

Kindon, S., Pain, R. and Kesby, M. (eds) (2007), *Participatory Action Research Approaches and Methods: Connecting People, Participation and Place*. Abingdon, Oxon: Routledge.

Kropotkin, P. (1996), 'What geography ought to be', in J. Agnew, D. N. Livingstone and A. Rogers (eds), *Human Geography: An Essential Anthology*. Oxford: Blackwell Publishers Ltd.

Lambert, D. (1999), 'Geography and moral education in a supercomplex world: the significance of values education and some remaining dilemmas. *Ethics, Place and Environment*, 2, (1), 5–18.

Leat, D. (ed.) (1998), *Thinking through Geography*. Cambridge: Chris Kington Publishing.

Leat, D. and Nichols, A. (1999), *Mysteries Make You Think*. Sheffield: Geographical Association.

Leopold, A. (1989), *A Sand County Almanac, and Sketches Here and There*. Special Commemorative edition. New York: Oxford University Press.

Massey, D. (1991), 'A global sense of place', in S. Daniels and R. Lee (eds), *Exploring Human Geography: A Reader*. London: Arnold.

—. (1993), 'Questions of locality', *Geography*, 78, (339), 142–149.

—. (1995), 'The conceptualization of place', in D. Massey and P. Jess (eds), *A Place in the World?* Oxford: Oxford University Press.

Mizzoni, J. (2010), *Ethics: The Basics*. Chichester: Wiley-Blackwell.

Morgan, A. (2006a), 'Argumentation, geography education and ICT', *Geography*, 91, (2), 126–140.

—. (2006b), 'Developing geographical wisdom: postformal thinking about, and relating to, the world', *International Research in Geographical and Environmental Education*, 15, (4), 336–352.

—. (2006c), 'Sustainable development and global citizenship: the "New Agenda" for geographical education in England and Wales', in J. Chi-Kin Lee and M. Williams (eds), *Environmental and Geographic Education for Sustainability: Cultural Contexts*. New York: Nova, pp. 187–203.

Morgan, J. and Lambert, D. (2005), *Teaching School Subjects: Geography*. London: RoutledgeFalmer.

Murdoch, J. (2006), *Post-Structuralist Geography*. London: Sage.

Naess, A. (1989), *Ecology, Community and Lifestyle*. Cambridge: Cambridge University Press.

O'Riordan, T. (1989), 'The challenge for environmentalism', in R. Peet and N. Thrift (eds), *New Models in Geography*. Boston: Unwin Hyman.

OfSTED (2008), *Geography in Schools: Changing Practice*. London: OfSTED.

Peters, R. S. (1970), *Ethics and Education*. London: George Allen & Unwin.

Proctor, J. D. (1999), 'Introduction: overlapping terrains', in J. D. Proctor and D. M. Smith (eds), *Geography and Ethics: Journeys in a Moral Terrain*. London: Routledge.

QCA (2007), *The Secondary Curriculum Review*. Available at http://www.qca.org.uk/secondary curriculumreview/

—. (2008), The National Curriculum On-Line. Available at http://curriculum.qcda.gov.uk/

Rawling, E. M. (2001), *Changing the Subject: The Impact of National Policy on School Geography 1980–2000*. Sheffield: Geographical Association.

Rediscovering Geography Committee of the National Research Council (1997), *Rediscovering Geography: New Relevance for Science and Society*. Washington, DC: National Academy Press.

Relph, E. (1974), *Place and Placelessness*. London: Pion.

Rittel, H. and Webber, M. (1973), 'Dilemmas in a general theory of planning', *Policy Sciences*, 4, (2), 155–169.

Rowley, C. and Lewis, L. (2003), *Thinking on the Edge: Thinking Activities to Develop Citizenship and Environmental Awareness around Morecambe Bay*. London: Living Earth Publications.

Shulman, L. S. (1987), 'Knowledge and teaching: foundations of the new reform', *Harvard Educational Review*, 57, (1), 1–22.

Slater, F. (2001), 'Values and values education in the geography curriculum in relation to concepts of citizenship', in D. Lambert and P. Machon (eds), *Citizenship through Secondary Geography*. London: RoutledgeFalmer.

Smith, D. M. (1999), 'Conclusion: towards a context-sensitive ethics', in J. D. Proctor and D. M. Smith (eds), *Geography and Ethics: Journeys in a Moral Terrain*. London: Routledge, pp. 275–290.

—. (2000), *Moral Geographies: Ethics in a World of Difference*. Edinburgh: Edinburgh University Press.

—. (2004), 'Morality, ethics and social justice', in P. Cloke, P. Crang and M. Goodwin (eds), *Envisioning Human Geographies*. London: Edward Arnold.

Sobel, D. (2005), *Place-Based Education: Connecting Classrooms & Communities*, 2nd edition. Great Barrington, MA: Orion Society.

Solomon, R. C. and Higgins, K. M. (eds) (2003), *From Africa to Zen: An Invitation to World Philosophy*, 2nd edition. Lanham, MD: Rowman & Littlefield.

Standish, A. (2007), 'Geography used to be about maps', in R. Whelan (ed.), *The Corruption of the Curriculum*. London: Civitas.

—. (2009), *Global Perspectives in the Geography Curriculum: Reviewing the Moral Case for Geography*. Abingdon, Oxon: Routledge.

Stapp, W. B., Wals, A. E. J. and Stankorb, S. L. (1996), *Environmental Education for Empowerment: Action Research and Community Problem Solving*. Dubuque, IA: Kendall/Hunt Publishing Company.

Sullivan, W. M. and Kymlicka, W. (eds) (2007), *The Globalization of Ethics: Religious and Secular Perspectives*. Cambridge: Cambridge University Press.

Tuan, Y.-F. (1976), 'Geopiety: a theme in man's attachment to nature and to place', in D. Lowenthal and M. J. Bowden (eds), *Geographies of the Mind: Essays in Historical Geosophy in Honor of John Kirtland Wright*. New York: Oxford University Press.

—. (1977), *Space and Place: The Perspective of Experience*. Minneapolis, MN: University of Minnesota Press.

UK-Parliament (1988), *Education Reform Act* (Chapter 40), ed. D.o.E.a. Science. London: HMSO.

Van Matre, S. (1990), *Earth Education: A New Beginning*. Warrenville, IL: Institute for Earth Education.

Walford, R. (1997), 'The great debate and 1988', in D. Tilbury and M. Williams (eds), *Teaching and Learning in Geography*. London: Routledge.

Ward, H. (ed.) (1999), *Acting Locally: Concepts and Models for Service Learning in Environmental Studies*. Washington, DC: AAHE.

Whatmore, S. (1999), 'Hybrid geographies: rethinking the "human" in human geography', in D. Massey, J. Allen and P. Sarre (eds), *Human Geography Today*. Cambridge: Polity Press.

Global Ethics, Sustainability and Partnership

11

Fran Martin

In the twenty-first century issues of economic, environmental and social sustainability, at a range of scales from local to global, are having a direct impact on our daily lives. In a world in which the pace of technological change continues to increase at rates formerly unthought of, the relevant knowledge bases of staples of the geography curriculum such as climate, population, migration, development and trade must also change if students are to develop appropriate knowledge, understanding, skills and attitudes to live successfully as responsible citizens in the future. The state of the world at present – climate change, global inequalities, the 'War on Terror' – all suggest that current ways of knowing and making sense of the world are not sufficient. Technology has, both spatially and temporally, brought the distant 'other' in close proximity and there is a heightened appreciation of how the world – economically, environmentally and socially – is interdependent. Some would argue that globalization has made geography irrelevant (Carey, 1989 cited in Sinha, 2002), but in this chapter I will argue that it is not geography that is irrelevant but the paradigms that currently dominate how world issues are understood and acted upon.

In England, the impact of globalization and the need for education to address global issues raised concerns that the curriculum was too narrow and Eurocentric. This led to the introduction of a global dimension across the curriculum (DfEE/DfID, 2000) and a citizenship curriculum (DfEE/QCA, 1999). The combination of the global dimension and citizenship can be seen in the notion of Global Citizenship, and the goal of developing global citizens now pervades education at all levels from primary to tertiary. Global Citizenship is one of the key dimensions of the UK sustainable schools framework (DfES, 2006) and is explicitly referred to in the Key Stage 3 geography curriculum programme of study (QCA, 2008). At institutional and government levels, the aim of producing global citizens is presented as a 'good', but an increasing number of educators (Andreotti, 2006; Burr, 2008) are questioning the practices that take place in the name of global citizenship, not least in the context of North-South[1] educational partnerships (Griffin, 2008; Martin, 2008).

On the face of it, the potential for North-South school partnerships to develop a wider range of perspectives on sustainability issues seems a positive way forward. In an interdependent world, solutions to sustainability issues based on Western perspectives are not going to be successful since they will arguably only perpetuate the inequalities that already exist. Analyses of policy documents that promote intercultural learning and global citizenship have revealed an overriding colonial discourse (Graves, 2002; Andreotti, 2006). This not only provides a significant barrier to learning, but also encourages actions that can be ethically questioned (such as fundraising, sponsoring a child), and which can only be overcome if an explicit awareness of the colonial legacy is developed at all levels of the British education system. Post-colonial theory, I wish to argue, offers an analytical framework that can enable colonial, hegemonic discourses to be revealed.

Post-colonial theory and sustainability

David Hicks (2006, 2008) has long argued that education has a missing dimension – that of the future – and that education for sustainable development should focus not on 'a' or 'the' future, but should involve students in predicting and envisioning a *number* of probable and preferable futures. This would enable students to consider their future actions according to the precautionary principle (Porritt et al., 2009). Similarly a focus on *the* past is not helpful. McQuaid (2009) argues that there are elements of the past that are missing, one of which is the legacy of colonialism.

> It is crucial we understand that our probable and preferable views of the future are constructed from the 'knowledges' we have absorbed from the past. This acknowledgement should allow us to deconstruct these views in order to understand their origins . . . Understanding the implications of a colonialist legacy on our education systems can facilitate learning from the past in order to guide the 'probable and preferable' futures towards congruency. (McQuaid, 2009, pp. 13–14)

In the sense that former colonies have moved to independence during the latter half of the twentieth century, we live in a post-colonial world. However, Young (2003) demonstrates how former imperial countries continue to dominate those countries they formerly ruled as colonies. He explains how in colonial times white culture was regarded as the basis for ideas of legitimate government, law, economic, 'in short, civilization' (2003, p. 2), and that this view remains implicit in the world today. There is an assumption that Western ideas about, for example, development and education are somehow universal. The effect of this is that when Western people look at the non-Western world what they see is often a mirror image of themselves and their own assumptions. Thus what is learnt from direct and indirect intercultural experiences between the North and South is often unwittingly affected by the former colonizer-colonized relationship. Post-colonial theory is useful in challenging dominant views because its starting-point views things 'from a completely different perspective – the other side of the photograph' (Young, 2003, p. 2).

Post-colonial theory[2] contains a number of key ideas which support understanding of North-South relationships. A few that are thought to be particularly apposite to the concerns of this chapter are shown in Table 11.1.

Massey (2005, p. 68) adds to our understanding of why colonialism built an image of the Other as 'savage' and 'inferior' by demonstrating how Modernity conceived of spatial differences in temporal sequence terms: Western Europe is 'advanced', other parts of the world 'some way behind' and yet others 'backward'. From this perspective, Africa is not different from Western Europe, it is behind. Massey argues that assigning (hidden) temporality has the effect of fixing things, leading to essentialist notions of places and identities, rather

Table 11.1 Key concepts from post-colonial theory, adapted from Ashcroft et al. (1998)

Key idea	Post-colonial meaning
Hierarchical, binary oppositions	Evident in most post-colonial writings is the idea that Western thought is based on binary opposites – Man/Woman, West/Rest, Rich/Poor, 'Us'/'Them' – which are hierarchically structured with one term being privileged over the other. Post-colonialism seeks to reveal and unpick these by showing that rather than being oppositional, binaries are relational; each is implicated in the other.
'Other' and 'Othering'	Said (1978), one of the first proponents of post-colonial theory, coined the term 'West and the Rest' to describe how colonizers divided the world; 'the Rest' was everything about the colonized that the West found uncomfortable or unsettling to its superior image. The inferior 'Other' is portrayed as uncivilized, undeveloped and savage – while the superior West is civilized, technologically advanced and developed.
Margins and centre	In colonial times, Western civilization was at the centre of a spread outwards to dominate and control other nations to the benefit of the colonizers. This created a situation in which Western culture, history, science, economy was (and is) seen to be at the centre of the world, and the basis for understanding the rest of the world. Alternative cultures, histories and economies were (are) relegated to the margins and devalued.
Essential	Essentialism is the idea that things have an essence or nature that is independent of their existence. Colonizers held essentialist notions about the 'Other'; the undeveloped 'savage' identity of the colonized was therefore seen to be a universal 'truth', fixed and stable. Post-colonialists call for a much more fluid, dynamic understanding of identity that is hybrid in nature, and allows for multiple identities.
Paternalism	Western responses to perceptions of the 'Other' as uncivilized and undeveloped have typically included the 'civilizing mission', and Modernist approaches to the development of third world countries. In both these discourses paternalistic attitudes of the colonizers are evident in the way the 'Other' is portrayed in a child-like fashion, unable to help her/himself without support or direction from the fatherly figure of the West.

than portraying them as open and constantly being made. Post-colonial theory criticizes the historicity of Modernity and, as expressed by Fanon (in Bhabha, 2005, p. 14) 'the black man refuses to occupy the past of which the white man is the future'. A deconstruction of the colonialist legacy in this way is seen as an essential first step in understanding the state of the world today, and in guiding our views on sustainable futures. How this might be achieved in the context of global economic poverty, as it is understood and represented in the English education system, will now be discussed.

Sustainability and equity

The most commonly cited definition of sustainable development comes from the Brundtland Report (1987) which defines it as 'meeting the needs of the present generation without compromising the ability of future generations to meet their own needs'. Porritt et al. (2009) show how this assumes two explicit elements: intergenerational equity (between generations; temporal equity) and intragenerational equity (that within a generation; spatial equity). Intragenerational equity is premised on the idea that it is 'wrong to further enrich the world's wealthy elites when the basic needs of the vast majority of humankind are still not met', and that this 'requires addressing the divides between rich and poor, both within and between nations' (ibid., p. 12). Porritt et al. argue that while intergenerational equity has almost universal consensus across cultures and wealth divides, intragenerational equity is more vigorously contested.

North-South partnerships provide the opportunity to enable students to begin to understand the factors affecting intragenerational equity and are seen as vital in contributing to a deeper understanding of sustainable development in a range of diverse contexts (DfID, 1999; DfES, 2004; UNESCO/BMBF, 2009). However, at the 2009 world conference on Education for Sustainable Development, it was stressed that

> we need to remove the stereotyping of the North-South relationships which mainly reduces the partnerships to an exchange of money from the North to South. We need to establish these relationships with an orientation of mutual benefits . . . to appreciate the different understandings of ESD. (UNESCO/BMBF, 2009, pp. 71–72)

Educational policy documents on global and citizenship education universally promote North-South school partnerships, but what are they *actually* teaching students about economic sustainability?

School partnerships and learning about sustainability

Two research projects at the London Institute of Education (Edge et al., 2009a, 2009b) provide evidence of how the global dimension and North-South school partnerships are affecting students' understanding of sustainability. The first of these investigates the global dimension in ten secondary schools. Edge et al. (2009a) report that five of the ten schools were engaged in charitable/fundraising activities, examples of which were:

- raising money to send children to school through a charity
- taking part in an NGO's Send My Friend to School Campaign
- raising money for education in deprived areas in South Africa
- buying goats for a link school in Africa.

When asked what they had learnt from global dimension activities – the most commonly identified topic after climate change was poverty. Asked about the impact of the activities on their attitudes and actions, students typically responded:

> It has changed how I feel because I think how lucky we are and they have nothing. (p. 80)

> I am more grateful about what I receive . . . I have donated more money and items to charity and am more grateful. (p. 33)

> It makes you feel guilty about what you have and take it for granted. (p. 67)

The North-South school partnerships report (Edge et al., 2009b) reveals a similar picture. Part of the research focused on six 'high momentum' schools – ones in which the partnership was seen to be particularly active and dynamic. Of these six, three connected the partnership to their school-level fundraising and charity priorities (ibid., p. 116). While data gathered from students were not available, several examples of teachers' views on the impact of the school partnership on students' knowledge and understanding were reported:

> Students get a greater sense of the people . . . they are people like themselves, exactly the same, same hopes, fears, memories, family situations, everything . . .
> When we brought students [partner school] over here, they didn't look like what they [our students] expected, like what they see on TV, so for them it had a big impact to see them wear baseball caps, or Nike trainers, and the fact that they [have] homes with computers – so it challenged the stereotyping of our own students quite substantially . . . (Edge et al., 2009b, p. 102)

Teachers' reporting of the impact on their own knowledge and understanding was not very different with one teacher stating: It has made me realize how lucky our children are over here and how lucky our education system is (ibid., p. 81). In another school, evidence showed that 'for some teachers it is challenging to see the school partnership with Zambia as an exchange of ideas, rather than fundraising only' (ibid., p. 56).

A post-colonial reading of the evidence presented above shows that the colonial legacy pervades teaching and learning about the world.

- Binary views of 'Them'/'Us', Poor/Wealthy, and Backward/Advanced are all too evident.
- Western views of development form the basis of a comparison between North and South that focuses on what 'we' have and what 'they' lack in comparison.
- This leads to Othering, because there appears to be no recognition of the West's implication in the intragenerational inequity that is evident.
- Disparities appear to cause feelings of compassion and guilt, but actions taken are paternalistic and focused around fundraising.
- This, combined with binary perspectives, appears to cause feelings of superiority: 'they' cannot get by without 'our' help.
- Essentialist views about the South as being poverty stricken dominate.
- When efforts are made to encourage students to move beyond feelings of pity and compassion to feeling connected to people in the south, this is done by focusing on those aspects of the Other that are the same as 'us' (Nike trainers, homes with computers), with echoes of the civilizing mission.

Dominant Western discourse about southern countries has an overriding focus on poverty and, as Graves (2002) and Brown (2006) have pointed out, while this appears to inspire a concern for others, the emphasis is on *material* poverty, with no mention of cultural, social and spiritual wealth and diversity. There is little evidence that any of the schools in Brown's or Edge et al.'s research included understanding of the global or historical causes of inequality. Griffin (2008) argues that 'the most obvious response to seeing that someone is in need is to give them money and in fact this is what we, as adults, are continually asked to do by all the major development NGOs' (p. 1). Furthermore, Disney (2004) notes that much of the advice from government and NGOs shows that school links 'are seen mainly from the UK perspective and raise the issue of the extent to which school linking [is] in danger of developing a new form of colonialism in which the experiences of people in poorer countries [is] used to resource the curriculum of UK schools' (p. 61). This identifies yet a further issue: that practice in schools is merely mirroring that of UK society, including government departments and non-governmental organizations. Are schools then to blame?

UK education policy and the role of NGOs

A number of educators have analysed education policy on global citizenship using post-colonial theory. In the context of US study abroad, Zemach-Bersin (2007) asks who does the writing, the describing, in educational policy and where are the southern voices? She argues that knowledge in the 'knowledge economy' is power and that under the rhetoric of intercultural learning, mutual respect and common humanity, lies an agenda of exploitation of the South for the purposes of enabling the United States to maintain its position as a leader in the global economy. UK education policy presents a similar picture. A key document on the global dimension (DfES/DfID, 2005) begins positively by observing that increased contact with diverse peoples enriches our lives, but goes on to say:

> However, although economic advances have meant huge improvements that have changed the lives of millions of people, one in five of the world's population still live in *extreme poverty*. They *lack* access to basic healthcare, education and clean water, with *little opportunity to improve* their condition. (p. 2; emphases added)

Objectives are stated as developing responsible and caring citizens, promoting equal opportunities and enabling students to challenge discrimination and indiscrimination, but this is overridden by the need to equip '*our* children, young people and adults for life in a global society and work in a global economy' (2005, pp. 2–3; emphasis added). The conflation of economic goals with the aims of developing 'good' citizens is a prime example of the paradoxical nature of government policy that schools have to negotiate. In another example, in 1999 the newly formed Department for International Development (DfID) identified the need to go

> . . . beyond attitudes to development based on compassion and charity, and [to] establish a real understanding of our interdependence and of the relevance of development issues to people's everyday lives. (p. 5)

Yet in guidance for schools on developing global educational partnerships, a message from the Chancellor of the Exchequer and the minister for International Development states:

> Through school links, UK students will learn just how limited the provision of education is in so many countries and discover that across the world almost 80 million

> children – most of them girls – don't go to school, today or any day. And many more go to schools many miles from their home, without enough textbooks, teachers and even simple things like toilets or classrooms. (DfID, 2006, p. 1)

This is a direct reference to Millennium Development Goals[3] (MDGs) One ('eradicate extreme poverty and hunger') and Two ('universal primary education for all'). Education, it appears, has been given the task of contributing to achievement of the MDGs. The deliberate conflation of development with education goals is highly political and I would argue contributes to the examples of student learning reported by Brown (2006) and Edge et al. (2009a, 2009b) earlier in this chapter. The MDGs are seen as universal because they have broad agreement across the United Nations. However, the interpretation of these goals within the United Kingdom indicates a modernization approach to development and a view of education based on Eurocentric concept of schools and schooling.

Global citizenship as conceived in Western nations thus represents a paradox borne of fear of losing economic status while at the same time having a moral obligation to those less fortunate; a paradox that echoes the 'European colonial project: control/uplift of a savage/primitive Other' (Jefferess, 2009, p. 30). The contradiction between human rights, citizenship and state sovereignty has led to a situation where

> Rather than interrogat[ing] the limitations of liberal democracy and capitalism, global citizenship extends them onto a global scale, thus perpetuating their hegemonic formations. (Carpenter et al., 2007, p. 5)

As a result, educators are increasingly questioning whether global citizenship is a citizenship of the privileged (see Andreotti, 2006; Zemach-Bersin, 2007; Jefferess, 2009).

Government educational policy on sustainability contributes to this discourse in its description of a sustainable school as one that is 'guided by the principle of care: care for oneself, care for each other and care for the environment' (DfES, 2006). This central principle of care is not new to schools but it is 'the addition of the reference to care for the environment and *its global citizens* as a whole school priority that moves a school from being a good school to a sustainable school' (Birney and Reed, 2009, p. 3; emphasis added). So while authors such as Porritt et al. (2009) are advocating for a greater emphasis on intragenerational equity, this is being interpreted as an ethics of 'care' with the implication of a moral obligation towards the 'Other' and reflecting the paternalistic attitudes discussed earlier.

There is a growing awareness of these issues within the education sections of some NGOs which, often in partnership with Development Education Centres are beginning to work with teachers to raise their understanding of global and development issues (DEA, 2009). One of the strategies is through study visits abroad. However, research shows that negative attitudes and stereotypes associated with colonialism are not automatically challenged or dispelled by 'exposure' to other cultures (Finney and Orr, 1995; Lee, 2006).

Geography, education and study abroad

Very little research has been conducted into the impact of study visits on teachers' world-views, and that which does exist provides a mixed picture. Hutchings and Smart (2007) conducted a study on the impact of extended placements in Namibia and Rwanda on UK primary headteachers and their schools. Their findings showed that an emphasis on fundraising was common to seven out of the eight placement schools, and it was noted that while some teachers 'hoped to move away from [fundraising] so that they were not seen as "white providers" . . . issues of power, discrimination, conflict, human rights, values and past injustices were rarely mentioned' (ibid., p. 9). In another study Merryfield (2000) found that experiences alone did not make a global educator. Depending on the nature of and relationship between power, identity and experience, different meanings would be ascribed to the same experiences by different educators. Merryfield concluded that crucial to a 'decolonisation of the mind' (2000, p. 439) was time to reflect and support to deconstruct previously held assumptions about the world; something that was not facilitated for the headteachers in the Smart and Hutchings study.

It might be expected that geography would have much to contribute with its long history of a focus on development, but McQuaid (2009) provides an analysis of how geography has perpetuated the colonial legacy, while Abbott (2006) offers a critique of geography fieldwork abroad from a post-colonial perspective. In some respects geography is part of the problem rather than the solution. Through organizations such as the Royal Geographical Society, geography as a discipline developed in colonial times in which white, middle class males travelled the world and viewed the Other as an object to study. Post-colonial theorists argue that in so doing, geographers relegated the study of those 'without history' to 'the dingy "ethnography corner" to which colonial discourse would wish them to remain cast for eternity' (Hoppers, 2009, p. 4).

However, the 'imperial gaze' is arguably the way many people still view other countries when they travel, and this gaze is 'sustained in many tourist and educational enterprises, representing a certain domestication of imperialism while continuing its staking out of the world as a classroom of instruction and delight' (Willinsky, 1998, cited in McQuaid, 2009).

Evidence that this continues today is provided by Abbott (2006) who argues for the need to disrupt the 'whiteness' of fieldwork in geography. Her analysis of literature on geography fieldwork shows that it is seen as neutral, that it can somehow be conducted through a homogenized approach no matter where the field study takes place, and that it 'disassociates the practice from its historical role in imperialism' (Abbott, 2006, p. 326). She raises the difficult question,

> What does 'cultural exchange' really mean when two groups (the local community and the students/tutors) are interacting in historically racialized spaces and places in the midst of conditions of material poverty? . . . Are we as geographers critically engaging in deconstructing the practice and pedagogy of long-haul fieldwork . . . or are we simply distancing ourselves from challenging questions by concentrating on the organizational and the practical aspects of these overseas trips? (ibid., pp. 329–330)

The same could be asked of North-South school partnerships. Therefore, if we wish to avoid repeating the geographical tradition of exploration that legitimizes whiteness, we need to be prepared to 'work towards a political analysis of long-haul field study activities, . . . and do better and more critical research about geography's historical role as the purveyor of boundaries on spaces of power and hierarchy' (Abbott, 2006, p. 337). Abbott is arguing for such an analysis in the context of geography field visits to ex-colonial countries, but as McQuaid has demonstrated, such an analysis also needs to be applied to policy and practice in Geographical Education.

Implications for geographical education

The overall purpose of this chapter has been to explore, at the points where geography, sustainability and school partnerships intersect, where current practice is problematic. In England, sustainability and school partnerships are connected through educational policy, such as the Sustainable Schools programme (DfES, 2006), which requires that education for sustainability has a global dimension, because the 'growing interdependence between countries changes the way we view the world and ourselves' (ibid.). A commitment to care is central to the Sustainable Schools framework, including 'care for each other across cultures, distances and generations' with schools being expected to act as 'models of global citizenship, enriching their educational mission with activities that improve the lives of people living in other parts of the world' (ibid.). When combined with North-South school partnerships, it is this commitment to care, and the explicit missionary approach to improving the lives of people in other parts of the world, that creates issues of a global ethical nature. Geographers cannot stand aside from these issues; they both profoundly affect, and are affected by, practice in geography education. In my view the post-colonial analysis presented above has clear implications for geography education that will now be discussed.

An argument 'for space'

Two of the core concepts of geography are those of Place and Space. As outlined earlier in the chapter, Massey (2005) showed how a Modernist approach to the 'Other' effectively assigned (hidden) temporality as the lens for making sense of what was encountered, which had (and has) the effect of fixing things in time, rather than portraying space (and societies) as open and constantly being made: 'The temporal convening of space thus reworks the nature of difference. Coexisting heterogeneity is rendered as (reduced to) place in the historical queue' (p. 69). Massey goes on to argue that migration from former colonies to the United Kingdom, in the second half of twentieth century and increasingly in the first decade of twenty-first century, not only represents the arrival of the margins at the centre, but is visible evidence that 'they' are not consigned to the past. The spatial eradication of distance between 'us' and 'them' has challenged the conceptualization of the Other in temporal terms and arguably contributed to the negative attitudes towards difference that are evident in the United Kingdom today (Brown and Smith, 2006).

The use of spatial analysis in this way can therefore aid understanding of attitudes towards difference, but Massey also argues that this in turn requires a reconceptualization of place: Place is not a thing, capturable as a slice through time in the sense of an essential section, it is 'the coming together of the previously un-related, a constellation of processes . . . not intrinsically coherent' (2005, p. 141). This, what Massey describes as the 'thrown togetherness' of place, demands negotiation and requires that we 'confront the challenge of the negotiation of multiplicity' (ibid.). Geography can make a contribution by developing a global sense of place which recognizes that 'the "lived reality of our daily lives" is utterly dispersed, unlocalised, in its sources and in its repercussions' (ibid., p. 184).

Critical global citizenship

This generation, encouraged and motivated to 'make a difference', . . . project[s] their beliefs and myths as universal and reproduce power relations and violence similar to those in colonial times. (Andreotti, 2006, p. 41)

In an analysis of the goals of global citizenship, Andreotti argues that rather than individuals becoming active citizens 'according to what has been defined for them as an ideal world', they should be empowered to 'reflect critically on the legacies and processes of their cultures, to imagine different futures and to take responsibility for decisions and actions' (2006, p. 48). Critical global citizenship requires critical literacy which not only advocates the adoption of critical perspectives towards text in order to uncover underlying messages, but also calls into question what counts as 'text' and what counts as 'literacy'. Traditional Western views of literacy are narrowly defined in terms of the ability to read and write; critical literacy extends this to reading not only the 'word' but also the 'world' (Gregory and Cahill, 2009). Based on Friere (1972), critical literacy starts with the desire to balance social inequities and address societal problems caused by abuse of power. A critical 'reading' of how words are used and the hegemonic meanings ascribed to them can help students to understand and act in the world differently. McQuaid cites an example from Morgan and Lambert (2003) of how this might apply to teaching of the geography topic of migration.

in teaching the 'facts' needed to gain knowledge about migration (both emigration and immigration), students may end up with essentialist understandings of place and culture where language of 'migrants' 'majorities' and 'illegals' may cover up the details of a complex issue. (2009, p. 16)

A focus on the concept of diaspora, linked to Massey's global sense of place described above, is suggested as being more useful in helping students to understand why some people have differing and complex senses of space, place and multiple belongings. Morgan and Lambert (2003) argue that understanding place as open, porous, products of other places, enables students to understand the interconnections between people rather than the distinctions between them. Yet it is important to be aware of the danger that focusing simply on interconnections rather than distinctions can lead to a denial of difference. For example, in another publication Morgan (2002) discusses how a critical literacy implies a pedagogy in which there is less of a concern to identify order and 'sameness' and more attention to 'difference'; it forces us to focus on the myriad of variations in the human condition and away from universalism (p. 18).

Knowledge or knowledges?

What was striking in Edge et al.'s (2009a) findings was that in the majority of schools teachers were presenting knowledge about the world as if it was universal and therefore certain and unproblematic. As a result, they were directing students to particular courses of action, rather than exploring a number of probable, possible and preferable futures and considering a range of alternative solutions to economic sustainability and intragenerational equity. The critical element so important in educating for sustainability was lacking. In his online teacher development resource David Hicks argues that to see the world only through one's own cultural lens is ethnocentric, whereas to begin to see a range of cultural values and perceptions relating to education and sustainable development offers far greater opportunities for dialogue and critical debate (Hicks, 2010, teaching unit session 11). Likewise, a dismantling of colonial discourse, requires bringing into the discourse arena 'totally different meaning and registers from other traditions' such as indigenous knowledge systems and related forms of agency (Hoppers, 2009, p. 5). For Andreotti (2006), this can only be achieved through a process of learning to unlearn (unpacking one's own historical and cultural 'baggage'); learning to listen (to multiple perspectives); learning to learn (taking on new perspectives, rearranging and expanding one's own); and learning to reach out (exploring new ways of being, thinking, doing, knowing and relating).

Conclusion

Teaching about sustainability through North-South school partnerships inevitably brings students into contact, directly or indirectly, with the 'Other' and there is an urgent need to develop an ethical approach to this work in order to avoid repeating patterns of thought and action that are redolent of colonialism. In summary, an ethical approach to learning about sustainability through

North-South partnerships might involve moving from traditional views of knowledge, the curriculum and pedagogy towards conceptualizations of these things that are based on a more relational ontology. Some suggestions for what such shifts in perception might look like are outlined below. It is possible to read these as binary opposites but the intention is that they should be viewed as proposals for movement along a continuum.

- *Partnerships*: Avoid South/Other as an 'object' of study as in colonial times; develop ways of working together through a process of mutual learning (Ballin, 2010) towards shared goals that are mutually beneficial.
- *Knowledge*: Move from a universal view of knowledge, to an understanding that knowledge is socially, historically, culturally constructed. Similarly, move from a view of knowledge that is certain and unproblematic, to one that reflects a relational, multiperspectival understanding concepts such as culture, identity, space, place, interdependence, sustainability – knowledges, not knowledge; futures, not future; geographies, not geography; histories, not history.
- *Subjects*: Rather than viewing knowledge as a set of discrete disciplines, Gilbert (2005) argues that it should be presenting as a series of systems that have particular ways of doing things (and particular strengths and weaknesses). Reframing our approach to knowledge in this way may 'allow us to work with students to develop the systems-level understanding, the big picture, [and the] connected ways of thinking they will need to function effectively in the knowledge society' (ibid., p. 175).
- *Curriculum*: Move away from conceptualizing 'curriculum as thing', a body of facts, ideas, skills and attitudes already decided by those in power to be 'delivered', to conceptualizing 'curriculum as encounter' (den Heyer, 2009, p. 28), to be created collaboratively between teachers and students who work towards shared sense making (Lambert, 2009).
- *Literacy*: Taking literacy in its broadest sense, and 'text' as including film, novels, popular music, art, and so on, den Heyer proposes moving from a 'readerly' to a 'writerly' approach to text. Readerly approaches assume that meaning resides in the text, whereas writerly approaches invites readers 'to make meanings through the context of their lives' (2009, p. 27). Any intercultural experiences, and encounters with texts will be interpreted through individuals' lenses; adopting a 'writerly' approach therefore requires recognizing that selves are implicated in texts and vice versa.
- *Pedagogy*: Morgan (2002) proposes a 'deconstructive pedagogy that begins to take apart the categories and meanings that have generally been thought of as fixed and stable' (p. 27). Things that Morgan suggests should be deconstructed in an explicit way with students are the various forms of representation that are used in geography classrooms (similar to den Heyer's 'texts'); taking such an approach will enable a move away from generalizations and a 'master narrative' to multiple

knowledges, perspectives and representations. However, in the context of discussing the sustainability issue of community cohesion, de Souza warns that when focusing on multiple perspectives the goal should not be to arrive at a consensus (which re-creates polarity). He proposes a pedagogy of dissensus as an alternative (de Souza, 2008), which requires an awareness of internal and external difference (self, individual, community) and an 'openness to new possibilities [rather than] substantial and universal certainties' (ibid.). This, as discussed in other chapters in this volume, calls into question the uncritical, 'ready-made' solutions approach to sustainability – buy Fair Trade, join the 'Send My Friend to School' Campaign, fund-raise for partner school.

Adopting an ethical approach to teaching about sustainability is a highly complex matter. Acknowledging that issues are complex is not just a matter of supplementing a standard curriculum with representative samplings from other points of view (e.g. through North-South school partnerships). It requires a fundamental rethink of the nature of education, curriculum and pedagogy and a willingness to not only bring difficult issues into the classroom, but also to reflect on one's own world-view.

Thinking in postcolonial terms about the topic of difference and multiplicity in education means thinking relationally and contextually. It means bringing back into educational discourses all the tensions and contradictions that we tend to suppress as we process experiences and history into curricular knowledge. It means abandoning the [essential] status of concepts such as 'culture' and 'identity' for a recognition of the vital porosity that exists between and among human groups in the modern world. It means foregrounding the intellectual autonomy of students by incorporating open-mindedness and inquiry that come from letting traditions debate with each other under the rubric that we learn more about ourselves by learning about others . . . [and] ultimately thinking across disciplinary boundaries and the insulation of knowledge. (McCarthy et al., 2005, p. 164)

Notes

1 Throughout this chapter the terms North and South will be used, as by Burr (2008), to convey common representations of the divide between the 'developed' and 'developing' world. It is recognized that these terms are contested, but they are used to facilitate discussion of the epistemological and pedagogical issues raised.

2 For those who wish to gain deeper insight into post-colonial theory, key theorists are Edward Said (1985), Frantz Fanon (1986), Homi Bhabha (1994) and Gayatri Chakravorti Spivak (1999).

3 The Millennium Development Goals (MDGs) are eight goals to be achieved by 2015 that respond to the world's main development challenges. The MDGs are drawn from the actions and targets

contained in the Millennium Declaration that was adopted by 189 nations and signed by 147 heads of state and governments during the UN Millennium Summit in September 2000 (www.undp.org/mdg/basics.shtml).

References

Abbott, D. (2006), 'Disrupting the "whiteness" of fieldwork in geography', *Singapore Journal of Tropical Geography*, 27, 326–341.

Andreotti, V. (2006), 'Soft versus critical global citizenship education', *Development Education: Policy and Practice*, Issue 3, Autumn 2006, Centre for Global Education, Belfast.

Ashcroft, B., Griffiths, G. and Tiffin, H. (1998), *Key Concepts in Post-Colonial Studies*. New York: Routledge.

Ballin, B. (2010), 'Mutual learning for sustainability: the Gambia and the UK', in Tide~Talk, Online journal. Available at http://www.tidec.org/Tidetalk/articles/thegambia.html

Bhabha, H. (1994), *Location of Culture*. New York: Routledge.

Bhabha, H. K. (2005), 'Forward: framing Fanon', in F. Fanon (ed.), *The Wretched of the Earth*. Boston: Grove Press.

Birney, A. and Reed, J. (2009), *Sustainability and Renewal: Findings from the Leading Sustainable Schools Research Project Summary Report*. Nottingham: National College for Leadership of Schools and Children's Services. Available as a download from www.nationalcollege.org.uk

Brown, K. (2006), 'School linking and teaching and learning Global Citizenship'. Available as a download from www.citized.info/pdf/commarticles/Kate_Brown.pdf

Brown, J. and Smith, A. (2006), 'Lies, damned lies and immigration', *The Independent*, 22 August 2006.

Brundtland, G. (1987), *Our Common Future: The World Commission on Environment and Development*. Oxford: Oxford University Press.

Burr, M. (2008), 'Thinking about linking?' Available as a download from www.dea.org.uk/thinkpieces

Carey, J. (1989), *Culture as Communication*. London: Unwin Hyman.

Carpenter, S., Chum, A. and Weber, N. (2007), 'Conflict and convergence: theories and practice for global citizenship and adult education'. Paper presented at SCUTREA conference, July 2007, Belfast, NI.

de Souza, L. M. T. (2008), 'A pedagogy of dissensus'. Keynote address at 'Shifting Margins, Shifting Centres: Negotiating Difference in Education in the 21st century' conference. Institute of Education, University of London. 17 September 2008. Audio version. Available at http://www.through-othereyes.org.uk/audio/index.html

den Heyer, K. (2009), 'Implicated and called upon: challenging an educated position of self, others, knowledge and knowing as things to acquire', *Critical Literacy: Theories and Practices*, 3, (1), 26–35.

Department for Education and Employment/Department for International Development (2000), *Global Dimension across the Curriculum*. London: DfEE.

Department for Education and Employment/Qualifications and Curriculum Authority (1999), *The National Curriculum for England*. London: DfEE.

Department for Education and Skills (2004), *Putting the World into World Class Education*. London: DfES.

—. (2006), *Sustainable Schools: For Pupils, Communities and the Environment*. London: DfES. Available online at http://www.teachernet.gov.uk/sustainableschools/

Department for Education and Skills/Department for International Development (2005), *Developing the Global Dimension in the School Curriculum*. London: DfES.

Department for International Development (1999), *Building Support for Development: DfID Strategy Paper*. Available as a download from www.dfid.gov.uk

—. (2006), *The World Classroom: Developing Global Partnerships in Education*. London: HMSO.

Disney, A. (2004), 'Children's developing images and representations of the school link environment', in S. Catling and F. Martin (eds), *Researching Primary Geography*. London: Register of Research in Primary Geography.

Edge, K., Khamsi, K. and Bourn, D. (2009a), *Exploring the Global Dimension in Secondary Schools*. London: Institute of Education.

Edge, K., Frayman, K. and Ben Jaafar, S. (2009b), *North-South School Partnerships: Learning from Schools in the UK, Asia and Africa*. London: Institute of Education.

Fanon, F. (1986), *Black Skin, White Masks*. London: Pluto Press.

Finney, S. and Orr, J. (1995), '"I've really learned a lot, but . . .": cross-cultural understanding and teacher education in a Racist society', *Journal of Teacher Education*, 46, (5), 327–333.

Friere, P. (1972), *Pedagogy of the Oppressed*. Harmondsworth: Penguin.

Gilbert, J. (2005), *Catching the Knowledge Wave? The Knowledge Society and the Future of Education*. Wellington: NZCER Press.

Graves, J. (2002), 'Developing a global dimension in the curriculum', *The Curriculum Journal*, 13, (3), 303–311.

Gregory, A. E. and Cahill, M. A. (2009), 'Constructing critical literacy: self-reflexive ways for curriculum and pedagogy', *Critical Literacy: Theories and Practices*, 3, (2), 6–16.

Griffin, H. (2008), 'Fundraising for people in economically poor countries: should schools do it?' *Development Education Centre South Yorkshire Newsletter*, Spring.

Hicks, D. (2006), *Lessons for the Future: The Missing Dimension in Education*. Victoria, BC: Trafford Publishing.

—. (2008), 'The global dimension'; 'A futures perspective'; and 'Education for sustainability', in S. Ward (ed.), *A Student's Guide to Education Studies*. London: Routledge.

—. (2010), Teaching Units Session 11, online learning resource available at http://teaching4abetterworld.co.uk/teaching.html (accessed 17 January 2010).

Hoppers, C. (2009), 'Development Education at the Transition from the Modern Triage Society to a Moral and Cognitive Reconstruction of Citizenship'. Keynote address International Conference on: Critical Thinking and Development Education: Moving from Evaluation to Research, National University of Galway, 3–4 October 2009.

Hutchings, M. and Smart, S. (2007), 'Evaluation of the impact on UK schools of the VSO/NAHT pilot scheme: "International Extended Placements for School Leaders"'. Unpublished report, Institute for Policy Studies in Education, London Metropolitan University.

Jefferess, D. (2008), 'Global citizenship and the cultural politics of benevolence', *Critical Literacies: Theories and Practices*, 2, (1), 27–36.

Lambert, D. (2009), *Geography in Education: Lost in the Post?* Inaugural professorial lecture, London Institute of Education, 23 June 2009.

Lee, M. M. (2006), '"Going global": conceptualization of the "other" and interpretation of crosscultural experience in an all-white, rural learning environment', *Ethnography and Education*, 1, (2), 197–213.

McCarthy, C., Giardina, M., Harewood, S. and Park, J. (2005), 'Contesting culture', in C. McCarthy, W. Critchlow, G. Dimitriadis and N. Dolby (eds), *Race, Identity and Representation in Education*, 2nd edition. New York: Routledge.

McQuaid, N. (2009), 'Learning to "un-divide" the world: the legacy of colonialism and education in the 21st century', *Critical Literacy: Theories and Practices*, 3, (1), 12–25.

Martin, F. (2008), 'Mutual learning: the impact of a study visit course on UK teachers' knowledge and understanding of global Partnerships', *Critical Literacy: Theories and Practices*, 2, (1), 60–75.

Massey, D. (2005), *For Space*. London: Sage.

Merryfield, M. M. (2000), 'Why aren't teachers being prepared to teach for diversity, equity, and global interconnectedness? A study of lived experiences in the making of multicultural and global educators', *Teaching and Teacher Education*, 16, 429–443.

Morgan, J. (2002), '"Teaching geography for a better world?" The postmodern challenge and geography education', *International Research in Geographical and Environmental Education*, 11, (1), 15–29.

Morgan, J. and Lambert, D. (2003), 'Place, "race" and teaching geography', in M. Biddulph and G. Butt (eds), *Theory into Practice, Professional Development for Geography Teachers*. Sheffield: Geographical Association.

Porritt, J., Hopkins, D., Birney, A. and Reed, J. (2009), *Every Child's Future: Leading the Way*. Nottingham: National College for Leadership of Schools and Children's Services. Available as a download from www.nationalcollege.org.uk

Qualifications and Curriculum Authority (2008), *The National Curriculum for Key Stage 3*. London: QCA.

Said, E. (1978), *Orientalism*. London: Penguin Books.

—. (1985), 'Orientalism reconsidered', *Cultural Critique*, 1, 89–107.

Sinha, A. (2002), 'Globalization: "making geography irrelevant"', *The Review of Education, Pedagogy, and Cultural Studies*, 24, 181–191.

Spivak, G. (1999), *A Critique of Postcolonial Reason: Toward a Critique of the Vanishing Present*. Cambridge MA: Harvard University Press.

UNESCO/BMBF (2009), Proceedings of UNESCO World Conference on Education for Sustainable Development. 31 March–2 April 2009, Bonn, Germany.

Willinsky, J. (1998), *Learning to Divide the World: Education at Empire's End*. Minneapolis, MN: University of Minnesota Press.

Young, R. J. C. (2003), *Postcolonialism – a Very Short Introduction*. Oxford: Oxford University Press.

Zemach-Bersin, T. (2007), 'Global citizenship & study abroad: it's all about U.S.', *Critical Literacy: Theories and Practices*, 1, (2), 16–28.

Teaching Ethical Citizens? A Geographical Approach

12

Jessica Pykett

Chapter Outline

The geography of citizenship education

Since 2002, many geography teachers in schools in England have had the responsibility for teaching compulsory citizenship lessons. These lessons are concerned with ensuring that young people are able to 'play an effective role in public life' and are organized around the concepts of 'democracy and justice', 'rights and responsibilities' and 'identities and diversity: living together in the UK'. These are said to enable young people to 'take action and try to make a difference' (QCA, 2007). The situation in Scotland and Wales is different. In Scotland, the Curriculum for Excellence launched in 2004 introduced 'social studies' which is described as 'developing [children and young people's] understanding of the world by learning about their own people and what has shaped them, other people and their values . . . and how their environment has been shaped'. This should help them in 'exercising informed and responsible citizenship' (Scottish Executive, 2006, p. 34). In Wales, there is statutory guidance on teaching sustainable development and non-statutory guidance on promoting global citizenship (ACCAC, 2002). This states that education for sustainable development and global citizenship 'enables people to understand the global forces which shape their lives and to acquire the knowledge, skills and values that will equip them to participate in decision making, both locally and globally, which promotes a more equitable and sustainable world' (2002, p. 6). Here, the emphasis is on interdependence, links between society, economy and environment, intergenerational equity, power relations, the distribution of resources, and the links between local action and global consequences.

This rapid and albeit partial review of some recent citizenship education programmes in the United Kingdom suggests that interpretations of the subject, its ethos and its geographical emphasis (local action, national values, global awareness) are highly variable. Consider further afield, a requirement in Texas to learn about 'the contributions of Texans who have been President of the United States' (Texas Education Agency, 1998, ch. 113, sec. 32), in Australia, an emphasis on understanding 'the impact of British colonisation on Aboriginal and Torres Strait Islander peoples and their pursuit of citizenship rights' (Curriculum Corporation, 2006, p. 3), or in France, the focus on universal and egalitarian rights, and the modern, enlightenment perspectives of the French Republic (Starkey, 2000, p. 41). This cultural specificity and variety indicates that citizenship education itself may have an implicit geography which any future geography should consider. The ethos underpinning citizenship education will have an important bearing on the conception of the ethical citizen promoted. Understanding the social, political and cultural context in which citizenship education emerges as a distinct subject, body of knowledge and set of classroom or whole school activities is therefore paramount. Doing so will enable us to interrogate some of the claims of, and justifications for, citizenship education and will help us to consider what is at stake in imagining the 'ideal' ethical citizen.

To this end, this chapter considers the historical antecedents of citizenship education in order to discern its future, and the related future of geography education. In the next section I trace some of the origins of citizenship education in the United Kingdom and discuss some of its rationales, how it defines a 'problem' to be solved, and the kind of ideal future citizens it seeks to promote. In the following section I examine the relationship between citizenship education and geography education, including the distinctions between citizenship and geography, what challenges may be faced by geography teachers responsible for citizenship education, and the potential contribution of a future geography education to a more critically engaged form of citizenship.

The final section works through an example of global trade and ethical consumption to explore the way in which values, emotions, motives and political activity are mobilized in order to make 'ethical citizens' in the classroom.

The long road to citizenship education

Citizenship education has a long history. David Heater (2004) comprehensively traces these origins to their classical Greek history, through the revolutionary and republican upheavals of early nation states, to a critique of more recent claims for European and World citizenship education. Children have been schooled in 'citizenly' behaviours since at least the inception of mass-schooling in the nineteenth century. For instance, Hendrick (1997, p. 73) notes that in 1885, the regulations of an Oxford school warned: 'All children must come clean, and with their hair combed, and must bring pocket handkerchiefs.' Since then, most, if not all, school subjects were – to a degree – concerned with the formation of a particular kind of citizen: Maths was to produce children with 'natural reason', in order that they be governed through their 'reasonableness' (Walkerdine, 1988, p. 6); English was to train children in the British literary canon and sensibilities; History was to give children a sense of a shared national heritage and common narrative, and Geography was concerned with developing a fixed sense of place and a rekindling of imperial power in an ever-changing world (Morgan, 2001, p. 58).

The recent promotion of citizenship education can be said to have begun with *Encouraging Citizenship* (HMSO, 1990). In this cross-parliamentary Speaker's Commission on Citizenship, Education for Citizenship was recommended as a cross-curricular theme and a distinct set of skills including debating, participating in elections, representing others, working collaboratively, team work and even protesting (ibid., p. 38). The commission argued that their recommendations should be seen in the context of:

> our rapidly changing society, the entitlements of citizens in the late twentieth century, and the obligations of public institutions, of which many are ignorant, the plight of the sick, the elderly, and the handicapped [sic], the contributions of the thousands of individuals who care for the environment or for their fellows on a voluntary or professional basis. (ibid., p. xvi)

But it wasn't until 1998, a year into the New Labour government, that citizenship education, was promoted as a distinct school subject. It had important interconnections with other subject disciplines, but its own specific curriculum statements, programmes of study and schemes of work. *Education for Citizenship and the Teaching of Democracy in Schools* ('The Crick Report', QCA, 1998) reported on the discussions and recommendations of an advisory group chaired by Professor (later, Sir) Bernard Crick. The report outlined a vision of citizenship in terms of the health of the UK's democracy and the education of young people as active citizens. The subject was designed to empower young people in their participation in both formal and informal political processes, and was concerned with fostering ethical relationships between people at multiple scales – both within and outside their immediate political communities.

Citizenship education has a geography as well as a history. The social and cultural geographical context of the introduction of citizenship education is indicative of some of its political rationales. At least three distinct rationales can be identified – each is presented from a geographical perspective which serves to challenge some of the underlying assumptions of citizenship education. The first is associated with media representations of youth and behaviour. Widespread panic following the murders of the toddler, Jamie Bulger and the Headteacher, Philip Lawrence led to grave concerns regarding the appropriate moral and legal status of children responsible for such violent crimes. In addition, a perception of general youth 'loutishness' informed the need for education in social and moral responsibility, as outlined in the Crick Report (QCA, 1998, p. 15): 'Truancy, vandalism, random violence, premeditated crime and habitual drug-taking can be other indicators of youth alienation.' The demonization of children and young people as lost innocents in this way reflects how they are reimagined and represented across different spaces and times (Valentine, 1996). This may be related to issues as constructed in the national media, local concerns, or a result of global economic restructuring which serves to recast young people's relationships with the economy, society, adults and each other (McDowell, 2003). In this way, both Valentine and McDowell show how 'youth alienation' is certainly not the root cause of a problem which can be solved through citizenship education, but instead results from the sensationalization of childhood morality and the disempowerment of particular groups of young people through their exclusion from the labour market. They have shown how the status (socially, politically and legally) of children as culturally imagined citizens is dependent not just on their historical status but on geographical factors.

Secondly, the Crick report was aimed specifically at improving the 'health and future of British democracy' (QCA, 1998, p. 8) – responding to a number of surveys and polls regarding the apparent 'apathy, ignorance and cynicism about public life', particularly among young people (ibid.). Levels of political engagement were said to be in decline – with few young people reading newspapers or taking an interest in parliament or investing trust in elected politicians. Voting turnout was at a low, and a need identified to improve the 'political literacy' of young people (ibid.). However, an interesting rebuke of this account of young people's sense of citizenship is offered by Weller (2007, pp. 162–163), who develops the notion of 'cumulative' and 'cosmopolitan' citizenship as a challenge to the idea that young people are not fully competent citizens. She explores how space and place are integral to young people's acts of citizenship – for instance, through their appropriation of particular spaces within the school and on the journey home, and through citizenship as it is practiced outside of formal education. She envisages a rich sense of 'citizen involvement' (ibid., p. 108) by young people in claiming to belonging to significant local spaces, campaigning for sociable spaces such as skate parks, and engaging in community activities such as football teams. A focus on the spaces inhabited and reproduced through the social practices of young people can therefore offer an important corrective to the account of citizenship presented in the justification of citizenship education – one which relies on the transference of the formal routes to citizen participation (voting, local government, voluntary work) into the lives of young people.

The final rationale concerns the realities of racism and a more explicit recognition of the UK's multicultural population. Responding to 'the worries' of increased cultural diversity, the Crick Report (ibid., p. 17) states that:

> a main aim for the whole community should be to find or restore a sense of common citizenship, including a national identity that is secure enough to find a place for the plurality of nations, cultures, ethnic identities and religions long found in the United Kingdom.

Arguably reflecting the concerns of 'majority' ethnic groups above others, and somewhat presuming cultural diversity as the problem rather than racism itself (Gillborn, 2006; Osler, 2000), this perceived need for citizenship education should also be seen in the contexts of the murder of teenager, Stephen Lawrence and the subsequent publication of the MacPherson report (MacPherson, 1999) on institutional racism in the Metropolitan Police. In addition to the later social unrest in Oldham and Burnley, Leeds and Bradford, which culminated in riots in the summer of 2001, these events led to the emergence of race and religion as a matter of 'public concern' as opposed to private identity (Ipgrave, 2003, p. 156). Later that year, the Cantle report (Home Office, 2001, p. 20) called in particular for an educational response coupling a common vision with an appreciation of diversity:

> A meaningful concept of 'citizenship' needs establishing – and championing – which recognises (in education programmes in particular) the contribution of all cultures to this Nation's development throughout its history, but establishes a clear primary loyalty to this Nation.

Within these specific incidences of unrest, as Amin (2002, n.p.) points out, was 'a discernible geographical pattern to sustained and everyday ethnic intolerance and conflict'. Amin also challenges the dominant policy conception of community cohesion which appears to be based on the idea that diverse people cannot get along because they are ethnically diverse, rather than as a result of long-running processes associated with economic deprivation, the spatial dynamics of segregation, and struggles over neighbourhood belonging. It is these trends he identifies which result in the emergence of a youth 'counter-public' (ibid., p. 964). His observations raise the question of whether children and young people can be held responsible for 'ethnic' conflict in a context in which their occupation of and orientation to particular places is limited by inequalities in the distribution of incomes, opportunities, access to welfare and chances for intercultural dialogue (ibid., p. 973).

The ideal young citizen imagined and promoted through the introduction of citizenship education is therefore someone who engages in community activities, participates in the electoral process and displays individual loyalty to a diverse yet common nation-state. Yet these aims and characteristics are derived from the framing of particular social problems during a specific historical period. As I have demonstrated above, these kind of solutions can be brought into question by a geographical perspective, which complicates the particular interpretations of such circumstances offered by education policy makers, the media and the government of the time, and are an important part of an informed and questioning approach to cultivating 'ethical' citizens.

While citizenship education paints a picture of the ideal citizen, related to the specific history and geography of its introduction as a new curriculum subject, these idealizations are far from fixed or secure. Where carefully and critically taught, citizenship education itself offers an agenda through which to challenge how such an ideal citizen (and its apparent 'other' – those viewed as less than ideal citizens) are imagined. Indeed it opens up curricular space for young people to deliberate a range of political concerns, and to consider the governmental, economic, social and cultural processes by which they themselves become governable as ideal citizens. In seeking out a distinctive approach to teaching citizenship through future geography, this consideration of the 'geographies of citizenship education' needs to be complemented with an excavation of the citizenship imagined through geography education. The next section thus examines the opportunities for developing synergies between citizenship and geography in the light of citizenship education's already existing geography, and geography's already existing sense of citizenship.

Citizenship and geography

There is an interesting and long-running history of education for citizenship in the school geography curriculum (Maddrell, 1996; Ploszajska, 1996; Walford, 1996). Through historical work, Maddrell (1996) rediscovers the role of school geography in encouraging a new sense of imperialism, via direct instruction on the worthiness of emigrating and the particular geographies of the British colonies between 1880–1925. School text books, learned societies such as the Royal Geographical Society and teacher journals all contributed to the imagination of the geography student as someone in preparation for an Imperial life ruling and civilizing culturally 'inferior' people deemed to be unable to rule themselves (ibid., p. 379). Learning about geography was therefore about developing a superior sense of national citizenship through the particular 'knowledge' of the place of the British Empire in the world, as well as learning about the geography of distant places so that children might be able to envisage themselves mastering such lands and their inhabitants. Though as Butt (2001, p. 69) points out, there were equally contributions from geographers such as Welpton and Fleure in the early 1900s, who promoted a more liberal and anti-imperialist kind of geography education (see also Kearns, 2004, p. 194). The association of school geography with a particularly gendered, racialized identification with the English landscape, and the rejection of the post-war urban environment have also been well-documented (Morgan, 2001, p. 61; Matless, 1996).

Some of the more recent geographies of citizenship found within school geography and citizenship education have been described in terms of the 'global citizen' (Morgan, 2001, p. 65) associated with the globalization of a competitive global education market (Dale and Robertson, 2008; Olds, 2007). Facilitated by new technologies, a discourse of global responsibility and mobility, the school geography curriculum has been said to play a part in the imagination of what Mitchell (2003) has termed, the 'strategic cosmopolitan' citizen – of which she is highly critical. To Mitchell (2003, p. 387), the ideal citizen produced through contemporary educational policy and practice is a globalized, neoliberal subject characterized by individualist and entrepreneurial tendencies – where diversity is no longer a lynchpin of democracy, but a source of 'competitive advantage in the global marketplace'. Others have considered the more informal, everyday citizenship experiences of young people going to school in particular geographically uneven contexts, within cities (Pykett, 2009), and at the global scale (Katz, 2004). Indeed Katz (2002, p. 248) argues that the nature of childhood has been changed by processes of globalization – in particular through the decoupling of social reproduction from particular forms of production and the reworking of the child, not as citizen, but as worker and consumer.

Hence, as David Lambert (2006, p. 30) has noted, our perceptions of citizenship have long been caught up with ideas about territory, space and scale; a very particular ethos which geography education could do better to question and contest:

> Geography plays a distinctive role in citizenship education through performing a type of 'mapping' function that enables young people to locate themselves in relation to other people and other places.

Elsewhere, Lambert and Machon (2001, p. 204) have argued for a need to constantly rework the meaning of geography education in a changing world, and to take a less fixed view of its disciplinary boundaries. In addition to their identification of important but implicit interrelations between geography and citizenship, there are clearly more formal synergies between the Geography and Citizenship curricula – in terms of skills, topics, understandings (see also Butt, 2001, p. 77 for further similarities). Table 12.1 outlines some of the parallels which can be drawn between Geography and Citizenship at Key Stage 3.

Both the Geography and Citizenship curricula are therefore concerned with developing young people's sense of public-mindedness, interconnectedness, global ethics and active responsibility – in some ways offering a corrective to the reproduction of Western children as consumers. Both subjects also provide opportunities to develop skills of investigation and critical inquiry, and encourage participation in citizenship- and geography-related issues. The range of contemporary topics which could be covered under both subjects is extensive, from migration, globalization, community, sustainability, environment, development, trade, conflict, culture and identity, the economy, cities, governance, and so on.

Table 12.1 A comparison of the Citizenship and Geography curricula in England at Key Stage 3, adapted from http://curriculum.qca.org.uk/

'The importance of Citizenship' curriculum statement, KS3:	'The importance of Geography' curriculum statement, KS3:
• Pupils learn about their **rights, responsibilities**, duties and freedoms and about laws, justice and democracy. • It helps pupils to become informed, critical, active citizens who have the confidence and conviction to work collaboratively, **take action and try to make a difference** in their communities and the wider world. • They learn to take part in decision-making and different forms of action. They play an **active role in the life** of their schools, neighbourhoods, communities and wider society as **active and global citizens**.	• Geography explains how a diverse range of economies, societies and environments are **interconnected.** • It builds on pupils' own experiences to investigate places at all **scales**, from the personal to the global. • Geography inspires pupils to **become global citizens** by exploring their own place in the world, their values and their **responsibilities** to other people, to the environment and to the sustainability of the planet.

In this configuration of the curriculum, there is a risk that the ideal twenty-first-century citizen imagined here shoulders the burden of responsibility for global problems associated with these issues. Indeed, it has been argued that a discourse of active citizenship and 'responsibilization' permeates not just the practices of schooling, but extends to social policies concerning welfare, health, personal finance and debt, education, housing and the environment. The implication here is that individuals are made responsible for their own problems, the future of the planet, for community and social problems – bypassing more collective solutions (Nolan, 1998). This has been described as a New Labour agenda for producing 'activated, empowered, responsibilized, abandoned' citizens (Clarke, 2005, p. 447).

This political movement towards personal responsibility raises the question of how particular groups/individuals get blamed for social problems and how policies promote the language of self-sufficiency, active citizenship, resilience and independence. Should active citizens be taking on more and more responsibilities, or should they be equipped with the knowledge and skills to demand that governments, corporations and more powerful organizations fulfil their responsibilities? Citizenship education and geography both arguably provide the opportunity to develop a more critical approach which contests notions of the ideal citizen imagined through political discourse and re-establishes the place of learning as a site from which to challenge conceptions of a globalized, individualized responsibility. While Citizenship raises the question of who is responsible for what, where and at what scale of action, a geographical approach to teaching future citizens will also ask 'who gets what, where and why?'

Asking these more geographically inflected questions allows students to consider a distinctly geographical ethics. A consideration of spatial patterns of inequalities of wealth, health and 'well-being', for instance, provokes students to consider justice and fairness. A geographical ethic of egalitarianism, as David Smith (2000, p. 204) has noted, involves understanding the absolute *absence* of responsibility that people should have for shaping their own original circumstances:

> The accident of birth – to whom, when and where – has a major bearing on individual life chances, yet there are no moral grounds for such an outcome. This is a matter of chance, over which people have no control, like race or gender which should similarly have no bearing on life chances.

Teaching students to be actively responsible for their own circumstances is not the same, however, as enabling them to take informed action to seek to challenge injustices or reduce geographical inequalities. This is a distinction that a geographical approach to teaching future citizen helps us to make. In order to elaborate on this distinction, the final section of this chapter develops the example of teaching fair trade.

Teaching fair trade, cultivating ethical citizens

As I have noted above, there is a need to develop a critical awareness of the historical and geographical context in which the ideal citizen is imagined through both geography and citizenship education. This can help us to problematize the role of the geography educator in reinforcing received and partial views of the child as global consumer, active citizen, agent of community cohesion, of personal responsibility and ethical behaviour. This can be demonstrated by working through the example of fair trade teaching which seeks to cultivate the ethical citizen in the Geography and Citizenship classrooms.

Teaching about the importance of fair trade is commonplace in both Citizenship and Geography lessons. Often related to work as part of the 'Global Dimension' cross-curricular theme, ethical consumption is often seen as one of the most hopeful and optimistic aspects of global trade, through the connection of young people's everyday consumption habits with the fostering of wider global equality. It is therefore an appropriate topic for geography teachers charged with teaching citizenship to consider. Teachers may use a number of resource packs available from educational and campaigning organizations (both governmental and non-governmental) such as the Fair-trade Foundation, Oxfam, regional Development Education Centres, Labour Behind the Label, Bananalink, Christian Aid, and so on. These resources may include trading games, videos, worker testimonials, websites and photos. They deploy a number of pedagogical techniques such as role-play, testimony and sequencing in order to promote certain ethical dispositions among students (Pykett et al., in press). The use of simulation games and role-play is intended to give students experiences of an unjust trade system, and to link particular commodities and their own consumption choices to workers' rights and conditions. Testimonials from workers and producers are used in order to develop students' sense of empathy with distant workers, whose lives are presented as much in their commonalities with Western consumers and school-aged students, as through their stark inequalities. Finally, sequencing is used in order to help students gradually come to their own realizations about the injustice of globalized commodity networks. The order of many fair trade simulation games is such that students' initial assumptions are questioned, and the particular commodity is eventually defetishized.

For some, the deployment of these emotional and affective pedagogical repertoires in the promotion of fair trade in schools is part of the very 'responsibilizing' ethos that this chapter is seeking to interrogate. Students are not simply given information about trade justice, but their very identities as global consumers are reinforced, and their sense of ethical citizenship is promoted as an individual virtue. Some commentators argue therefore that ethical consumption is intimately bound up with a neoliberal sense of self-interest and introspection, being more about developing the ethical identity of the consumer than ensuring justice for producers. Bryant and Goodman (2004, p. 359), for example, maintain that 'Fair trade knowledge flows thus act to re-work the fetish surrounding fair trade commodities into a new type of alternative "spectacle" for Northern consumers.' Others have argued that fair trade, environmental and social labelling 'look to be typical of neoliberal regulation' (Guthman, 2007, p. 457), in that they:

> attach economic values to ethical behaviors; and, finally, they 'devolve' regulatory responsibility to consumers. In other words, not only do these labels concede the market as the locus of regulation, in keeping with neoliberalism's fetish of market mechanisms, they employ tools designed to create markets.

The argument follows that the ideal ethical citizen promoted through fair trade education is part of the very same hegemonic rationality of the neoliberal globalized economy in which it purports to intervene. But this analysis can be contested on many fronts. The analysis of fair trade education as neo-liberal underestimates the agency of the teacher to enable critical investigation of fair trade practices and to promote learning which cannot be so easily dismissed. And as Cherrier (2007, p. 323) has pointed out, consumption practices are far more complex than the neoliberal market account permits. Consumers who are bombarded with an array of marketing messages, ecological, organic, ethical, social labelling do not make straightforward rational decisions based on full knowledge. In addition, consumption is not an individual market-place decision but a social practice, and people develop their consumer identities from a variety of shared identifications outside of the market-place – for instance, from religious organizations or social movements (see also Cloke et al., 2009). Furthermore, fair trade education is not just based on the affective and emotional pedagogical tactics of role-play, testimony and sequencing, but is also often part of a more active consciousness-raising and politically motivating pedagogy (Pykett et al., in press); students may be encouraged to think about and take part in campaigns and enterprises for trade justice. This might be a school-based campaign looking at procurement in the canteen and vending machines, or setting up/joining a fair trade group, becoming a fair trade school, town, county or even country, and becoming involved in wider social movements for change, such as the Make Poverty History campaign or World Social Forum. Although fair trade can therefore be criticized as being responsibilizing, at the same time, it opens up the potential for more ethically engaged consumption and political practices which, rather than being neoliberal, are concerned with trade justice and the promotion of trade regulation.

So how can we teach a topic like fair trade without falling back on idealizations of the individual ethical consumer-citizen? How do we avoid reinforcing the view that the school student is entirely responsible for global inequality – in addition to their responsibility (as set out in the Crick Report) for 'unchildlike' behaviour, political disengagement and local 'ethnic' conflict? Being mindful of existing critiques of fair trade education such as these, and of the citizen imagined through Geography and Citizenship is a good starting-point to help teachers avoid some of the potential pitfalls of teaching fair trade as 'a controversial issue'. A critical geographical approach to teaching fair trade would not treat fair trade simply as a private consumption choice but instead, as a means to political engagement, motivation and social forms of organizing towards trade justice. Fair trade would be presented in light of an understanding of the global economic system, the international and supranational regulatory architecture governing trade, and a consideration of the geometry of power (Massey, 1993) which shapes global interdependence and dependencies.

Teachers would be given the opportunities and training required to question the moral (and moralizing) imperatives of a lesson's aims and objectives and the resources used. It is important to consider what kind of virtues are promoted and where these come from. Reflecting on our own ethical dilemmas as a teacher, consumer, citizen will also help us to better understand the different pushes and pulls on our ethical behaviours – possibly by doing some research into philosophical debates concerning ethics, egalitarianism, justice and fairness. And we must always expect the unexpected! We can help students develop their own interpretations of the need for fair trade but they may also wish to experiment with valid counter-arguments, delving deeper into the politics of global trade. While this might not fit with our own aims and values, such critical inquiry must surely be encouraged.

Conclusion

As a topic with obvious connections to the geography and citizenship education curricula, fair trade can therefore be taught with geographical ethics in mind. This chapter has explored the characteristics of this geographical sensibility as it relates to the ideal citizen imagined through the geography and citizenship classrooms. Unpacking the cultural politics behind this imagined citizen is an important task for geographers, and one which should arguably be extended to geography students in schools – through a critically reflexive look at the social contexts and political assumptions behind both geography and citizenship education, their historical antecedents and geographical specificity. In a world in which the pressures and responsibilities put upon young people as (largely disenfranchised) citizens are rapidly multiplying, a future geography education must question not only who is responsible for what, at what scale, but who gets what, where and why.

References

ACCAC (Qualifications and Curriculum Authority for Wales) (2002), *Education for Sustainable Development and Global Citizenship. Guidance*. Birmingham: ACCAC Publications.

Amin, A. (2002), 'Ethnicity and the multicultural city. Living with diversity'. Report for the Department of Transport, Local Government and the Regions and the ESRC Cities Initiative. Available at http://www.pucp.edu.pe/ridei/b_virtual/archivos/Amin_ethnicity.pdf (accessed 21 September 2009).

Bryant, R. L. and Goodman, M. K. (2004), 'Consuming narratives: the political ecology of "alternative" consumption', *Transactions of the Institute of British Geographers*, 29, 344–366.

Butt, G. (2001), 'Finding its place: contextualising citizenship within the geography curriculum', in D. Lambert and P. Machon (eds), *Citizenship through Secondary Geography*. London: RoutledgeFalmer, pp. 68–84.

Cherrier, H. (2007), 'Ethical consumption practices: co-production of self-expression and social recognition', *Journal of Consumer Behaviour*, 6, 321–335.

Clarke, J. (2005), 'New Labour's Citizens: activated, empowered, responsibilised, abandoned?' *Critical Social Policy*, 25, (4), 447–463.

Cloke, P., Barnett, C., Clarke, N. and Malpass, A. (2009), 'Faith in ethical consumption', in L. Thomas (ed.), *Religion, Consumerism and Sustainability: Paradise Lost?* Basingstoke: Palgrave Macmillan.

Curriculum Corporation (2006), *Statements of Learning for Civics and Citizenship*. Curriculum Corporation, Carlton, Australia. Available at http://www.curriculum.edu.au

Dale, R. and Robertson, S. (2008), *Globalisation and Europeanisation of Education*. Oxford: Symposium Books.

Gillborn, D. (2006), 'Citizenship education as placebo. "Standards", institutional racism and education policy', *Education, Citizenship and Social Justice*, 1, (1), 83–104.

Guthman, J. (2007), 'The Polanyian way? Voluntary food labels as neoliberal governance', *Antipode*, 39, (3), 456–478.

Heater, D. (2004), *A Brief History of Citizenship*. Edinburgh: Edinburgh University Press.

Hendrick, H. (1997), *Children, Childhood and English Society, 1880–1990/Prepared for the Economic History Society*. Cambridge: Cambridge University Press.

HMSO (1990), *Encouraging Citizenship. Report of the Commission on Citizenship*. London: HMSO.

Home Office (2001), *Community Cohesion: A Report of the Independent Review Team Chaired by Ted Cantle*. Available at http://resources.cohesioninstitute.org.uk/Publications/Documents/Document/DownloadDocumentsFile.aspx?recordId=96&file=PDFversion (accessed 21 September 2009)

Ipgrave, J. (2003), 'Dialogue, citizenship and religious education', in R. Jackson (ed.), *International Perspectives on Citizenship, Education and Religious Diversity*. London: RoutledgeFalmer, ch. 8, pp. 147–168.

Katz, C. (2002), 'Stuck in place: children and the globalization of social reproduction', in R. J. Johnston, P. J. Taylor and M. J. Watts (eds), *Geographies of Global Change: Remapping the World*, 2nd edition. Oxford: Blackwell, pp. 248–259.

—. (2004), *Growing Up Global: Economic Restructuring and Children's Everyday Lives*. Minneapolis, MN: University of Minnesota Press.

Kearns, G. (2004), 'Environmental history', in J. S. Duncan, N. C. Johnson and R. H. Shein (eds), *A Companion to Cultural Geography*. Oxford: Blackwell, ch. 13, pp. 194–208.

Lambert, D. (2006), 'What's the point of teaching geography?' in D. Balderstone (ed.), *Secondary Geography Handbook*. Sheffield: Geographical Association, pp. 30–37.

Lambert, D. and Machon, P. (eds) (2001), *Citizenship through Secondary Geography*. London: RoutledgeFalmer.

McDowell, L. (2003), *Redundant Masculinities. Employment Change and White Working Class Youth*. Oxford: Blackwell.

MacPherson, W. (1999), *The Stephen Lawrence Inquiry*. London: The Stationary Office.

Maddrell, A. M. C. (1996), 'Empire, emigration and school geography: changing discourses of Imperial citizenship, 1880–1925', *Journal of Historical Geography*, 22, (4), 373–387.

Massey, D. (1993), 'Power-geometry and a progressive sense of place', in J. Bird, B. Curtis, T. Putnam, G. Robertson and L. Tickner (eds), *Mapping the Futures: Local Cultures, Global Change*. London: Routledge, pp. 59–69.

Matless, D. (1996), 'Visual culture and geographical citizenship: England in the 1940s', *Journal of Historical Geography*, 22, (4), 424–439.

Mitchell, K. (2003), 'Educating the national citizen in neoliberal times: from the multicultural self to the strategic cosmopolitan', *Transactions of the Institute of British Geographers*, 28, (4), 387–403.

Morgan, J. (2001), 'To which space do I belong? Imagining citizenship in one curriculum subject', *The Curriculum Journal*, 11, (1), 55–68.

Nolan, J. L. (1998), *The Therapeutic State: Justifying Government at Century's End*. New York: New York University Press.

Olds, K. (2007), 'Global assemblage: Singapore, foreign universities, and the construction of a "Global Education Hub"', *World Development*, 35, (6), 959–975.

Osler, A. (2000), 'The Crick Report: difference, equality and racial justice', *The Curriculum Journal*, 11, (1), 25–37.

Ploszajska, T. (1996), 'Constructing the subject: geographical models in English schools, 1870–1944', *Journal of Historical Geography*, 22, (4), 388–398.

Pykett, J. (2009), 'Making citizens in the classroom. An urban geography of citizenship education?' *Urban Studies*, 46, (4), 803–823.

Pykett, J., Cloke, P., Barnett, C., Clarke, N. and Malpass, A. (in press, 2010), 'Learning to be global citizens. The rationalities of fair-trade education', *Environment and Planning D: Society and Space*.

Qualifications and Curriculum Authority (QCA) (1998), *Education for Citizenship and the Teaching of Democracy in Schools*. London: QCA.

—. (2007), *National Curriculum Citizenship Key Stage 4*. Available at http://curriculum.qca.org.uk/ (accessed 3 April 2009).

Scottish Executive (2006), *A Curriculum for Excellence. Building the Curriculum 1. The Contribution of Curriculum Areas*. Available at http://www.ltscotland.org.uk/curriculumforexcellence/ (accessed 3 April 2009).

Smith, D. M. (2000), 'Egalitarianism', in R. J. Johnston, D. Gregory, G. Pratt and M. Watts (eds), *The Dictionary of Human Geography*, 4th edition. Oxford: Blackwell, p. 204.

Starkey, H. (2000), 'Citizenship education in France and Britain: evolving theories and practices', *The Curriculum Journal*, 11, (1), 39–54.

Texas Education Agency (1998), *Texas Administrative Code* (TAC), Title 19, Part II: Chapter 113. Texas Essential Knowledge and Skills for Social Studies. Available at http://ritter.tea.state.tx.us/rules/tac/chapter113/ch113c.html (accessed 3 April 2009).

Valentine G. (1996), 'Angels and devils: moral landscapes of childhood', *Environment and Planning D: Society and Space*, 14, (5), 581–599.

Walford R. (1996), 'Geographical education and citizenship: afterword', *Journal of Historical Geography*, 22, (4), 440–442.

Walkerdine, V. (1988), *The Mastery of Reason. Cognitive Development and the Production of Rationality*. Routledge: London.

Weller, S. (2007), *Teenagers' Citizenship. Experiences and Education*. Routledge: London.

Discussion to Part 4
Clive Barnett

For as long as I have been a grown-up geographer – studying, teaching and researching in university geography departments – there has been an ongoing debate about how to reconnect school-level and university-level geographies (e.g. Castree et al., 2007, Hill and Jones, 2010, Jeffrey, 2003). One recurring aspect of these debates is the perceived need to revitalize school-level curricula with insights from the frontiers of University research – the ghost of the 1960s Madingley lectures often haunts these discussions. The three chapters in this part throw into relief some of the difficulties that arise from any attempt to bridge the putative divide between school-level geography and university-level geography when it is framed as an exchange between teaching-focused practices (in schools) and research-focused knowledge (in universities).

The issue of 'ethics' cuts straight to the heart of how the relationships between teachers and students is conceptualized, bringing into view the contested terrain of just what wider public purposes geography education is meant to serve and how these can be best pursued in the routines of everyday teaching spaces. There is a slipperiness about the term 'ethics' in many discussions of 'geography and ethics'. On the one hand, there is the idea that geography education has a mission to cultivate broadened ethical horizons among students and broader publics. This is most often understood in terms of ideas of responsibility, and articulated around topics such as environmental sustainability, climate change, trade justice or human rights. On the other hand, there is a sense of the pedagogical relationship itself being an ethical one, in which the professional responsibilities of geography educators (at school and university) are infused with the task of facilitating the 'becoming-ethical' of student-subjects in the first sense.

Of course, the first 'externalist' sense of geography and ethics threatens to generate a version of what the literary theorist Bruce Robbins has called 'the sweatshop sublime' – by demonstrating to students how their most mundane daily activities (e.g. having breakfast, flushing the loo) are contributing to enormous global problems; there is always the possibility that geography can render its audiences into passive cynics rather than active agents of change, overwhelming them with too many responsibilities while providing only scant alternatives for practical action. It is this threat that makes the second sense of geography as ethics, embedded in the pedagogical relationship, so crucial of course. What is at stake in the sliding together of these two senses is a shared professional self-identity of geography as a subject charged with the important public responsibility of broadening horizons – spatially, temporally, and perhaps most ambitiously, imaginatively and empathetically too. This is an honourable image for any profession to have of itself, and while we have become experts in unpacking the historical origins and sometimes unhappy outcomes of this image of geography education, we should be loathe to abandon it too hastily (see Bonnett, 2003). In fact, it seems to me, that it is not so much the expansive, global ambition of geography as ethics that is most worrying. Certainly, geographical knowledge is easily 'deconstructed' to reveal hidden power relations and political investments. But this hermeneutics of suspicion always has to be suspended for geographical education to proceed. Otherwise, all that we would be left with is the idea of geography as an adjunct of cultural criticism, revealing layers of *geographical* meaning to unsuspecting students while constantly deferring the task of describing or explaining what the world is actually like (or worse, smuggling in unacknowledged assumptions about what the world is really like to bolster the rabbit-from-a-hat authority of the deconstructive manoeuvres).

It is the second sense of the 'ethics' of geography education – the image of the pedagogical relationship through which geography educators are meant to instil expansive geographical responsibilities in their students – which might require much more careful attention than it is often given. I have become more and more uncomfortable with the representations of self-effacing ethical authority which circulate in discussions of the responsibilities of geographers to enact certain moral lessons in their daily practices. One reason for this is that I now work in a distance education institution, The Open University. It is very difficult (actually, impossible and unhelpful) to imagine that one can have the sorts of influence over one's students' deepest commitments or sense of themselves as citizens of the world that many discussions of the tasks of geography education presume, when the pedagogical relationship is structurally attenuated by the gaps, delays, slippages and loops which characterize the pedagogies of distance education. But of course, there isn't actually anything odd about distance education in this respect. Students in school classrooms or university lecture theatres aren't prisoners, after all; their attention to and engagement with geography and geographers is only ever partial, temporary and folded into all sorts of other activities. My point is that the spaces and temporalities of educational relationships, if we pause to think about them for a moment, should lead us to question the strongly transformative image of geographical pedagogy as an instrument for broadening the scope and content of students' responsibilities which one often finds in the debates about what geography is good for.

In their respective emphases, the three chapters in this part nicely illustrate three aspects of what might make up a more modest self-image of the tasks of geography education. Fran Martin presents a compelling case for appreciating the ways in which geography education can serve as an instrument of reproducing unequal and discriminatory power relations, for example, of class, race, gender or colonialism. She recommends a view of geography as a field for teaching *critical literacy* to enhance students' capacities to spot and challenge these discourses of power. Jessica Pykett reminds us of the degree to which geography education always has been, and likely always will be, embedded in broader programmes of citizenship-formation in which geography pedagogy is imagined as a scene for the shaping of ethical subjects with various sorts of dispositions to the world. She recommends the vigilance of *reflexivity* as a means of negotiating the potentials and pitfalls of geography's changing 'citizenly' responsibilities. Alun Morgan also focuses on the contentious qualities of geographical knowledge, and he draws out the *dialogic* pedagogies of argumentation which have been developed to address this feature of geography's global, environmental and societal canvas. It is here, in fact, that there might be significant potential to reverse the direction of fit usually assumed to pertain between school-level and university-level geographies (see Pykett and Smith, 2009). University-level geographers like me are trained experts at doing critical literacy in appropriately reflexive ways, but this often lends itself to a style of teaching (and an image of geography more broadly as having 'political' relevance) which conflates the fact that professional educators know certain things about the world with a view of the *mistaken* beliefs that ordinary people hold about it and which we need to correct. Morgan's discussion of the emergence of dialogic pedagogies is important not least because it brings back into view the importance of having something to dialogue over and argue about – a shared world not so much of geographical facts as of geographical puzzles and enchantments that provoke the curiosity and concerns of students. Geography might be usefully understood as actionable knowledge about a shareable world, knowledge around which people can gather together, and over which they can laugh, cry, reach agreement or perhaps agree to disagree.

Trying to find the proper combination of all three dispositions developed in the three chapters in this part – critical suspicion, reflexive knowingness and dialogic openness – is the real challenge in developing a modest image of geographical education which is equal to the disciplines' inherited global responsibilities and ambitions. And if I had to suggest a simple principle to guide the task of finding this combination, it would be to always try to teach what you know as something which you learned.

References

Bonnett, A. (2003), 'Geography as the world discipline: connecting popular and academic geographical imaginations', *Area*, 35, 55–63.

Castree, N., Fuller, D. and Lambert, D. (2007), 'Geography without borders', *Transactions of the Institute of British Geographers*, 32, 129–132.

Hill, J. and Jones, M. (2010), 'Joined-up geography: connecting school-level and university-level geographies', *Geography*, 95, (1), 22–32.

Jeffrey, C. (2003), 'Bridging the gulf between secondary school and university-level geography teachers', *Journal of Geography in Higher Education*, 27, 201–215.

Pykett, J. and Smith, M. (2009), 'Rediscovering school geographies: connecting the distant worlds of school and academic geography', *Teaching Geography*, 34, 35–38.

Conclusion

Margaret Roberts

[T]he what, the how and the why of teaching is always up for grabs. There is no one correct set of things that students should know; there is no one 'proper' way of learning; there are no 'self-evident' goals of education. Instead there are only ever choices about what to teach, how to teach and to what ends.

Castree, 2005

In this final part I would like to explore some of the challenges implicit in this book.

The challenge of the future

Bart, one of the students in Hopwood's research project, considered the future 'simply too unpredictable to enable any kind of firm knowledge' (Chapter 2). Of course, the future is inevitably uncertain. Yet, despite the uncertainties, there are some aspects of the future about which we can be fairly confident. We know that students at present in schools in England will live lives which stretch towards the end of the twenty-first century. We know that the world has changed massively politically, economically, environmentally and socially during the last 50 years (Chapter 6) and will continue to change and provide new contexts in which we live our lives. We know that the rate of technological change will continue to accelerate; students are growing up in a world which is transformed from the one in which their parents and teachers grew up. We are educating people who will encounter enormous changes.

Thinking about the future is particularly pertinent for those involved in geography education because many current trends have geographical dimensions. World total population will continue to grow. The percentage of people living in cities will continue increasing. The population of the United Kingdom will continue to age. The world's economic centre of gravity is shifting to Asia. The processes of globalization already taking place will continue to make the world increasingly interconnected and interdependent with flows of capital, goods, culture and people criss-crossing the world. New developments in communications technology will enable rapid movement of information and ideas across the globe. What is interesting geographically is that none of these trends are producing the 'flat world' that some writers proclaim (Friedman, 2006); they impact differently on different places. There are different patterns of globalization: of finance, tourism, economic production and consumption and culture; the impacts are unevenly distributed as is the power to influence the process of globalization (Massey, 2006). It is because all these changes impact in some way on everyone's lives that it is important to help young people make sense of them.

Bart said, 'the future is unpredictable' but it is precisely because of its unpredictability that it is worth thinking about. If the future was fixed, then it would simply have to be accepted; but human beings have the capacity to think about the future, to consider what kinds of future they want and to try to influence what happens. Many of the big issues of our time, about which we can make informed judgements and take action, have geographical dimensions. Here are just a few examples. What should be done about the increase in carbon dioxide emissions? How can the world provide for its future energy and water needs? How can the world feed its growing population? What kinds of transport are appropriate for the twenty-first century? How should we respond to Europe's increasing diversity? By studying trends we might determine what kinds of future are probable but it is also possible to consider alternative possible futures and preferable futures.

Young people come across ideas about the future from all kinds of media. Many are familiar with doomsday scenarios or uncritical hi-tech representations of the future. They have hopes and fears for the future (Hicks and Holden, 1995). A recent MORI poll indicated that they are interested in the big issues of our time and think that geography is the school subject most able to help them understand them (Chapter 2). Given their interest in issues, their exposure through the media to various representations of the future and their hopes and fears, it seems important to provide young people with ways of thinking of the future, for example, through using scenarios to envisage, evaluate and identify possible and preferable futures (Hicks, 2007).

The challenge of geography as a subject discipline

All subject disciplines can make claims about their relevance, but the claim of geography is particularly strong because it is an integral part of our everyday lives (Chapters 1–3). We experience directly the places we inhabit, we experience weather and we travel. What we experience directly in local places interconnects with people and places in a much wider global world; a world of food and energy production, distribution and consumption, a world of weather and climate patterns, a world of travel and population movements. We also, from a very young age, experience the world indirectly. Preschool children encounter the world through stories, songs, TV programmes, DVDs and through what people tell them about other places. We continue, throughout our lives, to be bombarded with representations of both the real and imagined worlds on television, in music, film, books, newspapers and advertisements. Communications technologies have enabled us, through the internet, email, webcams and social networks to have instant contact with people and places all over the globe. These direct and indirect experiences together contribute to our own 'personal geographies' our own knowledge of the world. Because we all have different experiences, influenced by gender, class, ethnicity, nationality, age and by the opportunities to interact with different people, we all have different personal geographies. They are also different because of our viewpoint; the places from which we see the world are different: 'we see the world from here rather than there' (Allen and Massey, 1995). From the earliest age we use all these experiences to try to make sense of the world. Massey (ibid.) refers to the set of ideas people develop to interpret the world as their 'geographical imaginations'. Geographical imaginations matter because they influence how we see the world, what we pay attention to, what we neglect and how we act within the world.

Geography is part of our lives, not simply because we experience the world and develop ideas about it. We also all contribute to making the world what it is, through what we do in our daily lives and through the decisions we make. Because of the interconnectedness of the world even our smallest actions, such as buying a particular product or making a journey, has both local and global impacts and can affect local and global environments as well as people all over the world. So geography is not something simply out there, but something which we help constitute.

The task of the academic discipline is, according to Bonnett (2003), 'to inform, challenge and conceptually re-wire people's understanding of the world'. Its scope, encompassing the earth, its natural environment and its people is 'absurdly vast' (Bonnett, 2008). Although some academic geographers are concerned with the big picture, most choose to specialize, focusing their curiosity on certain aspects. So geography can appear fragmented as indeed can other disciplines with diverse content areas, such as science or history. The scope of geography is framed by the questions that geographers ask and by the ways in which geographers investigate the questions to produce geographical knowledge. The nature and focus of the questions have changed over time, influenced by changes in the world and by the prevailing intellectual climate. Geographical knowledge is not fixed; its knowledge and its ideas and ways of seeing are always open to challenge, contestation and change. In the last 30 years geographers have paid increasing attention to the values and ideologies underpinning decisions that have impacts both locally and globally.

Geography, because it straddles the science/humanities divide and uses the methodologies of both, is by its nature interdisciplinary and has been referred to as the 'awkward discipline' (Bonnett, 2008), not fitting in neatly with either the sciences or the humanities subjects. Because of the different approaches geographers use to investigate the world, 'geography produces a diversity of knowledges' (Castree, 2005), all of which contribute to our understanding. Whereas some people regret fragmentation, Jackson (1996) welcomes the 'plurality of method and approach' because there are 'multiple ways of seeing the world, and 'all forms of knowledge are selective'. Developments in the subject have made it yet more interdisciplinary as research has been carried out on the perceived margins of the subject, where it overlaps with art and literature (Chapter 4), science (e.g. in the study of sustainability and climate change), psychology (e.g. in the study of how children understand their environment) and ethics (Chapters 10–12). Geography cannot be confined within tight boundaries without severely restricting what it can contribute to our understanding of the world. Furthermore, although geographers have a big contribution to make, some of the big questions of our time, such as those needed to investigate climate change and sustainability, demand collaboration between several disciplines.

The way geography pervades our lives, the vast scope of the subject and its interdisciplinary nature create opportunities and challenges for education. Young people are entitled to have access to the ways in which geography sees the world, ways which will help them make sense of both their own personal geographies and also information and ideas about the world and its people that they will encounter in the future.

The challenge of geography's place in the curriculum

Geography's place in the curriculum needs to be understood in relation to the purpose of education generally. Is its main purpose to serve the economic and social needs of society or to develop the individual's potential? Is it more important to equip students with skills than with knowledge and understanding? Is education about socializing young people to fit into the existing culture or should it equip them to challenge current thinking, policies and practices? The purposes of education are not self-evident; setting out alternatives draws attention to the fact that they are open to debate and choice. Although many would express purposes in a way that combines the above alternatives, the emphasis given to either end of the spectrum reveals underpinning values and views about what kind of society and future is preferred.

During the last 30 years in England, many decisions about the curriculum have been made centrally, influenced by thinking at the time, as different underpinning ideologies have gained political currency (Rawling, 2001). Currently, government discourse emphasizes the needs of the economy rather than those of the individual and skills rather than understanding. There is emphasis on a technical, managerial approach in which language such as 'targets', 'standards', 'objectives' and 'delivery' are commonly used. The word 'education' appears less frequently in official documents. This kind of discourse is important because it influences not only educational practice but also the way people, including young people, talk and think about education; matters of choice can become accepted as 'commonsense' (Castree, 2005).

In these years of central control there has been disjunction between visions of what geographers think the subject has to offer and the contribution it has been allowed to make (Rawling, 2001; Lambert and Morgan, 2010). Nevertheless, it is important to think about possible and preferred futures for geography in the curriculum and to develop ideas and arguments that could change the situation. The central curriculum question is 'what should be taught?' If it is accepted that young people are entitled to increase their understanding of the world and of their place in it, then what geographical knowledge would be worth including in a curriculum for their future in the twenty-first century? For geography, as for many other subjects which have a vast scope, this question is problematic. If the 'what' is thought of in terms of content, in terms of facts and information, then there is simply too much to know and there is a need to decide what to select and why. Also the world is changing so what seems important and relevant now might seem less so in future. If the purpose is to increase understanding, then it is more important to give students access to ways of thinking geographically, to enable them to see the world in different ways. The powerful big ideas of geography can transform the way young people see the world.

A further curriculum question, if it is accepted that geography has something worthwhile to offer, is whether geography should be taught as a separate subject or as part of a wider grouping of subjects (Chapter 5). Again the choice is influenced by the perceived purposes of education. If education aims to give young people access to ways of thinking developed over the years by subject disciplines then there are risks of incorporating geography into integrated courses. First, a course might be nothing more than an assembly of idiosyncratic bits of information on the same topic, where the emphasis is on information rather than developing ways of thinking about the world. Such a course might be used to develop skills but not understanding. Second, if the geographical aspects of a course are being taught by non-specialists, then it is unlikely they would have sufficient subject 'expertise' (Chapter 9) to draw on to take young people's thinking forward. It seems vital if students are to have access to the kinds of thinking that will help them make sense of the world in the twenty-first century, that the people who teach them have sufficient subject expertise on which to draw (Chapters 8 and 9).

The challenge of teaching and learning geography in the twenty-first century

The curriculum can be thought of in three ways: first, in terms of national curriculum policy documents; second, in terms of curriculum plans produced by schools and third, in terms of the curriculum experienced by students. Although the first two are influential, it is through the experience of the curriculum by young people that the purposes of geography education are to be achieved or not. If the main purpose of geography education is to increase understanding, what has to happen for this to take place? Understanding cannot be achieved simply by transmitting information. Geography is not about fragmented bits of information but about the ideas and conceptual frameworks that link them together. If it was simply a matter of finding information to answer questions, given easy online access to vast amounts of data, then many students could find this for themselves without much help from a teacher. Very few, however, would have the capacity to get access, without the guidance of the teacher, to ways of thinking which would help them make sense of the information; the teacher has a significant role in supporting understanding.

In order to carry out this role the teacher needs 'expertise' (Chapters 8 and 9): a developing professional resource on which to draw when teaching. Expertise comes from the developing capacity of teachers to make connections of many kinds: between academic geography and their own personal geographies (Martin, 2006); between academic geography and school geography and between how subject knowledge is conceptualized and presented and pedagogy (Chapter 8). Teachers' expertise is not something static and fixed; it is dynamic in that it can develop through study, through professional dialogue and through the practice of teaching itself. By reflecting on their practice 'in action' (Schon, 1983) while they are working with young people, good teachers are continuously making connections in their minds and this can enrich the geography subject resources on which they can draw.

It is not only teachers who have to make connections. Understanding cannot be 'delivered' into students' minds. Children and young people have to do something with the knowledge to make sense of it. Several authors in this book emphasize the need of students to relate new information and ideas to existing knowledge. The Young People's Geography Project encourages children in primary schools to link their everyday lives with school geography (Chapter 1) and secondary school students to see connections between their lived experiences with the big ideas of the academic discipline (Chapter 3). Students need to be able to apply ideas in new settings (Chapter 2) and fit new information into conceptual frameworks (Chapter 7). If their understanding is to become coherent, students need to connect knowledge gained from different knowledge domains: school, their own experience and the media.

It is not enough, however, for teachers to develop expertise and for students to engage in activities that encourage them to make connections. There needs to be a 'meeting of minds' for 'an exchange of understanding' between teacher and learner if learning is to take place (Bruner, 1996). The making of meaning through the meeting of minds is the essential challenge of teaching. A prerequisite for making this connection is respect for what students bring to school in terms of their experiences and their ideas. Young people have considerable geographical knowledge from their direct and indirect experiences but it might be quite different from what is expected by the national curriculum, by the teacher or by society. So they might appear spectacularly ignorant. Also, as all human beings are continually active in interpreting the world, they will have made sense of it for themselves but in ways which might be confused or erroneous. Bonnett (2008) recognizes this when he comments: '*Even if geography were to be dropped from every school and university curriculum, some kind of illiterate geographical consciousness would blunder on*' (p. 99; emphasis added). Students' knowledge and understanding might seem to be 'illiterate', but their knowledge needs to be recognized, respected and accepted as the starting-point for developing geographical understanding; it is important for teachers to value and take into account what students do know as well as being aware of what they do not.

Examples from the Young People's Geography Project show that there can be a meeting of minds if there is respect for students' knowledge and ideas, if their own interests are taken into account, if they are encouraged to participate in the curriculum making process, if there is collaboration between teacher and learners and if there are conversational dialogues between teachers and students as part of the learning process (Chapters 1 and 3). In these conversations it is as important for teachers to learn to understand what young people are thinking as it is for learners to understand what is in the teachers' minds.

There needs to be more geography education research into the kinds of conversation that help teachers elicit students' embryonic geographical understanding and into the kinds of experiences and conversations that help students understand the subject's big ideas. It is also, as Hopkirk's research has shown

(Chapter 2) valuable to know what sense students are making of what they are studying and of its significance to them.

The challenge for geography education

Perhaps the biggest challenge for geography education is related to the fact that much of what is valued by the authors of this book is not encouraged by the prevailing culture of education. All the emphases are different. There is an emphasis on skills rather than understanding, on predetermined objectives rather than a more open enquiry approach, on performance rather than developing minds, on acceptance of authoritative information rather than critical engagement and on tasks rather than conversations. Little value seems to be placed on what the subject disciplines have to offer (Lambert and Morgan, 2010). If educational purposes are seen to be mainly utilitarian and if there is a technical, managerial approach to education then how can the vision of geography education implicit in this book be realized? The challenge is two-fold: first, to argue for and work towards policies and practices that are truly educational rather than utilitarian and instrumental; second, to find the spaces to manoeuvre within existing contexts. Both these challenges need to be supported by research, by projects which show what can be achieved to increase young peoples' capacity to know and understand the complex world in which they are growing up. The future is not fixed: as Castree (2005) states we still have 'choices about what to teach, how to teach and to what ends'.

References

Allen, J. and Massey, D. (1995), *Geographical Worlds*. Oxford: Open University Press.

Bonnett, A. (2003), 'Geography as a world discipline: connecting popular and academic imaginations', *Area*, 35, (1), 55–63.

—. (2008), *What is Geography?* London: Sage.

Bruner, J. (1996), *The Culture of Education*. Cambridge, MA: Harvard University Press.

Castree, N. (2005), *Nature*. London: Routledge.

Friedman, T. (2006), *The World is Flat*. London: Penguin Books.

Hicks, D. (2007), 'Lessons for the future: a geographical contribution', *Geography*, 92, (3), 179–188.

Hicks, D. and Holden, C. (1995), *Visions of the Future: Why We Need to Teach for Tomorrow*. Stoke-on-Trent: Trentham Books.

Jackson, P. (1996), 'Only connect: approaches to human geography', in E. Rawling and R. Daugherty (eds), *Geography into the Twenty-First Century*. Chichester: Wiley.

Lambert, D. and Morgan, J. (2010), *Teaching Geography 11–18*. Maidenhead: Open University Press.

Martin, F. (2006), 'Knowledge bases for effective teaching: beginning teachers' development as teachers of primary geography', in D. Schmeik (ed.), *Research on Learning and Teaching in Primary Geography*. Karlsruhe: Pedagogische Hochschule Karlsruhe, pp. 149–184.

Massey, D. (2006), *A Global Sense of Place*. Available at http://www.unc.edu/courses/2006spring/geog/021/001/massey.pdf (accessed March 2010).

Rawling, E. (2001), *Changing the Subject*. Sheffield: Geographical Association.

Schon, D. (1983), *The Reflective Practitioner: How Professionals Think in Action*. London: Temple Smith.

Index